Gifted Children Growing Up

Gifted Children Growing Up

Joan Freeman

CASSELL

HEINEMANN
Portsmouth, NH

Published in Great Britain by
Cassell Educational Limited
Villiers House
41/47 Strand
London WC2N 5JE, England

Published in the United States of America by
Heinemann Educational Books, Inc.
361 Hanover Street
Portsmouth, NH 03801–3959

First published 1991

British Library Cataloguing in Publication Data
Freeman, Joan *1935–*
    Gifted children growing up.
    1. Gifted children
    I. Title
    155.455

ISBN 0–304–32408–6 (Cassell hardback)
        0–304–32428–0 (Cassell paperback)
        0–435–08706–1 (Heinemann paperback)

Phototypeset by Intype, London
Printed and bound in Great Britain by Dotesios Ltd, Trowbridge, Wiltshire

Contents

Acknowledgements

My first thanks are to the people who told me about their experiences and feelings, the young people and their families. It was a privilege to visit their homes and I am particularly grateful for the way everyone made me feel very welcome. The research was funded by the Calouste Gulbenkian Foundation, United Kingdom and Commonwealth Branch, which has given great encouragement to this study from its inception. It could not have been done without its financial support and I am truly grateful for it.

The largesse of material produced by the 'naturalistic' approach of this research called for considerable organizational skills, for which my sincere thanks go to Della Alvarez; and also to Penny Wadsworth for typing the hundreds of hours of transcripts. My everyday appreciation has been for Satellite Software International's superb word-processing program, Word-Perfect, and to Manchester University's mainframe facilities. My sincere thanks go to Naomi Roth at Cassell, whose help was vital; and to Hugh my husband, who gave me steady encouragement, especially when things looked black, much love.

Joan Freeman
London 1991

Preface

The major aim of this follow-up has been to see how some highly able children have grown up into young adults compared with those of more average ability. In doing this, I have tried to open some windows on their personal worlds, to throw some light on how very high-level abilities develop in terms of people's social and emotional lives. So little attention has been paid to it, as, for example, when children's behaviour is observed in school without reference to the rest of their lives, or when they are categorized as gifted and particular characteristics and expectations of behaviour are then attributed to them, which can be far from the truth.

The ethical aspects of working with people hold true for any professional – to safeguard confidentiality unless permission is given, and to give respect to everyone concerned. All those who were interviewed gave their permission for me to record and use what they said, and some even allowed their real names to be used. But there were still times when it did not seem right to disclose intimacies: I have then changed names and tried to disguise any identifying features. Though some may well recognize themselves in this book, I hope it is less likely that anyone else would.

I have made liberal use of the description 'gifted', simply because it is easier at times than all the circumlocutions. However, this is always to be understood as relative, implying that it is but one end of a spectrum of ability among a variety of abilities. In the introductory brief descriptions of the young people, I have sometimes used a convenient shorthand – 'highly gifted' denotes ability at around the top 1 per cent and 'gifted' implies youngsters in the top 5 to 1 per cent. 'Above average' is used for those between the top 20 and 5 per cent, and 'average' for those within about 20 per cent of a national average, on either side of the mean. The difficulties of even such rough definitions are compounded by overlapping talents and abilities, in areas which are not reliably measurable. Therefore, these terms should only be taken as rough guides for present use.

In this book the variety of views and feelings of the young people, their relationships with parents, teachers and friends, how they experienced their education, and their reasons for doing what they did, are given at their most illuminative, in their own words. Their valuable psychological insights provide a basis for clear and much-needed changes of direction in the care and education of the gifted. Before long I shall start to look for them again, to see how many of their aims and hopes have been realized. Interest in the most able children is growing, but it is also important to see just how much is actually changing for those who need some help to make the most of themselves throughout their lives.

The Studies

FIRST TIME ROUND – 1974-8

In the first part of this study, the 210 children I researched were aged 5 to 14. Each of the children whose parents had identified them as gifted was matched with two Control children – the first for intelligence (though the Control child was not seen as gifted), and the second taken at random. All three were from the same school-class so that their education was held as constant as possible. This meant that it was easier to see not only differences between school approaches, by comparing schools, but also differences in the children's personal lives within each group of three. The children's teachers were interviewed in the schools, and the families interviewed and children tested in their homes.

The major difference between the children seen as gifted and those of equal ability but not seen as gifted was in the children's social behaviour. The first were more frequently described as 'difficult' and, indeed, were found to live in more unusual circumstances. All the children's achievements were found to be directly related to educational provision (whether at home or school) and to the example rather than the expectations of their parents.

THE FOLLOW-UP – 1985-8

The uniqueness of the follow-up was again in the deep one-to-one conversations with the (by then) young people, and separately with their parents. Of the original sample, 81 per cent were interviewed in their homes across Britain.

Not all the young people had fulfilled their extremely high promise. The reasons were partly due to their personal circumstances, but also to inadequate educational provision. However, some schools had abused their pupils' potentials by force-feeding them for examination honours, and most did not provide an adequate preparation for university life and work. Teachers often seemed unwilling to be close to their pupils, and an improvement in counselling seems vital. Such matters as self-confidence and personal relationships can be as important in education as the often excellently taught mastery of skills and knowledge.

The experiences, opinions and achievements of these gifted young people are important. The conclusions are unquestionably pertinent to gifted youngsters in other cultures, and should be affecting educational policy-making for such children now.

Chapter 1
What Was Done

Golden lads and girls all must,
As chimney sweepers, come to dust.
WILLIAM SHAKESPEARE, *CYMBELINE*

Concerns about exceptional gifts in children include the special educational and emotional problems involved in helping them reach their potentials. This chapter gives a general outline of the longitudinal study, in which children growing up gifted were compared with others of more average ability. There were two stages in the study, the 1974 original Gulbenkian Project, which laid to rest some myths about gifted children, and the detailed results of the follow-up, ten years later, which is what this book is about.

AN INTRODUCTION TO THE IDEA OF GIFTEDNESS

Concern for the gifted is important because of the inherent quality of each individual's life. Yet high ability is also a national resource, and the future course of society depends on the developed potential of its young. No country can afford the loss of their exceptional ability. It is unfortunate but true that relatively few of the most able children in the world are recognized and educated appropriately. The beneficial educational spin-off which comes from recognizing and catering for the highly able has often been to raise the overall standard of all children's work in schools; this also adds to the variety and excitement of all their learning.

The first difficulty is how to find those children in need of special attention because they are gifted. The search needs to be made with care, because the way the children are selected and the reasons for searching for them will affect the kind of children who are chosen. For example, if children are selected for special education by examinations, they are likely to be different in outlook from others who are keen to develop their painting to a high level of excellence in their own time. If provision for the highly able is ultimately to benefit others, there are many human attributes to be considered and developed for gifted individuals. There is commitment to ideals, for instance, sensitivity to ethical issues, inspiring enthusiasm, or a creative outlook.

Modern concern with the highly able began when Sir Francis Galton published his book *Hereditary Genius* in Britain in 1869. It was the United States, though, which took the first practical steps in 1900, by providing Rapid Advancement Classes for high achievers in New York City. The characteristics of those early high achievers in school have provided the image of what people today often recognize as giftedness in children.

The next major move was Lewis Terman's *Genetic Studies of Genius* (1925–9) in Stanford, California. This was the first large-scale, longitudinal study of the gifted, and is still continuing. However, Professor Terman selected children who conformed to those early, already outdated, ideas of giftedness. He picked the children by adapting the intelligence test designed by Alfred Binet in Paris to find children who were failing in school, and renamed it the Stanford–Binet Intelligence Test. (See p. 10 for details about this test.) Using a minimum score of IQ 140 on his new test, Terman looked for those 'with a degree of brightness that would rate them well within the top one per cent of the school population'.

However, like Galton, Terman was never concerned with how this form of high achievement came about, or with the effects of their home backgrounds on his sample of 'genii'. In fact, most of his sample were the children of white university lecturers, who had enjoyed the best of most things, including good food and education. It is well recognized that IQ (like height) rises as a country's standard of living goes up, but Terman neither took proper account of his sample's exceptional standard of health nor made comparisons with any other children. Yet his generalizations that intellectually gifted children were superior in most things have held sway for half a century in America.

We now know that not all gifted children possess the wide range of outstanding abilities of Terman's sample, and that sometimes a single characteristic can indicate a special gift or talent in an otherwise unexceptional child. Though the more ephemeral concepts such as creativity, social awareness, or leadership are included today in definitions of giftedness, there are still many unanswered questions. Is precocity the same as giftedness? Is creativity a part of general high intelligence or independent of it? Is there such a thing as emotional giftedness, and how might it be related to social intelligence, if that exists? How is it possible to discover unexercised ability?

The difficulties and complexities of answering these questions are inherent in the children's stories in this book. There are some general conclusions to be drawn, which are outlined in the final chapter on educational policies for the gifted. But as always in life, each individual can only be provided for in the best way the local circumstances will allow.

Unfortunately, there is some animosity in many countries towards the idea of any special attention for the gifted. Part of the problem lies in the word itself – because it implies that others are not gifted and so are somehow less worthy. Because of the power of the image behind that word, when a child is labelled gifted it not only has an effect on his or her self-concept, but alters the attitudes and behaviour of others towards the child. It is a label to be used sparingly and with great care. Indeed it is often replaced by less provocative, fuzzier descriptions such as 'exceptionally able' or 'highly able', really meaning much the same thing. These other terms at least intimate that everyone is able, though, to paraphrase George Orwell's pigs in *Animal Farm*, some are more able than others.

In addition, the way the term 'giftedness' is used depends on the context, so that even in the same area of activity, children can be called gifted at different levels of ability and achievement. In a district where school-type learning is not held in high esteem, for example, pupils may be seen as gifted who would be considered dim in a highly selective school. If children are identified as gifted just in terms of their precocity, they may appear to have 'burned out' when they lose that advantage – just as a boy who is tall at 12 years old may not be at all outstanding at 16, when the others mostly catch up. But there are always some individuals who will stay at a higher ability level than others, just as some will stay taller than others.

Carl Friedrich Gauss is an example of someone who started life as a genius and stayed that way, a maker of the modern scientific world. He was born into a relatively poor family, who let him find his own intellectual way. He taught himself to calculate before he could talk and corrected a mistake in his father's wages when he was only 3. At 8 he found the sum of the first 100 integers, astounding his teacher. When he entered the Brunswick Collegium Carolinum at the age of 15, he had already independently discovered Bode's law of planetary distances, the binomial theorem and the arithmetic–geometric mean. His mind in childhood was capable not only of astonishing calculation, but of the most advanced mathematical insight.

André Marie Ampère too, born in Lyons in 1775, was an infant prodigy. It was Ampère who discovered the way that magnetism is related to electricity – that it is caused by electricity in motion – though the discovery was made at the relatively late age of 45; it is his name we use for the unit of electric current. His father was an educationally enlightened merchant who was influenced by Rousseau's book *Emile* and encouraged his boy to read as and when he chose. André, however, was fascinated by numbers and taught himself number theory. His prodigious mathematical powers were noticed by the time he was 4, but he was discouraged because he was seen as too young for the subject.

Both Gauss and Ampère were also highly literate, and they saw their scientific proofs as beautiful, as well as accurate. Great scientists like them are often remarkably good at visualization, and also possess equal powers of description. Charles Darwin, for instance, was one of the best writers of English in the nineteenth century; and Sigmund Freud's books are far more enjoyable to read than most of the millions of words written about them.

It is strange that some gifts in children are more acceptable within their societies, and therefore better provided for, than others. In the main, the more physical the activity, the more likely it is to be approved of. Who has ever heard of talented footballers being obliged to keep their kicks at the average level so as not to embarrass the other boys? Far from it: they are normally given extra tuition outside school hours, including arrangements to meet and engage with other gifted footballers. Something similar happens to the musically talented too, in that specialist teachers may come round to schools to provide extra lessons, and there are out-of-school musical activities where they can meet others like themselves.

But the intellectually gifted and the talented fine artists are not always so fortunate, although aesthetic talent is particularly dependent on cultural encouragement. In many countries, special schools exist for music and dance, though fewer for drama and fine art. Extra provision for foreign languages or mathematics may be found in school societies, and there are national and international mathematics contests and get-togethers. But the idea of a Saturday morning practice for keen chemists must be rare, if it happens at all.

It may be that highly able entertainers receive special privileges because they are seen as non-threatening in their gladiatorial skills. They do not threaten the status quo, as they often learn by an initiation technique, engaging in the mystery of their skills by an apprenticeship to one of their own kind – gymnasts, musicians, sports. They are in a sense licensed jesters, and sporting children also provide a good image for the school.

Gifted footballers are not of course identified by any test; instead, they are encouraged and given practice provision so that those who are able may shine and be seen to shine. But many educators feel that the problems of defining most intellectual giftedness are so difficult that they stop trying. For example, identifying the intellectually gifted with different styles of test which claim to be measuring general intelligence can result in the selection of different children as gifted. And if the gifted are chosen entirely subjectively, well . . . it all depends on what you mean by giftedness. An alternative reaction is simply to deny that the needs of any gifted pupils are sufficient to merit precious teaching resources, involving a dip into the education budget.

The widespread charge of elitism acts as a barrier to special provision for the highly able. Local education authorities, pressed for more money from many sides, often find pleas for provision for the gifted the easiest to refuse. The key to altering that negative, old-fashioned, elitist view of giftedness is to change the perspective from achievement to potential. Instead of gifted children being considered as different or even superior to others in terms of their examination passes or musical performances, they should be recognized as the carriers of much greater than normal potential. Indeed, thinking of children in terms of future rather than present performances encourages teachers to raise their expectations for all pupils. For the gifted especially, it alerts teachers to look out for those who are just coasting along at average level, to recognize them as capable of better work, and to help them develop their abilities more fully.

Intelligence

Not all one's native intelligence is put to work, and in fact it is not required in most people's everyday lives. Some may choose to use only a habitually superficial layer, while others never learn to make good use of what they possess at all.

Intelligence may be considered as being either working or measurable.

In its broadest sense, working intelligence is an individual's power to cope with his or her personal world. This might be the immediate objective of getting enough to eat, or a more distant one, such as passing exams. Intelligence assesses the choices available and then works out the potentially most effective action in the circumstances. Measurable intelligence can be increased to a limited degree by training in the kind of learning that is tapped by intelligence tests, and also to some extent by the very act of study, of almost any subject. This idea that study, of itself, can improve intelligence is sometimes given as the reason why the measured intelligence level of Japanese schoolchildren is going up steadily. They stay at school longer than any other nation's and work harder while they are there. Certainly, most people's intelligence can be used more efficiently and effectively (see Chapter 4). No one, though, has yet discovered how to increase the power of people's innate mental abilities to the extent that would, for example, help the mentally handicapped to function at an average level.

The differences between people's abilities are due to the interaction of heredity (the capacity they are born with) and environment (circumstances after birth). Give or take 10 per cent, the usually accepted figures are that about 70 per cent of the variance between people in intellectual ability is due to inherited differences, and the rest to environmental effect. But for the intellectually gifted, the situation is rather different. Though their genetic endowment cannot be changed, the environmental influence on their intelligence quotient (IQ) score is greater because of their extra mental power to take in and make more effective use of information and ideas (Freeman, 1983). It is a sliding scale – the brighter children are, the more they can absorb, and so, if this potential is to be fully developed, the greater the need for appropriate educational provision.

Children's intellectual development is not a smooth, continuous process. The many interacting aspects develop neither at the same time nor necessarily in the same direction. Theorists such as Howard Gardner (1985) or Robert Sternberg (1986) have proposed that instead of one general intellectual ability, such as IQ, there are in fact different kinds of intelligence. They point out that when the brain is damaged, general intelligence usually remains intact, though specific abilities may suffer. But whether specific or across the board, gifted-level intelligence often unfolds early, so that to teach very bright children entirely at the same level as their age peers is to keep them learning at a lower level than one which would be more stimulating and beneficial for them.

How well children develop their abilities depends greatly on the environ-

ment they live in, and most importantly on that vital mediator of intellectual growth, the language they hear and use. Babies start to learn how
to cope with their environments from birth. There is some evidence that
'difficult' infants trigger special family attention and resources by demanding them, and that this extra interaction can stimulate their intellectual
development. But the option is not open to all babies – only to those whose
parents themselves are good communicators (Rutter, 1985).

Stimulation alone is not an impetus for intellectual growth. In fact,
loud clashing noises or screaming at a baby can be simply confusing or
even detrimental. The result is that demanding babies in poorly responding, insensitive homes are not advantaged, but such babies in responsive
homes can benefit. In good homes, a highly intelligent child often demands
and gets more stimulation from the family, for instance, by initiating
conversation. Even by age 5, a child's measured intelligence is clearly
related to the quality of language spoken in the family. In this way, a
child can actually contribute to his or her own environment.

The efficient use of intelligence also depends on feelings of self-esteem.
These are shaped by emotional security and by protection from stress,
since adventures into new ways of thought call for confidence. Intellectual
growth therefore thrives best in a setting of steady, balanced relationships,
rather than a series of disconnected emotional encounters.

At the turn of the century, when the serious study of intelligence took
shape, new tests were designed to measure academic potential, the ability
to do well in school learning, which at that time was considered to be
fixed for life. IQ is a statistical comparison of an individual's test results
on that kind of intelligence test with those of the whole population of the
same age. Though IQ is just a number, it is in fact the end-result of the
orchestration of very many distinct mental activities. If that orchestration
could be improved, then so would the performance. Intelligence tests are
hard to beat as an estimate of how well a child is likely to cope with
school learning. But though they are unlikely to overestimate ability, they
can underestimate it, and for that reason alone need great care in use.
Such tests continue to proliferate in number and variety, but they are not
used in the design of appropriate educations for children who are scoring
at different levels on them. Although children are selected for different
courses by them, notably in America, the detailed information they provide
about study strengths and weaknesses are not incorporated into individual
teaching programmes.

Who Are the Gifted?

Identifying the gifted and knowing how they go about their gifted business is important in deciding what we should do for them. But the term is flexible and always relative. Some say that children are only gifted if they are in the top 1 per cent of the population on any measure, others use the top 5 per cent to define giftedness – or the line can be almost wherever one cares to draw it. There is no fixed rule. The British Department of Education and Science chooses to take the top 1 per cent of schoolchildren, as measured on intelligence tests, and considers that 10 per cent of these are underachieving. Yet some American states describe the top 30 per cent as gifted. In some of the Southern US states, black (minority) children are assessed separately from whites, taking into account their poor diet and local vocabulary. The result is that some who would actually score below average on a national test are selected for special 'gifted' education in their home territory.

If the aim of education is to develop all children's potential, then it must include those with more potential than the majority. Yet finding such exceptionally high ability in children who are not showing it in their achievements calls for a broad approach. As with any condition, the sooner it can be identified, the soooner it can be helped, and to do that, parents and teachers need correct information.

One method of looking for gifted children, which local education author-ities sometimes favour, is to draw up a checklist of their 'characteristics' for teachers. These lists may start with a short selection, such as independ-ence of mind, early talking and early reading, but as there are always children who do not fit the pattern exactly, further areas are added until the lists eventually become so all-embracing as to fit almost any child. Although checklists can usefully serve as pointers, parents and teachers should know that some items are very misleading. It is often said, for example, that gifted children need less sleep than other children, and so this item usually appears on checklists, although there is absolutely no scientific evidence to back the assertion. An equally unreliable example is that the child asks a lot of questions, which is a decided outcome of how a child is brought up – where questions are encouraged, children are more likely to ask them. It is always important for parents and teachers to coordinate their understanding and efforts with children because children's behaviour can vary at school and at home.

The results of my long-term study, which follow, have thrown consider-able light on this tricky area of identification by showing how, for example, some children can be mistakenly seen as gifted and so can never satisfy anyone, and yet others with outstanding potential can be missed and so fail to develop their gifts.

THE GULBENKIAN PROJECT

In 1974, I began investigating attitudes to giftedness. I wanted to know why some children were seen by their parents as gifted, whereas others, who were equally able, were not. Fortunately, I was given access to the records of 4,500 children whose parents had joined the National Association for Gifted Children (NAGC) in Britain. At that time, membership did not require any test for the children, which meant that by the very act of joining, parents had made a clear statement of their belief in their child's high ability.

I took a sample of 70 of those NAGC children as my Target group, after checking that they were typical of the whole membership. The sample criteria were that they lived in the north-west of England, were aged between 5 and 14 years old, and that their parents had joined within the last four years. My purpose was to compare them with equally able children whose parents had not joined the association, as well as with a random sample of children from the same social circumstances.

At the start of the research, the real abilities of the NAGC children were unknown. Acting on the assumption that they were indeed gifted and that such children were exceptional in any classroom, I devised a complicated cross-school research design. But it proved to be quite unnecessary. The first important finding to come from this study was that there is normally a spectrum of ability in every school, which results from the social population it draws on. There is not, therefore, a wide gap between the very brightest in a class and the rest. This means that the gifted are rarely, in fact, in a position of intellectual isolation among their classmates. The differences between schools are often greater than the differences within schools. Consequently, I was able to match the Target children for ability perfectly, each within his or her own school-class.

The whole of the Target child's school-class was measured for general intelligence on a pattern test, the Raven's Progressive Matrices. This is a useful test for large numbers of children in groups. In it, children have a choice of six possibilities to make up missing parts of a pattern. The only learning it demands is that of handling the printed page, and so it is accepted as relatively 'culture-free'. It provides a general measure of mental ability by which each child can be compared with others in that age-group. Sometimes, in order to give useful information to the head-teacher, the whole school was included, so that eventually nearly 3,000 children were involved in that initial search.

Using those test results, each of the Target children was then matched up with two Control children – for age, sex, socio-economic status, and school-class. But there was one important difference between the two Control children in that the first, Control–1, was matched for measured ability, but the second, Control–2, was taken at random in that respect. The ability matching was remarkably accurate: the average Raven's raw score for the Target children was 34.60, which barely skimmed the Control–1 children's average of 34.53, but was significantly different from the Control–2's average of 28.75. Eventually, there were 210 children, 210 sets of parents and 61 schools in the sample.

The children were tested on a wide variety of measures including intelligence, personality, musical ability, and general creativity, and they and their parents were interviewed in their homes. The class teachers completed a standardized questionnaire on the children's behaviour in class (Stott, 1976), and they and the headteachers were interviewed in the schools. The children's environmental circumstances were noted. The essence of this project was that each child was regarded as an individual, rather than a statistic. This involved a greater familiarity with them and their families than is usual in psychological research. In fact many were visited more than once, and for hours at a time, so that I was able to get to know everyone reasonably well.

Two kinds of intelligence test were given to the children to provide a more rounded picture and also a basis for comparison between the different results. The second, the updated Stanford–Binet Intelligence Test, is given individually, which sometimes takes a couple of hours. It demands some previously learned information, including vocabulary, and so to some extent it reflects a child's educational environment. The test results are given in terms of an intelligence quota or IQ score. This is a calculation of the child's chronological age divided by the mental age of the test-score and multiplied by 100. The average IQ is around 100, and about 60 per cent of all children in most of the world have IQ scores within 17 points either side of that. Only about 2 per cent have scores above IQ 130, and less than 1 per cent above 140. Those scoring above IQ 150 are in a tiny minority – one in a thousand children.

Of the 210 children in the whole sample, 65 were of about average ability at IQ 97–120, 63 were above average at IQ 121–40, and 82 were in the top 1 per cent of the population at IQ 141–70. This was clearly not an average sample of children, because of the way it had been taken, from children presented as gifted by their parents. Consequently, the sample average IQ was very high – in the top 2 per cent of the population, at IQ 137.36. Two-thirds were boys and one-third were girls. The resulting matrix of 210 children and 230 pieces of information about them was statistically analysed by factor analysis, analysis of variance with ortho-gonal comparisons, and various non-parametric methods with the smaller subdivisions. This work is described in my book *Gifted Children* (Freeman, 1979), and summarized here.

Heredity and Environment

As each of the trios of one Target and two Control children were pupils in the same school-class, their school education was held as a constant. This meant that the specific home educational influences could be more readily distinguished. The Raven's pattern test scores were used as a guide to basic general intelligence, and the detailed Standford–Binet IQs as a measure of the children's intelligence which had taken up learning. In this way the IQ score was regarded in part as an achievement score. The two intelligence test scores were then compared statistically, along with all the other data collected from parents, teachers, and rated obser-vations.

Calculated statistical comparisons showed conclusively that some of the children who had been measured as having virtually identical intelli-gences on the pattern test scored significantly differently on the detailed IQ test. These differences were directly related to their home circum-stances. The children in educationally better circumstances had accord-ingly higher IQ scores. It was a sliding scale – the brighter the children, the more they had taken in from their surroundings.

This study, which had taken home and school settings into account, had demonstrated that a bright child living in an educationally poor environment could score the same IQ as a child of more modest abilities in a really good educational environment (Freeman, 1983; underlined by Howe in a review of the literature, 1990).

No previous study had ever taken account of the interaction between exceptionally high ability in children and the amalgam of wider edu-cational influences, and these findings directly affect three concerns about the IQ score:

- The proportions of the relationship between heredity and environment are seen to differ in their effect on intelligence for the gifted, and are very dependent on circumstances.
- The selection of children as gifted – when made solely on the basis of the IQ score – will miss all those gifted children who have not had the opportunities in that kind of school-type learning. I concluded that a cut-off point of not more than IQ 130 could be used, always with the proviso that other measures were considered along with it which were as culture-free as possible, and with an understanding of the child's circumstances.
- When children are compared in terms of their IQs, it is essential to be aware of the input to their scores from their home backgrounds.
- In practical educational terms, because brighter children can take in and use more information and ideas than less bright children, their education has to be both broader and more intense to develop their potential for learning to the full. When the intellectually gifted have poor educational nourishment, they will be more deprived in this respect than less able children, because their potential to make use of such nourishment is so much greater. It was clear from this research that the gifted do have special educational needs.

Personal Differences

Compared with their Control groups, the Target parents proved to have distinct differences. For example, although the mothers of each trio had received similar educations, far more of the Target group mothers had reached high-level occupations – and yet they remained much more dissatisfied with their own educations. Target mothers often took much more responsibility for their children's education than the fathers. However, both the Target parents put greater educational pressure on their children than did the parents of either Control group.

Although all the children in each trio were pupils in the same school-class, the parents of the Target children had made a significantly greater number of complaints about the school – 23 per cent, compared with the equally able Control-1's 16 per cent, and the Control-2's 8 per cent. In addition, the Target children were significantly more often described as difficult, both by their parents and their teachers, on a Social Adjustment Guide (Stott, 1976). They were also more troubled by problems of a 'nervous' type, such as poor sleep, poor coordination, and asthma, and were markedly overactive in school. This Target group had a measured higher level of maladjustment at school than either of the other groups, and far fewer friends.

At this point in the research it did look as though many ideas about gifted children were correct – their frustration in a normal school, their inability to make friends, their poor sleep, and so on. But this did not ring true. Both Target and Control–1 groups were matched for general intelligence, and just about everything else, and yet they were not functioning in the same way. How could it be that children who had been measured as so equal should be so different in their school behaviour?

The next move was to take all the children out of their original categories of Target and Controls and make some more comparisons. But this time it was the IQ scores alone which were looked at in terms of all the other factors in the children's lives – more than 200 of them. The picture then changed dramatically: the specific behavioural problems of the Target group mostly vanished. The children's problems were not related to IQ alone, but rather they were due to other causes.

Laying Some Myths

These comparisons of IQ with the vast body of collected information about the lives of all the children disposed of a few myths about children with gifted-level IQ scores.

Physical development

There were no differences in physique or pattern of health across the whole sample range of ability from average to gifted. On the other hand, the stereotype of the gifted child as being more likely to wear spectacles than other children was found to be true. As with all children, physical coordination was found to be related to general psychological adjustment and not to IQ. As is also usual, boys had more difficulty than girls with fine motor control, which was most likely to show up in their poor handwriting, but again this was not associated with IQ.

Emotional development

The children of exceptionally high IQ proved to be just as emotionally stable as any others. And they were also as badly affected by life events as any others, such as warring parents. Of itself, a high IQ score cannot be said to bring about emotional problems. However, other people's reactions to it, such as constant 'put-downs', can wear at a child's self-concept.

There had been no differences either in the children's measured personality (Cattell and Cattell, 1973), other than a tendency to extroversion in the music performers. It could not be said that the intellectually gifted children had any special personality traits. Even traits such as ambition or curiosity, which are often described as features of high intellect, are really due to culture and upbringing. It was perhaps the intensity of their curiosity which distinguished the gifted, although at times they appeared to their teachers to be not so much curious as 'know-all'. The brightest children were often aware of their superior abilities, and were also more sensitive to their own and others' feelings.

The intellectually gifted were not found to sleep less or more fitfully than other children, although parents had been questioned very carefully on this matter. The length of a child's sleep was directly related to age. Nor were they usually loners. They had as many friends at school as other children, but fewer at home due to the nature of their out-of-school activities, such as music practice, hobbies, and more homework. Even those children at the highest possible IQ levels did not describe themselves as significantly more bored in school than the other children.

Mental development

The brightest children were very often precocious in the three symbolic skills of talking, reading, and writing. Parents often noticed their high verbal ability, sometimes within months of birth. As they got older, they became wider and more avid readers than the other children, and this included comics. Though they did not make more collections of things, or play with any different kinds of toys, they seemed to be more intense about them. They did have a greater variety of interests, and usually enjoyed television, though they were more discriminating than the other children in their choice of programmes. Most outstandingly in their mental development, the exceptionally high IQ children had much better abilities to concentrate and memorize. They were usually able to derive great educational benefit from those mental faculties from an early age.

Gulbenkian Project Conclusions

There were many valuable lessons to come out of that first survey. The most important was that IQ of itself was not associated with emotional disturbance. Both the teachers' and the parents' complaints about the behaviour of many of the Target children were spread throughout that group, irrespective of their IQs, which spanned a wide range. The children with the problems tended to have unusual home backgrounds. It had to be concluded that many of the children who had been identified as gifted by their parents (whether they were really so or not) were those who were somewhat difficult to live with. There was also a high proportion of boys, two to each girl. Well-behaved children who simply did well at their lessons, notably girls, were far less likely to be given the label of 'gifted'.

The idea that highly able children were bound to be 'odd', and accordingly unhappy, was found to be rife. Parents often looked for (and found) early signs of differentness, such as when boys were called 'the little professor' at school. Yet always, playing close by, there would be children of identical ability who would not be seen as gifted. In fact, it seemed that the label was often attached to a bright child's social behaviour rather than to his or her ability. There were, however, some real problems in schools, such as a teacher's disbelief in a child's capacities, when a gifted 5-year-old, who had been reading fluently, was kept at the same reading pace as the rest of the class—a frustrating and upsetting matter for the child.

The educational home environments which were seen as giving the greatest lift to a child's IQ score and success at school did not come only from the parents' attitudes to education, nor even from their high expectations. There were two outstandingly important home influences:

- The material provision the children had to learn with – books, space, musical instruments, paper, and so on. This tied up with an earlier study, in which children who were outstandingly talented in music or fine art had been compared with their non-talented classmates (Freeman, 1976). That had showed clearly that most of the impetus for the practice and development of those arts had come from the parents. Though the schools did sometimes initiate interest, they were not usually successful in bringing standards of work up to an outstandingly high level without the parent's cooperation and provision. The roots of children's proficiency in almost every respect normally begin long before they start school.
- Parental involvement with their children. This included the way parents behaved, the example they set, and the cultural milieu they provided. Where the environment was rich and varied in opportunities to learn, then each child could respond according to his or her abilities. In

simple terms, it was not a very effective move for a parent to say to a child, 'Here is a book about flowers; go out and identify some!' What was effective was when a parent said, 'Let's use this book to find out the names of the flowers – together.'

The publication of these findings (Freeman, 1979) caused some anger among people who had drawn conclusions about the gifted from only their own personal experiences. It seemed strange to me that this evidence of a gifted child's emotional normality was so unwelcome. However, the work did help to shift attitudes to the gifted away from the focus on their problems and towards a more balanced and positive concern with the whole child. Intellectually gifted children clearly needed both an appropriate education and the life chances to make the most of their innate potential – just like all other children.

The real differences between the gifted and other children lie in their abilities. How far these gifts will unfold naturally and how much they depend on help could only be seen by looking at the way those of very high ability develop in their different circumstances. I had often been asked how the children from the study had progressed – what happened next? – so, again with very welcome assistance from the Calouste Gulbenkian Foundation, I decided to find this out in the follow-up study.

THE FOLLOW-UP STUDY

The primary purpose of following up these children was to find out what had happened to them and their parents in the ten years since we had last met. I was looking for threads in their lives which could indicate ways in which the gifted might be growing up differently from the others, for any influences in common to which they might have responded, and for the impact of chance. I aimed for the best of all possible research worlds – in-depth interviewing for the quality of the young people's reactions to what they had experienced, and statistical analysis to deal with the measurable quantities of their progress.

The major value of any longitudinal study is in providing a long view across time, based on reports and measurements as events happen, rather than being entirely dependent on people's only too fallible memories. Single studies without that continuity may miss vital information, but the longer the study is continued, the more it should be possible to see the stability of the original characteristics. In this one, for example, there should be some answer to such frequently asked questions as whether early giftedness burns itself out.

In psychology, studies which involve talking to people in their homes are rare, because it is time-consuming and therefore expensive. But as life is not normally lived in either a clinic or a laboratory, I was determined to reach a closer understanding of the fabric of the young people's lives, not least by talking with them where they spent their time. This worthy intent, however, proved to be no small feat to carry out. Although the children had all lived in the north-west of England ten years earlier, they had moved across Britain, from Inverness to Jersey, and from Exeter to Harwich. And worse, the young people did not always live with their parents any more, so that about half the cases involved two journeys per family. Car travel alone amounted to 8,000 miles, not counting rail and air. It was physically hard going at times, but always tremendously interesting and worthwhile.

The follow-up began in 1984, but as there had been no contact for ten years, it took nearly six months to find the children again. This involved a variety of devious methods and dogged, foot-in-the-door persistence. All long-term studies are subject to human vicissitudes – particularly to losing contact with some of the subjects – although compared with most, the loss in this one was minimal. Some families had vanished without trace. Just a few of the original people refused – one because of illness, two because their parents told me that their sons had become drug addicts and were not capable of responding intelligently, two youths because of their depression which they put down to their unemployment, and one because he said he was working and 'There's nothing in it for me.'

The interviews were conducted in places as different as the governor's office in a women's open prison, a brewery laboratory, sitting on beds in student accommodation, a corner of a shared kitchen, a café in a department store, the back of a taxi, and the head's office in a school. There was a Georgian mansion in a national park, a freezing slum, rich homes in acres of grounds, a farmhouse high on a bleak hill, and a seventeenth-century cottage in a vale of spring daffodils. Most, though, were in the typical British dwelling – a three-bedroomed, semi-detached house in the suburb of a city.

In the end, 81 per cent of the original sample of both children and parents agreed to take part, in proportions which were truly representative of all the original groupings (see Tables 1.1 and 1.2).

The interviews had a prepared questionnaire as a base (see Appendix I), but they were really more like conversations or even at times like

Table 1.1 *The Two Sample Make-ups*

	1974%	1984%
Boys	64.3	64.5
Girls	35.7	35.5
Target	33.3	32.0
Control–1	33.3	34.9
Control–2	33.3	33.1
High IQ (140+)	39.0	42.0
Moderate IQ (under 140)	61.0	58.0

Table 1.2 *Follow-up Sample*

Grouping		Spread	Mean
Age		14–22	18
IQ		97–170	135.4
Raven's percentile		50–99	90
Gender: Boys	109		
Girls	60		
Total in sample	169		

counselling. These bright young people were often very articulate and keen to discourse – often into the small hours, an excellent time for good communication. At times the same story, when seen through the eyes of children and parents, took on quite a different slant. Even the effects of grandparents on their grandchildren were clear to see. The audio-taped interviews, averaging several hours each, were transcribed on to computer disc. Eventually, 338 filled-in questionnaires as well as over 500 interview and report transcripts were rated and statistically analysed. The personal experiences of the young people – during the most important, formative parts of their lives – were teased out from the hundreds of hours of recorded conversations. Though I have edited and woven them into a whole, it is their own words which have provided the information and the vitality, offering a true picture of what the gifted teenager's world looks and feels like.

The Research Outlook

It is important to know about the approach taken to any study because it sets the mould in which data are discovered and analysed, and from which conclusions are drawn. Using my style of investigation, working on the fringes of what is measurable and reaching out to what looks like impressions, was a dangerous game for a respectable psychologist. As with any scientist, I am expected to be able to distinguish what I see in my subjective world from the worlds of the people I am trying to understand. It would have been far easier to hide in jargon and statistics, in the way that I had been trained, and present a picture of objectivity than to run the risk of appearing to be both unscientific and unsophisticated. Oscar Wilde put the danger succinctly in *Lady Windermere's Fan*, saying, 'To be intelligible is to be found out.'

There is no escape from the importance of the environment in all aspects of children's development. It is not something 'out there', but almost as much a part of the children themselves as the working out of their genes. Though an individual's abilities and character are mainly developed in the family's micro-culture, they are also open to the influences of the broader society. To try to understand children without concern for their personal worlds is rather like a zoologist examining fish behaviour without considering water – yet it is often done.

But in attempting to unravel the predicaments of everyday life, there are few standardized measures. Instead, the observer has to be sensitive to atmosphere and to the emotional meaning of other people's lives. Clues may have to be picked up on the spur of the moment, and relationships interpreted as they flow. So often in psychological research, people's own words are set aside as interesting but unusable, when in fact they are often vital to understanding that person. But there is always the risk that by the very act of asking the person to look inwards – introspection – the intellectual process itself and the report on it could become distorted. For that reason, some psychologists prefer only to study what they can measure – behaviour. This restriction, however, cuts out some of the most exciting aspects of mental life – why people perceive the world as they do, their hopes and concerns, and the way they assimilate their experiences. The practical problem in this kind of research, though, is how to cope numerically with the infinite variety and quality of the everyday events which impinge on an individual's development.

An important aspect of good communication is sharing a common cultural consciousness. This is difficult, though, both between people of different cultures and between those of the same social culture but very different intellectual abilities. My major advantages were in being from the same part of the country as the young people I was studying, and in being a research psychologist who had also been trained in counselling. Highly gifted people may use concepts and ideas which are beyond those of the non-gifted, including at times this interviewer. More than one gifted mathematician among these young people found it hard to understand the difficulties normal people face in following what they themselves saw as simple. I had the impression that Sarah Mortimer (highly gifted, aged 20, studying computer systems engineering at university) rather enjoyed the difference:

In class, I might suddenly say, 'Oh, this is wrong,' rewrite the program, churn it through and find it works. Someone will ask, 'Why did you do that?' and I reply, 'Well, it's obvious. We didn't do this, that and the other,' and sometimes they can't follow, because I jump too many steps at once. In the time they've taken to think what they're going to do, I've written down the whole formula, and then the next line.

While the observer tries to remain as neutral as possible, some form of interaction always develops in any human meeting, so that the process can never be as objective as a laboratory experiment or a test score. Yet the outcome is always richer in quality than with any other method. Although I made conscious efforts not to influence the people I met, two of the young people were inspired to go on to study psychology at university, and who can say what other repercussions may have occurred from our getting together in this research?

This book is mainly concerned with the findings from the follow-up study. But it also aims to tie these up with what was learned from the first Gulbenkian Research Project on gifted children, and to draw conclusions about the young people's development over the whole fourteen-year span in which I was working with them. The issues raised are basic to the individual development of all children, not just the gifted, and to the system which seeks to educate children.

Chapter 2
Some Problems in Being Gifted

No man is an Island, entire of itself.
JOHN DONNE. *DEVOTIONS*

Although children do not have problems just because they are gifted, they are vulnerable in some specific ways. Because they are exceptional, stereotypes and biased attitudes in others can act as brakes to their identification and development. Children may, for example, take their role of being 'gifted' too much to heart, or parents may try to live through them. There is also the problem of lopsided gifts, when emotion does not keep pace with intellect, or when a child is gifted in a limited area. Identification is made more difficult because deprivation and handicaps certainly inhibit gifted development.

THE STEREOTYPE OF GIFTEDNESS

To be brilliant is in a sense an affront to good manners, to the ordered way of things. A particular problem in being termed gifted is that it places a child into a special psychological category of exceptionality, so that he or she is then expected to have particular characteristics and problems. But popular stereotypes of the gifted child vary considerably from place to place. For example, current descriptions on either side of the Atlantic, in the United States and Britain, are almost entirely in opposition.

The American stereotype is of a superchild: he (for it is always he) is a brilliant sportsman, a natural leader, and a straight-A scholar. He is expected to be physically well formed and probably good to look at. But the British stereotype is of a weedy lad: he (for he is still male) is bespectacled, lonely, and much given to solitary reading. This stereotype is in fact of a juvenile intellectual, at times referred to by his schoolmates and maybe his teachers as 'the little professor'. He will look old-fashioned, move awkwardly, be difficult to bring up, and will find it hard if not impossible to make friends. He is certainly not a leader, for in Britain talent in leadership and sport are assumed to be the province of non-intellectuals.

However different they may be, such expected characteristics bring problems to the gifted in other people's expectations of them. For example, if gifted American children do not conform to that superboy stereotype, if they are undersized, or shy, or only shine in one area, they can be missed by teachers. Added to that is the burden of living up to the perfect image, so that an A grade which drops to a B is seen as failure. In my study, a significant number of the Target children were described by their parents as 'typically' gifted, of course in the British mould. Parents would list the child's 'symptoms', which were seen as making difficulties in the family's life – such as overactivity, making excessive demands, needing little sleep, and not fitting in at school.

In following up those children, I was able to look at their longer-term reactions to having that mantle of giftedness, and its anticipated problems, laid on their young shoulders. The first comparisons between the Target and the ability-matched Control–1 groups had shown that differences in family outlook were related to the children's social behaviour. This could not have been due to the children's abilities, as these were the same for both groups. Children described by both parents and teachers as gifted and difficult had had significantly more unusual home circumstances. Their parents may have separated, moved home constantly, or tried to live vicariously through them, or they might have been late babies, when the rest of the family's children had grown up. The possibility was that the bright child had simply failed to learn adequate consideration for other people, this being mistaken for the 'symptoms' of giftedness, although such behaviour can in fact be found in children of all abilities.

Ten years later, many of the Target group seemed still to be carrying the burden of their stereotype, particularly in terms of poor relationships, and maybe they will do so for life. Other problems, though, such as poor sleep, had vanished, probably because they were really problems of childhood and had simply been grown out of. As in the first part of the study, the Target group still described themselves as more sensitive than the Control–1 group, and they were also distinctly more lonely and depressed, their bouts of misery being far worse than for either of the other groups. This emotional disturbance may also have knocked the edge off their school achievements, because they had somewhat lower examination marks than the equally able Control–1 group (statistically significant at 5 per cent). Yet they had more frequently jumped a class at school, and so felt better recognized for their high ability, even though this move could have lowered some of their exam results.

However, although a significantly larger number of the Target parents (37 per cent) had expressed keen ambitions for their children than in the other two groups (Control–1, 23 per cent, Control–2, 6 per cent), and had put pressure on the child to fulfil these ambitions (Target, 30 per cent; Control–1, 13 per cent; Control–2, 6 per cent), this difference in parental pressure quite disappeared in the follow-up. The great majority of parents then said that they simply wanted their children to be happy whatever they did.

One cannot say with statistical certainty that early stereotyping of the Target children as gifted had been the cause of their emotional problems: it could have been that those children were indeed difficult. But as the families of the Target group had been more troubled and the parents had shown significantly different attitudes to their children from those of the equally able group, it was likely that they had been influential in their children's behaviour and outlook, especially in 'labelling' them as gifted children. When compared in measured IQ terms, there had been no link between children's exceptionally high scores and their difficult behaviour. There were many and often complex reasons why the children had acted in that way, which can be seen clearly in the children's life stories which follow.

Career Giftedness

One of the reactions from some of the less happy young people in the Target group had been to try very hard to live up to the characteristics of the stereotype of the gifted child as they saw it. The problem had usually begun early in their lives, since they had learned, as do all children, to adapt to their circumstances. But adaptation which is appropriate at one time of life can be harmful and inappropriate later. For instance, a child who is outstandingly brilliant at primary school may be showered with approval and praise from adults, classmates too looking on in admiration. What an attractive, satisfying role in life it seems to be – being gifted. But then the child moves on, perhaps to a selective school, and discovers with shock that he or she is no longer the best at everything. What sometimes follows is a lowering of self-respect – if you had been labelled 'gifted' and staked your all on the image, but now are no better than all the others, where does that leave you? Who are you then?

If a child decides (usually unconsciously) to cling to that early role of being the most brilliant, there are two major ways to avoid the risk of slipping off the pinnacle. One is to work extremely hard to stay at the top, the other is to avoid any testing situations as much as possible. The second way also involves keeping a set of excuses to hand to explain poor performance in those tests which are unavoidable. The most common excuse among the gifted in this sample for not doing well was to make a show of disdain for the work required, saying effectively, 'Of course I didn't do well, because I didn't work.' Unfortunately, that ploy often has the side-effect of stunting the very ability to study; in addition, the down-ward spiral of excuses and general failure produces a state of dissatis-faction, if not depression, in pupils who know in their hearts that they are not fulfilling their potential. So they can end up in the worst possible position – second best – further alienated by nagging from confused par-ents and teachers, who do not understand what is happening.

I have called the youngsters whose sense of self-worth seems to be dependent on being seen as brilliant – whether actually so or not – Career Gifteds. A notable feature of such people (children and adults) is that they often 'dine out on it', informing the world both of the difficulties of being gifted and how tiresome it is having to cope with normal (mediocre) people. Parents sometimes play along with this. Some Career Gifteds do work hard, achieve superbly, and accept their laurels as their just deserts; but others, equally able, insist that were it not for . . . (insert excuse) . . . they could show their true and brilliant colours.

Behind the façade and the bravado of the Career Gifteds, whether achieving or not, lies fear. It is fear of being a nobody, of being undeserving of attention, of appearing unworthy to oneself, and of being exposed as fraudulently gifted. Such fear has inhibiting spin-offs, both to academic study and to creative expression. In this follow-up study, the Career Gif-teds were seen to have had their reasons for choosing that way of life, usually the combination of their high ability with their psychological circumstances. Now, locked into their unactable roles and unable to fulfil their potentials either emotionally or intellectually, the Career Gifteds were often in need of help.

Gaynor Pattison was a Career Gifted. Within minutes of our meeting, talking without a break, she had told me how nobody could understand the depth of her philosophy, and how uncomfortable she felt with her life among students with lesser brains. The barrage of words struck me as a combination of a hook to hold my attention and a defence against hurt. She seemed desperate to be different.

As a very small child, in an uncomplicated, loving family, she had enthusiastically adopted the stereotyped image of 'the gifted child who finds it difficult to live in a mediocre world'. At the time, it seemed to suit everyone. Then, to protect herself from losing this glory, she had carefully avoided any real test of her abilities by demonstrating contempt for the educational system. She had refused, for example, to revise for school exams, and had therefore done badly. As an unqualified school-leaver, she then found herself doing unskilled work, where the hours were long and hard for very little reward. It had stimulated her to scrape together enough qualifications to take a teacher training course at a small college. She told me, 'When this college said I could have a place, I didn't bother about it very much, occasionally remembered I was taking the exams, got them and came here.' It would have been emotionally too difficult for her to encounter her intellectual equals at a university. As part of her self-styled performance as a brilliant philosopher, Gaynor produced what she described as 'deep unanswerable questions', with which she taunted her teachers. But trying to follow her non-stop, undisciplined flow of words was in fact like chasing a zig-zagging rabbit that was trying to throw the pursuer off the scent.

Gaynor Pattison (highly gifted, aged 21, at college):

It's difficult for people like me with a very high intelligence, because we think we know so much and are influenced by bigger things. I say a lot of things that other people would never say, and do things that other people wouldn't do. I live how other people wouldn't live. I've got a lot of thoughts that other people can't possibly begin to understand because they've probably never thought that hard before. It's unfortunate, but they just don't know what I'm going on about. Last week, I thought about truth – nothing's real because what you see one day may be seen the next day as totally different. So reality is always real, but it changes and it's a different reality. When I say things like that, they say, 'Yes ... I think I'll go and have a cup of coffee.'

I can't help myself crying if I'm depressed. It's a natural reaction. But I can't stop it. I can cry and cry and really get myself into a state, and then I stop and sort it out; then the depression will just go. I'm never going to be happy until I've got what I want, which is a very small farmhouse with a farmer. That's all I want, with a four-poster bed to make love in. I want to make my four-poster bed and carve it and make my patchwork quilt, and build the house too, stone by stone.

There seemed to be far more reason for Stephen Kaye to become a Career Gifted. Life had already put many rocks in the path of this sad teenager, who had reacted by withdrawing into his own world – at some cost to his happiness. He attributed his emotional problems entirely to his undoubted giftedness. In his mother's words: 'It's probably what you find a lot with gifted children, isn't it? They just don't mix. Stephen's too academic, a bit like an absent-minded professor; just so oblivious of human beings all around him.'

He put a brave face on things. His mother had gone to live with another man; his father was given to listening to classical music in his own room for hours, often even eating alone there. Stephen never once spoke of him spontaneously, and though they shared the same house, the father hardly seemed to exist. Added to that, his younger brother seemed to have reacted in a very different way as an apparently carefree extrovert, who filled the house with many noisy friends.

Measured as one of the brightest boys in the whole study, way over the top of any scale, Stephen's greatest gift was mathematics. Although his junior school had accelerated him just for that subject, which he had found a great relief, his present unselective school had never recognized or provided for his educational needs. He was not in a happy position, without support from home, school, or companions, and his immensely powerful intellect was almost lying fallow. He needed the emotional security and steady reassurance that he was valued for himself.

Stephen Kaye *(highly gifted, age 14, at school):*

However bad I think I am, I'm one of the top scorers in most tests in every subject. The teachers don't tell me I'm doing well because it's obvious, and the others only get jealous. It used to hurt me, but it doesn't any more because I've developed a hard skin, and now it's just annoying. I wouldn't lower my marks on purpose to please them; it would be silly. My study habits are not studying. I normally remember things as they're coming through in the lesson, but my memory's not as good as it used to be. Lessons have to hold my attention more and I can't really remember what I felt like a few years ago, though I remember things that have happened to me in the past very well. I don't read around, because in general I won't be tested on it, so what's the point?

Probably because I'm an introvert, I don't like going out. I've never read a newspaper, and I'm quite happy to do nothing without being bored. When I'm with other people I immediately find things that I don't like about them. I know I'm very sensitive; I get annoyed quite easily and irritated and upset. I often feel with other people when people get at them, sort of cringe in sympathy. I just don't trust anyone any more because of the number of times people have tricked me just as a practical joke, and it depresses me. The way people react to me is very stupid; they don't understand me and think I'm weird or mental: sometimes it's on purpose, even if I say something really simple, because that's what they're expecting to do with somebody more intelligent than them. All my viewpoints seem to be different from everybody else in my year. I seem to be the only person who isn't a racist, or bopping along to the latest pop album.

I've realized that I don't have to try to stand in with the crowd because it doesn't really matter. I never seem to get the time to rest: I don't know why, because it's what I'd like to do most.

Career Gifted Families

There were several families in the sample that could also be described as Career Gifted families. I should have been warned when Carl Hadley's mother described herself as 'loquacious': I was in that house for five hours – fixed like a fly by a couple of spiders. Both she and Carl provided exhaustively detailed replies in response to the simplest of questions, using words as complicated as they could find. Carl seemed to be very dependent on recognition as gifted for his sense of self and dignity, and he was finding some difficulties with relationships at university, where he had met many who were his intellectual match. His mother described how difficult it was for him to be gifted: 'Before he went to university, he very frequently used to say how he felt different from other people and that they were mainly stupid. He is always on about PBs – personal bests – so he tries to beat himself – runs himself into the ground.'

It was hard for highly gifted Richard Neville when he went to school and found that the other children there did not give him the same devoted attention as his parents, which was, as his mother said, 'regardless of anybody else'. She did recognize, however, that his behaviour could appear to be selfish:

He had always been encouraged to talk to grown-ups and ask questions, and he will go on and on and on till he's got to the bottom of it. I could see why teachers might want to let off steam about that arrogant kid who thought that he could run the lesson, and that this wasn't going to be good for personal relationships all round. But if a child is top amongst fairly competitive children then he's going to provoke jealousy, which is why the junior school class ganged up on him. So that he wouldn't always be top, we then sent him to a high-powered school for the extra stimulation. But even when he was 16 his chemistry teacher said, 'God, he drives me mad sometimes!'

Sometimes the child was able to reject the gifted role which parents had placed them in. Though she had little education herself, Mrs Jacobs had been a powerful force behind her gentle son, guiding, cajoling, and verbally battering his teachers to push him on, because she saw him as gifted. She said:

I made an appointment to see the junior headmaster, who I couldn't stand at all, to get him to put Vincent up a year. When we'd finished, he said 'I've never had a parent speak to me like you've spoken before.' I said 'Well, I don't frankly care.' He put Vincent up.

She had devoted her life to her son. The only photographs in the house were of him, and since he'd been a small child he had been allocated two rooms, as study and bedroom. Even at the age of 4, he was having four lessons a week, and when I first met him at age 6, it had increased to seven subjects – chess, swimming, elocution, French, Hebrew, etc. – one a day. The stereotype of the problem gifted child dominated his mother's thinking, even to the extent that she couldn't have any more children, as this one was so demanding: 'All my friends, they were very amazed!' Even ten years later she was still complaining about his poor sleep and his insatiable curiosity.

Not only, however, did Vincent seem to me decidedly incurious, but I had heard more interesting views on life from much less able youngsters. He had taken a very 'laid-back' attitude to his mother's view of him as a stereotyped gifted child, seeing it as her opinion, rather than his obligation. His sense of esteem was clearly not dependent on his capacity for learning, so that he had no need either to make excuses or to strive frantically, but was working steadily at his own very high level. He had plenty of friends and a good social life. He did appreciate, though, his mother's faith in him, and they understood each other well.

LOPSIDED GIFTS

All children can have problems if their abilities develop unevenly. But when it happens to the gifted, the results for both child and parents can be much more extreme and difficult to cope with. The most common problem is when intellectual ability far outstrips emotional or practical development. The disturbing lack of harmony can cause a child to retreat into babyishness, more than others of the same age, and especially at bedtimes. This is because emotional distress, such as that from normal childhood anxieties, is not easily dismissed by reason, so that however powerful the child's intellect, it is unsuitable as a means of coping. Additionally, a young gifted child may pick up information which other children might miss, which he or she is not yet mature enough to deal with, causing stress which needs help to be resolved.

The main alternative reason for lopsided development is that the child is not gifted all round but in a specifically limited way. This is how it was for Laura Grunberger (gifted, aged 16, at school), who had an outstanding facility for languages. Her mother told me that Laura had a vocabulary of 200 words by the age of 12 months. This gift, though, had had to be shelved for the time being to allow her life to be balanced, happy, and normal except for her voracious reading – a book a day. Her mother is the best person to explain why:

> You remember that when you first saw Laura, when she was seven, she was speaking fluent Hebrew, so you suggested Greek lessons. Well, I rang the Greek Orthodox Church, and they recommended someone who teaches the children of mixed marriages, and she used to teach Laura with her own children. Laura was doing fantastically at Greek, she was adoring it, and the teacher was most impressed. Then the children at school found out that she was learning Greek and they teased her so unmercifully she wouldn't go any more, and she stopped. It was such a shame.
>
> In the junior school, she was completely shutting off. What she used

to do, was to go off in a corner on her own and read, because she really was quite bored with the whole system. She read her way through the whole library of her own classroom and three other classrooms as well. She'd still read and read to the exclusion of all else if we'd let her. Now, she'll take a shopping bag to the library for twelve or fourteen books at a time. If there wasn't a library, we couldn't keep her in books; her room is filled with them, and she reads almost anything that she can get hold of.

There were several youths in this sample who were unquestionably brilliant in their field of science, but otherwise socially immature, uncultured, unthinking, and inarticulate. Their lopsided development had resulted in less happy outcomes. The following two provide excellent examples.

For Michael Grayling (gifted, aged 20, studying science at university), it was only science that he was capable of taking to gifted level. He was a slight fellow, who looked about 14 and was extremely shy. His mother said, 'He hasn't brought one person to this house since we moved here fourteen months ago. He stays alone in his room.' Although he had scraped through the necessary school English lessons, his ability to string sentences together was decidedly limited. Nor did his solitude appear to have been spent thinking about things; in response to many of my questions, he said that he'd never given the matter any consideration before. In the first study, his intelligence scores had been wildly different on the two kinds of tests. The non-verbal, pattern test of logical thinking had identified him as well within the top 1 per cent of the population, but the IQ test, which includes the use of language, had found him just above average. The intervening ten years had proved the accuracy of those earlier measurements.

In John Whitcombe's case, it was neither he, nor his family, but his father who played the role of Career Gifted. His father provided me with a great variety of reasons why he had not done well at school himself, and was now living somewhat vicariously through his son's singular brilliance. The headmaster of John's primary school told me how he had been regularly buttonholed by this extremely verbal man, whose great love was poetry. His son's strength, however, was entirely numerical, to the extent that he knew he found great difficulty in expressing himself in words.

John Whitcombe's father:

There are brilliant members of the family on both sides. I was gifted myself. John was like blotting paper as a child. I was alerted to his potential giftedness when he told me one day at 4 years old, 'I don't sleep, I dream,' and he possibly slept only four hours a night. So I had him tested. With the confirmation, I fed him books and taught him 'body language'. When he was little, he'd told me that his mother didn't talk to him, and I was furious. He was accepted for Millfield [an expensive private school], with a scholarship, but I wouldn't let him go, as his accent and the divorce would have handicapped him. I've remarried, you see, but I kept the kids, as John needed my brain.

He was sent to the comprehensive school a year early. But things were bad then ... the divorce, it wasn't good for him and he had to settle back with his age-group. He lives and breathes maths; saved up and bought himself a computer, and used to crack the codes of the computer games for fun. When he got on to Advanced levels at school, that's when he really woke up and got all A grades. His handwriting is atrocious – looks like a child's. But he's left-handed. Spelling is damn' good – he'd be cross with himself if it wasn't perfect.

He's gifted, but I told him not to boast, just to get on with it. Now that he's at Cambridge, he is able to stand on his own feet amongst his peers, a crowd of bright students. He has made friends and loves his work. His tutor thinks he'll get a first. He may have to go to America when he qualifies.

John Whitcombe *(gifted, aged 19, studying mathematics at university):*

At school, I used to be very shy but very conceited. I thought I was better than everyone else – at everything really – but I was actually only top in maths. I think the problem of getting on with people was due to my ability, because I was more intelligent than them; they didn't trust me. I felt they were all suspicious of me. It wasn't my whole problem, but it made me feel isolated. Now I've got to know people better, started actually caring about people more, I usually go round to visit someone else every day after I've stopped working. But I could quite happily work all hours God sends, and still not have enough time to work all I wanted to.

THE EFFECTS OF DISADVANTAGE

Whereas some children may be pushed into the role of gifted child, others, because of individual or social disadvantage, may not show signs of their very high potential, and so are easily overlooked. Of the many kinds of disadvantage which can hamper children, even within my relatively small sample I found physical, emotional, cultural, and economic problems which had clearly inhibited the growth of some of the children's exceptional potential. There is a difference between those who do not show their gifts because of psychological reasons, such as lack of motivation or social pressures, and those who cannot because of poor nervous functioning. Obviously, it is important to know the cause if the child is to be helped appropriately.

Individual handicaps can be, for example, poor verbal ability due to mild deafness, or developmental delay in fine motor skills, which affects handwriting and many school activities. Emotionally, children who are crippled with shyness, so that they never answer questions in class or strive towards the goals the teacher sets, are also handicapped in their learning. The disability may be social, as for children of minority cultures, who have to adapt both to home life and to school, and whose self-expression may be considerably better in a home language than in English. This also applies to inner-city children, who may have limited school English but excellent 'street language', or maybe a culture which is dead set against school and all it stands for. It is not unreasonable for parents or teachers to look on a child who has difficulty in following simple directions, controlling the impulse to talk, concentrating on work, or completing tasks on time as far from gifted. The problem for teachers is lack of information, and the answer is in getting to know the child completely as a person, especially being in close communication with parents.

Physical Disadvantage

Gifted minds trapped in bodies which will not obey instructions from the brain make children appear to be stupid. Neurological damage can be genetic or can happen during a difficult birth, leaving babies with spastic handicaps, perhaps even without speech. Until recently, children with severe physical disability were often treated as though they were also mentally retarded. But with advances in technology, such as word-processors workable by feet or head movements, it has become possible to see that physical damage does not imply intellectual damage. Separating the two has meant that children imprisoned by their handicapped bodies are gradually being released from a lifetime of torment.

A less dramatic problem coming more and more to notice is a child with difficulties in learning to read and write, as in dyslexia. This confuses and sometimes irritates teachers when they can see that a child is very bright, though not producing the expected level of work. Both Thomas Edison and Leonardo da Vinci had literacy difficulties which today would be called dyslexia.

It was noticeable the first time I saw Scott Kendall, at 6 years old, that he had a problem with pronouncing words clearly, and that was still true ten years later. In 1974, his reading standard was well below where it should have been, and though his teachers could see his problem, they felt that the school could cope with it in the remedial class. His parents had accepted their authority and not taken action themselves, even though they felt uneasy. When I saw Scott ten years later, he was about to visit a psychologist for the first time for help on this matter, as he approached the age of 16. The effects of his problems with words, and the long delay in treating them properly, had been educationally disastrous for this very bright boy.

Scott Kendall *(gifted, aged 15, at school):*

> Sometimes I can spell a word right, then the next time I'll spell it wrong, but it looks right to me. Sometimes I can write essays and not get any spelling mistakes, and then sometimes I write one and nearly every word will be a spelling mistake. It comes and goes. Sometimes when I'm reading, one letter out of a word will make me stop: just that one letter will stand out, and I don't know what's wrong. I can see the word, but I just can't say it.

No one in this sample suffered from severe nerve damage, but even among these apparently normal individuals, there were some who had difficult physical handicaps to overcome. Not only were the families' medical practitioners often less than helpful, but several mothers told me they had been called 'neurotic' because of their concern, and that this had resulted in delays of a year or more before vitally important remedial action was taken. Only the determined mothers really won through to get help, and there must be many more whose bright children were simply treated as of poor potential, when they were in fact gifted. One mother was sharp: 'He was ill at 6 months, so we took him to the hospital, and they said it was allergy because he was very intelligent – to which I replied that intelligence is not an illness.'

Philip Bessant had been tall for his age when I first met him at 9 years old. But he had real problems of muscle control. At 20 he was still tall, with a delicate, little-boy face. His movements were obviously clumsy, and he had a constant tremor, which caused him problems in making us coffee. Interestingly, he was studying chemistry, a subject needing fine motor control. Listening to him was not easy, because he had difficulty controlling his mouth sufficiently for clear speech. He told me that he talked too fast for people to follow, though I suspected that they became impatient waiting for the end of the sentence. He also had problems with social relationships, but it was difficult to distinguish how much was due to his own personality and how much to the hardships he had endured with his muscle clumsiness. Fortunately, he had a mother who had not waited for medical authority to find help for him.

Philip Bessant's mother:

Our doctor had seen Philip going upstairs at about the age of 3, first one foot then together, like a younger child, and I hadn't realized that was unusual. Without any concern, he turned to me and said, 'You know you've got an ESN [educationally subnormal] child there.' I said, 'He may be anything but he's not ESN,' because I could remember all sorts of things he'd done. Once, when he was under 2, he and his grandmother weren't speaking because he said a certain car was a Minor and she said it was a Mini! He's probably ten years ahead of what he would have been if I hadn't seen to it all.

They really didn't know what to make of Philip when they assessed him at the Children's Hospital. Coordination-wise he was way down, clumsy, but he'd got great concentration, and was intellectually gifted. I found a remedial teacher without qualifications, who did a lot for him, and I taught him how to write myself. His worst difficulty was with reading, because he couldn't coordinate his eyes along the line, so he was reading encyclopaedias with short lines for the information, but he couldn't manage stories. The school was very kind, but they couldn't understand it.

We chose private, more disciplined, traditional sort of education, because we felt that with his problems, he would flounder in a free-expression kind of school. He needed to know where he was. At first the less able boys teased him, but when he was put with boys of similar ability, he seemed to cope pretty well. His writing was appalling, so the teachers didn't upset him. Most of them used to just tick it, and say 'Yes, that was fine.' The English master gave him real confidence when he said, 'I don't care how you write; I love your ideas.' He did so well with him.

He's helped himself enormously, because he's got determination, and discipline; if he has to do something, he gets it done. If he had an assignment in the holidays, he'd do it the first two or three days. Of course he can't be sporty, but he doesn't seem to mind that at all. He can hold his own in company, but when the time comes for him to look at jobs, I worry that he's not had enough practice in dealing with people.

Philip Bessant *(highly gifted, aged 20, studying science at university):*

I do care that people think well of me, but there are certain things that I wouldn't be prepared to change. The reason why I disregard people is that I've had to build up some sort of shield for myself over the years, and it's made me very much more of an individual. I do worry, which I suppose could be partly anger, and I tend to find my hands perspiring a lot. I'm also a slightly withdrawn person: I don't enjoy parties, or pubs, or restaurants nearly as much as most people in my age-group. On that count, principally, I consider myself to be different. But no matter how unlucky I am – I am very, very lucky compared to lots and lots of other people.

This type of story was not only true for the highly able. Mrs Collins went time and time again to her doctor, who told her she was creating a fuss about nothing. She told me:

I went to the hospital without any appointment, sat down in the waiting room and said, 'I'm not going to go until somebody looks at this child, because I know something's wrong.' The staff were rolling their eyes a little bit, thinking, 'Stupid woman, that child, she should just take him home.' He was on phenobarbs; they'd put him on phenobarbs.

I was lucky the consultant saw him and ran every test in the book on him. He found an epileptic problem, and his fits were soon under control. He couldn't speak, and they sent him to a school for very handicapped children, you know the locked doors and the special bus variety. But there was always a twinkle in James's eye, and his comprehension was very great indeed, it was just that he would not respond. You know when you're talking to someone, you know they understand in their eyes. Nothing was working, so I resorted to bribery. Smarties at that point were the passport to everything for James, and we decided to do one final testing, simply to please me, when he was about 6. Before we went I'd bought very big tubes of Smarties – bought about a dozen, tipped them all into a washing-up bowl, and said 'Do test,' because he refused to do anything, you see, 'and then when you come home you can have those.' So he did the test. With the result he was transferred into ordinary school, into the annexe. Having not been able to read and write, and just to speak – within, oh, a six-month period he was reading and he was writing. He's now just left school, he's on a work opportunity thing, can make anything with his hands, can read and write as well as anybody else, is obsessed with maps, cartography. Of all my children, if I was going to put them on a scale of worry, James would be at the bottom of it, because James is a very self-contained person, he loves music and it doesn't matter what James ends up doing, he'll be all right – he's comfortable with himself, is what I mean.

Cultural Disadvantage

Not all the gifted young people in the follow-up had developed steadily over the years. Some who had been well advanced and full of promise ten years ago were found to be working at only average level. Could this have been 'early ripe, early rot', the burn-out syndrome? But there was no evidence of that; rather, for some children, progress had been impeded by the circumstances of their lives. There was never an instance of parents who did not love their children or want to help them, but there were parents who were simply not able to provide what their gifted children needed. It was at that point that the school could and should have stepped in, but even when it offered the help, the family culture was not always open to it and so the child missed out.

Families which operate at a low intellectual level show it most notice-ably in the lack of breadth and flexibility in their use of language. A broad language base is vital for building knowledge, yet for some families it seems almost a time-wasting luxury to 'play' with it. For them, com-munication is more practical, sufficient for everyday needs and feelings, but not enough for problem-solving and creativity. Where intellectual stimulation of the young child has a low priority, his or her curiosity is less likely to be appreciated, and spending time reading books and think-ing can be unacceptable behaviour.

It was in this context of being pulled between the two cultures of home and school that nature had played a mean trick on Ann Youngman (gifted, aged 17, at school). She had been born to parents who loved her, but were very different in ability and temperament from her. As communication had become more difficult, she developed some resentment towards them, simply because they could not give her the support and direction she so desperately needed. She knew it, and did not like herself for those feelings, but she was slowly beginning to give in to her home culture. Her grammar school teachers had tried to help this obviously highly able girl, but failed. She told me bluntly:

> I don't like school, so I don't always bother turning up. I used to disrupt the classes, and I was banned from most of them in the end, but I've stayed on because I knew there would be no job otherwise. I've never revised for exams, I don't know how to, so everything I know is from what I remember during class. I just go and do them, and I always do well. I've never had any problems with them.

His home culture had also moulded Duncan Sutherland's low opinion of academic work, though on his intelligence test score he was clearly gifted. His sailor father and his mother, who had left school at the earliest opportunity, worked hard to make their home extremely comfortable. But Duncan said that the television was on all the time and he had to escape to his room to find the peace to think in. His parents loved Duncan dearly and took great pride in his achievements, expecting that he would go far. They told me, however, that they had no idea how they could help him. To cover up his gentler side, Duncan had adopted a tough, macho image, was aiming to serve in the navy, and hoped to fight a war. But as he came to trust me, he told me more about himself.

Duncan Sutherland (gifted, aged 18, leaving school):

> A lot of the teachers had the sense of humour of a rat; they hated me. Simple as that. If someone comes at me, then there would be absolutely no backing down, I wouldn't give one inch. I like going shooting with air rifles. Anything that moves. The television's on most of the day, and I spend most of my time being bored. But if it's something that really needs thinking out, I'll spend about 90 per cent of my time thinking about it. Could be about a week – 90 per cent of a week just thinking! When I was little, I used to remember a story by putting it into a poem or a rhyme. Even though I'll say it with scorn, poetry is the most powerful way of saying something. The last few generations of poets have been really good. You can get more from some of the short poems than you can from a book.

The tradition of Liverpool toughness had also touched Nicholas Fawcett, though he was well aware that his great physical and mental gifts were underused, and that at 21, with already more than fifteen dead-end jobs behind him, he was in desperate need of vocational guidance. His poor self-confidence and lack of sophistication had kept his ambitions very low. His reading was minimal, his television watching desultory, and his only areas of activity were running hard and girlfriends.

Nicholas Fawcett *(highly gifted, aged 21, out of work):*

I always felt that I was one of the school's better pupils, because I was usually in the top set without trying. I never studied, but I knew I could do better than most of them. It might have been the old ego thing, you know. If I turned into a studier and a boffin, all my friends might look at me and think ... maybe it was just a pride thing. It wasn't that I hated school, I just couldn't be bothered. I'd come home and try to revise, but after half an hour I was bored. I'd be sat there looking through a book, and I'd prefer to be outside, physically active. Even so, I still was one of the best in the class, but I thought ... well, sod it ... so I left school.

I know I'm intelligent and capable of doing anything really, with the right guidance. People recognize I'm intelligent. If I'm interested I can concentrate for hours, like when I go training at the gym, I give it all I've got. I didn't leave all those jobs because I didn't like them, I left because I felt that I could have done a better job than the person who's above me was doing. It just didn't seem right. I want to be somewhere at the top. I'm starting to realize that the next job that I get, I'll make a career of it.

P.S. Nicholas answered an advertisement to be an assistant in a small antiques business, learned fast, and loved it, before the firm folded. After that he joined the Foreign Legion, but is now once again unemployed and bored.

Disadvantage through Poverty

Even in a modern industrial society, there are pockets of poverty, and where wealth enables, poverty disables. In a cold, damp home, where the quality of food is poor, illness and low spirits are frequent visitors. All children in those situations suffer, but it is an added detriment to a child of high potential that intellectual stimulation is often inadequate too.

For Dennis Foster, it was the physical aspects of his poverty that were pulling him down. He seemed to have glazed over his exceptional gifts and was working at just above average level. Poignantly, his goal at 8 years old had been the most ambitious of all the sample – to be a tycoon.

The Fosters' house was part of a poor terrace by the railway shunting yard. All the windows were permanently covered with grey rags, admitting just a little daylight. Inside, the floors were bare of any covering, as were most of the walls. Loose strips of wallpaper hung down, and the few ceiling tiles that remained up hung at angles by their corners. Old pink rayon curtains were pinned on the walls here and there, maybe to cover damp patches, and a few family photographs decorated a shelf. Everything was clean, but furniture and possessions were torn and decrepit, and the old display cabinet was quite empty. The room was extremely damp and cold, though they had done their best to warm it, and even during the few hours I was there, I began to feel drawn and listless. Dennis suffered constantly from bronchitis, sinusitis, and other respiratory problems. At 19, he was thin, pale, and a little stooped, with a particularly sweet face.

His parents were courteous and articulate; disregarding their very poor surroundings, they made me feel very welcome. Though they were both heavy library users, neither had sought higher education. Now, Mr Foster was too ill to work, but assured me with pride that he was 'not a scrounger' living off the state, and so was refusing most of the social benefits to which he was entitled. They did what they could for their son with what they had, encouraging him, loving him, and being concerned for his future, but they felt they had little support from his school, which had clearly not recognized his great potential: 'They didn't seem to be bothered about his continuous absences, or his level of work. They seemed to think that because he was keeping up it was all right,' his father said.

Dennis Foster *(highly gifted, aged 19, at college):*

I was always terribly ill. All winter I'd get constant streaming colds and flu, and I'm still not a healthy boy, so I missed a lot of school. And I sleep a lot. At school, I used to turn in the odd decent piece of work to prove that I could, but there was nothing else they could have done with me; it wasn't their fault. School and life were completely separate things to me, though I think my parents feel they've failed me too. I can't remember actually having revised. The exams I did well in were those you can get by on a very small amount of information, things I'd heard in class when I was there. Still, I did get average marks for the class.

I write poems in spurts. Every few months, I write about twenty or so, then come back six months later, rip half of them up and write a few more. I never show them to anybody except a few of my friends; certainly not school. I did send some to Faber and Faber [the publishers] and they sent a letter back saying they might publish some in an anthology, but I haven't heard from them for over a year, so I've given up hope on that. I can't think of anything I want to do, so mostly I lie in bed and think. Then I get really angry because I'm bored.

I hardly ever express anger as I'm terrified of violence of any kind, and generally there's nothing worth getting angry about at a personal level. But I'm depressed a lot of the time, about once a week, and sometimes lonely as well. But I only get really badly depressed about three or four times a year, when I get to an almost suicidal, 'end-it-all', hopeless state. I don't want sympathy off anyone. Deep down, I've still got the feeling that it's going to pass, but it's still not very pleasant. Sometimes I get sucked away in my depression and think, 'Is there no end to it and no hope for the future?' Not on this planet at any rate.

I'd much rather have been a middle-class kid, Edwardian or 1950s. I've got a stereotyped idea from old black-and-white films of lots of rosy-cheeked, post-war boom kids running round brand-new schools and housing projects, all well fed when rationing was over, and it was always sunny and really nice and cosy and middle class.

MISTAKEN IDENTITY

The labelling of children as gifted may be mistaken. Yet it is bound to happen at times, for example, when they are so heavily tutored that they appear to be advanced for their age, or because of their parents' hopes. Such a mistake means that a child is put into the terrible situation of trying to follow a prescribed but impossible role. The awful choices he or she then faces are about the best ways of failing. There are two major options: either to strive ferociously to meet expectations and fail; or to find excuses and fail. Several in this sample had indeed become worker bees, striving against heavy odds for modest results. In one girl's case it had begun to interfere with her health, so that her worried parents had placed an upper limit to her voluntary study of four extra hours a night.

Of the original Target group whose parents had joined the association for gifted children, a few of the children (5.4 per cent) were not found to be measurable as gifted in any way, nor did there seem to be any mitigating reasons for their average-level performances on the tests or at school. The conclusion could not be avoided that they were not in fact gifted. Their parents had joined the association for a variety of reasons: mostly because they thought it would do something for their child, but also because the child was difficult to live with and seemed bright, so they had assumed the cause of the behaviour problems to be giftedness.

Bernard Harrison was certainly of above average ability (aged 20, at technical college), but he had accepted his mother's belief that he was more intelligent than almost everybody else he knew. She referred to him quite simply as a 'genius'. Bernard did his best to comply. But his 'incredible promise' was dealt a blow when he failed the entrance examination for the selective secondary school. His mother told me, 'At the junior school, the teachers treated him as though he was backward. A private education was the only way out. I started going out to work to pay the fees, and continued for nine years. I just couldn't stop thanking them because he was so happy there.'

Bernard's modest school-leaving results were excellent in terms of his measured ability, but he knew in his heart that it was the best he could do. His mother was very proud of him, accepting that the reason for his non-gifted examination performance was that he'd never revised, though she did not say why he had not. Although superficially his self-esteem appeared to have benefited from his being put on a pedestal, he said he'd never had many friends because he was an 'intellectual snob'. He had a very subdued emotional life, living at home, and at 20 years old often fell asleep while watching television.

There were no excuses about her poor examination performance from Anne Charlton, however (above average, aged 16, at school) – her mother provided them all. She could not accept that her belief in her daughter's giftedness could have been a mistake, which had put Anne on the receiving end of constant conflicting messages. At home she was seen as brilliant and failing her mother, but at school she was seen as of average ability with a troublesome mother. Her resulting confusion about her sense of self probably had a negative influence on her growing up, for it was far from smooth.

Mrs Charlton had joined the association for gifted children believing her daughter to be in a state of considerable intellectual frustration at the junior school. Anne, coming from a bookish home, had been an early reader, but that lead did not last. Her failure to get into the selective secondary school, her mother believed, was due to the poor teaching and attitude of the junior school, and to Anne's flu the week before. If they had had enough money to send Anne to the small private school, it would probably have been better for her, but as it was she had opted out of all educational endeavour. Her only thoughts were of boys, clothes, pop music, and the disco every night of the week. It took a lot of persuasion for Anne to take part in the follow-up, and she soon lost interest in considering her answers, though she didn't quit. Since her mother was hard-working and competent, it was becoming very difficult for them both to live together. 'Sometimes,' her mother said, 'I think that somebody swopped babies at the hospital.'

Chapter 3
Growing up Gifted

All young people are likely to face challenges in growing up, but it is somewhat different for the gifted simply because they are exceptional. Although in this sample they were seen to be neither more nor less stable nor morally different, at times they did have to find subtle personal skills to see them through some specific and delicate situations – such as always coming top. The great majority delighted in their high-level abilities of all kinds, but some saw their gifts as responsible for their emotional problems, which had often resulted in poor relationships with others of the same age.

ADOLESCENCE

Learning to be at ease with others starts with the first communication between mother and baby, then develops with increasing contact with the world outside the family. On the whole, human beings stay true to themselves over great lengths of time, continuing to develop the special habits and style they had begun in infancy. At first, children copy the behaviour and attitudes of adults, but as they move into the teenage years, they also blend in the outlooks of their contemporaries. Adolescence, though, is a time of sharpening and defining personal ways of dealing with such matters as work commitment, sexual life, and above all the need for a sense of self in one's family and in society. The greater the feeling each individual gains of being in control of his or her own life at that time, then the more effective he or she will be as an adult. For those with no friends to learn from, the gap in development can be hard to close later.

Every family has a style of operating, in which all the members learn to negotiate for themselves. But the normal restraints in these negotiations may be strained to breaking during adolescence. The reasons are not so much because the young person's moods are different from before, or from an adult's, but because they can alter rapidly and swing to greater extremes of dejection or exhilaration. Adolescents may experience a wider range of short-lived states, more like flashes of emotion. Unlike adults, they are less cushioned in these experiences by the memories of past ones. In the words of one teenager in this study, 'One time, when we went up in the hills, walking, the air was fresh, and I just suddenly felt that it was a really beautiful place. That's all.'

The anthropologist Margaret Mead often pointed out the conflicting messages given to young people in western society: that they should be responsible yet fun-loving, childlike yet mature. Similarly, Erik Erikson (1963), the psychoanalyst, suggested that adolescence was a time of facing the challenge of 'identity' versus 'identity confusion'. The main problem, he said, was the lack of signposts as to how to behave (in western society), which made the aim of 'finding oneself' very difficult. The rocky path from childhood to adulthood is often climbed through hazy parental expectations – 'We don't mind what you do, we just want you to be happy.' Not easy when one is gifted and can do so many things.

For most of the young people in this follow-up study, their growing up was smooth, and their general opinion was that the old *Sturm und Drang* idea of adolescence was highly overrated. Typically, I would be told, 'It's been a lot easier than I was led to expect. At the age of 12 or 13, I thought I'd feel . . . this puberty and all the rest of it . . . what's it going to be like? But I've never even noticed that I was growing up.'

RELATIONSHIPS

Almost all the problems between the gifted young people and their parents were due to the normal reasons of growing up and breaking away. But, as in so many things, the gifted do tend to head for the extremes, and it was not always easy or possible for parents to provide the attention demanded of them. Their children's urgent ideas, which must be discussed the instant they burst forth, did not always come at convenient times. Also, when the highly intelligent get their teeth into an argument, especially with parents who are just as lively, there can be a particularly stimulating intellectual confrontation.

Sharp, articulate words sparked, for example, between Justine Williams, a mature, gifted 17-year-old, and her mother. To Justine, life was a vivid palette of deep issues of morality, justice, and beliefs, which she desperately wanted to talk about at home, especially since her teacher showed little interest in her ideas. The situation had reached a point when neither Justine nor her equally intelligent and outspoken mother felt able to communicate easily. But each knew the situation, her mother saying, 'I appreciate Justine – I don't know whether she does likewise – but I think she finds me very difficult.' On her part, Justine asked me to funnel some of what she wanted to say to her mother because, 'She can't accept that I'm growing up.' I suggested they talk it over directly. Justine's words encapsulate the everyday frictions of growing up gifted; she is wise, understanding, curious, eager to learn, and frustrated.

Justine Williams *(gifted, aged 17, at school):*

> As I get older, I get on less and less with my Mum. I want her to be perfect and she's not because she's a human being. But as she runs my life to a certain extent, it's important to me what she thinks and does. She doesn't know how I think; she's been too busy. She comes home from work and reads the paper, and I resent that she doesn't ask me what I've been doing. If I say something thoughtful, she's so sarcastic – 'Stop trying to be profound.' If I tell her that she's been bad about bringing me up in some ways, then she calls me arrogant. I don't know where I'm up to really.

Feeling Different

Throughout this study, those in the top 1 per cent of the IQ range had said they felt different, at a high level of statistical significance. For most, the gifts which made them different were a source of pride and pleasure, just like any other blessings of nature: 'To be quite honest, I'm quite proud of the fact that I'm brighter than most others. If you've got good looks you might as well enhance them, so if you've got intelligence you might as well let everybody know it.'

Parents saw the feelings of difference as starting very early in life and suggested that the bad aspects were due to other people: 'Alison was always top at school, so some parents counted their child's order in the class as though she wasn't there. She used to keep her hand down in the class, things like that, so she wouldn't stand out.' But those less happy aspects usually diminished with growing up and the increased freedom to choose companions more like themselves: 'When I was about 15 or 16, it was the academic side that made me different, but now I'm a student with other students. OK, there are some of us who are at polytechnics and some at universities, but we're all going for degrees, so I don't come into contact with many people that make me feel noticeably different any more.'

For just a few of the gifted young people, though, life had compounded those early feelings with some extra problems, and the combination was much harder to cope with. The outcome was not so much dependent on reasoning power, but on circumstances, such as how early in their lives the trouble had started, and how long it had taken to erupt.

Andy Spurgeon handled his many differences with skill and sophistication. He was an intriguing youth of 17, with grey eyes, long dark lashes, and an easy, friendly smile. He was dark-skinned and thick-set like his African father, though his brother and sisters were slender, pale, and very blond. Andy and his mother were good for each other, and she had given him enormous emotional and intellectual support, as well as an exceptionally long rein of freedom to be himself. The family had come up in the world: three generations out of the workhouse, through the grammar school, to his mother's Master's degree. And now there was Andy, brilliant in everything he touched.

Andy Spurgeon's mother:

From about the age of 3 he was very difficult, tremendously aggressive; it was dreadful if he was crossed. The child psychologist said he was just very frustrated. But he was living in a household that was offering him books, music, theatre visits, stately homes, swimming, tennis, people who talk and are lively. I think that when our marriage was going downhill, I had been trying to keep him quiet, avoiding the issues which were more between his father and him really than with me. He certainly got better once we were divorced.

Now he's just argumentative, mostly about what he considers to be my very untidy and illogical mind. He has no false modesty at all about his. I end up shouting at him that he's overbearing, arrogant, etc., etc.

But I don't think it's as much to do with adolescence as to do with him and me. He said that he was living in a nest full of feminists and he would report us to the social services for maltreating him – not valuing his male personality!

It's not only the supreme self-confidence and his brightness that makes him different; it's also the fact that he's black, half-caste as it were. And also in the past year, he's decided that he's gay – and his is a very macho, male school. When he first told me, my reaction was 'Don't be so silly, of course you're not.' But it's OK now; it isn't a problem to me any more, though I am anxious about the AIDS thing, and the exploitation of young people. You'd think it would be quite a load, with his colour and his sexual preference, but in fact, he hasn't presented me with that problem at all. He's perfectly happy.

Andy Spurgeon *(highly gifted, aged 17, at school):*

I'm not very black, so sometimes people don't notice, and their reaction is surprise because I'm coloured when everyone else in my family is white: it is a bit weird. It's not a nice position to be in, half-caste; I get the whole range of insults that go with it.

But I'm difficult to hurt emotionally. Going through life as somebody who's very good at things, but coloured, I've had to build up defences. When I get to school, I've learned to isolate myself mentally from anything that might hurt me; I just sort of close the door. My music is a useful emotional outlet, and it's also something that I gain emotion from, so it's an input as well. I can please myself quite easily playing the piano, and if I'm angry, it'll help me to control myself and bring myself round.

My home is free. If I bring somebody back to this house, a friend or a lover, they always say, 'Isn't your house amazing, there's so few restrictions?' Even at a younger age where there are often more restrictions, my mother was very loose and let us do what we thought was best. We are all fairly bright and intelligent and trustworthy, and she trusts us. There's a really nice atmosphere here.

What gives me pleasure? You ready for this? Have you got any more tape? Playing the piano, playing the recorder, playing the clarinet, talking to people, reading books, learning new things, experiencing new things, playing tennis, playing badminton, playing squash, playing rugby when I get the chance, playing table-tennis. Going to new places in my personal and everyday life, seeing new sides to people that you didn't know were there before. Everything, everything's something new, there's nothing that I dislike. Watching the leaves on the trees shake about, watching a fly trying to get to the bottom of a flower – just literally anything, because everything has its own relevance, so it's always interesting. Even if I was to go to jail for doing something that I didn't do, that wouldn't be bad, because it would be another experience, another new thing to be interested in, new people around you, and such things.

I used to find it very frustrating that there wasn't anyone at school that I could really sit down and talk to, but now I accept it. I refuse to conform, and I don't like to get drawn into conversations where the limit is sex. Homosexual people are just ordinary people in my experience. Being good at a lot of things seems to be disturbing to other people, and though I might play down 'me' in the introduction into a new group, making myself less obtrusive than I really am, really I'm strongly independent. I'm the type of person that's going to do something, somewhere along the line. Hopefully quite a few things. Yeah, I think I will.

Caroline Hardman (highly gifted, aged 20) must have had two fairy godmothers in attendance at her birth. The good one had given her an intelligence over the top of any scale, and great beauty – a girl with potential to do almost anything in the world – but the bad fairy had given her a terrible burden. In her sensitive early years she had been dealt an intense blow to her sense of worth, when she was effectively orphaned for years by her mother's constant illness, and was cared for by whomever was to hand, while her father worked.

Being intellectually gifted, she had been advanced a year at her highly academic school, but without having the maturity to cope. In addition, travelling to and from school was exhausting – out before 8 a.m., and sometimes not home until nearly 6 in the evening. At the first stirrings of adolescence, her latent distress had erupted to shatter the family's peace. She left school at 16, for a briefly free but disastrous life. Even though she had now come some way back to the educational path, studying at a small teacher-training college, she never studied alone, but always in the company of friends. Although she well knew that they were much below her own level of ability, she seemed frightened by the latent power of her mind, and they helped her to rein it in. Were she to release it, she feared losing their friendship and, perhaps worse, having to face up to herself. But she had learned much from her wild life, and the signs were promising: 'I know I'm on my last chance; if I blow it this time, then that's it.'

Parental Break-up

Since the first part of the study, several of the young people had lost contact with one of their parents through divorce, the boys appearing to take it more to heart than the girls. Two highly gifted boys had been suddenly deserted by their fathers at educationally crucial times. In both cases, the boys' exceptional abilities appeared to have played an important role in those events, certainly in their timing, and possibly in their happening at all.

Richard Neville's father was a college lecturer who had struggled hard to reach his position, and who must have been keenly aware of the importance of examination hurdles, yet he disappeared when Richard was 15 – just two weeks before his son's first vital set of public exams. Indeed, Richard's mother suggested that 'One of the chief reasons for him leaving was perhaps having a son who's bigger, stronger, cleverer and generally more socially effective.'

It was all true. Richard was over six feet tall, handsome, thoroughly charming, and over the top of the intelligence scale. He burned to do better and better, always working to his limits. In spite of being two years advanced at school, and with the handicap of almost three hours' travel a day, he had achieved all A grades in his A-level exams. Although this didn't allow him enough time for friends, it didn't seem to bother him. He had found a girlfriend at Cambridge University who was very like him, even to the extent of cutting down the Christmas vacation break to a few days. He seemed to have the ability, not only to adapt to his environment, but also to get other people to adapt to him.

Richard Neville (highly gifted, aged 19, studying physics at university):

I hadn't known he was going to go. He just said, 'It's like this, son, I'm going away.' It wasn't particularly good timing, but he wasn't going to ruin my chances – they were more important. I retreated into my room, into my revision, and it probably made me do more work, which kept my mind off it. But it was quite difficult for me. All of a sudden I had to do a lot of things myself, and I'd been presented with all the responsibility of my Mum. It was his job and he ought to have done it. For a very long time I was quite angry. But it's a bit like water under the bridge now, though my sister still rather misses her Dad. It had a knock-on effect on personal relationships for a while afterwards, particularly with girls. I became rather sceptical and cynical about the whole idea of marriage and relationships, thinking, 'What's the point, they don't work anyway.' But I've grown out of that now.

Tom Dewhurst used his powerful mind to cope with his father's traumatic disappearance by means of a strongly rationalized defence system. His mother described them as alike – determined and strong-willed – and explained, 'Tom had been really close with his father, and he was only 12. My ex-husband phoned and said he wasn't coming home, and we've never seen him since. I don't suppose I'll ever quite know what really happened.' At 21, Tom was studying medicine, and I could see him as a rather gruff practitioner, well loved by his patients, but not allowing himself much overt sympathy for their worries – a 'pull yourself together' man.

Tom Dewhurst *(highly gifted, aged 21, studying medicine):*

When my father disappeared, I became a bit detached and couldn't concentrate properly at school, but I got used to it. The family – me, my Mum, and sister – we became closer and that helped. I suppose I'm a bit of an insensitive person, things don't normally hurt me, though I have to admit it really did at the beginning. Now, when I look at my life, I don't suppose it's made that much of a difference to me. Just that I feel that I ought to be really sure before I marry someone.

The effect of Adrian Lambert's (highly gifted, aged 22) parents' stormy marriage and eventual break-up had been to cripple his high-level creative and intellectual potential severely. He was a big, cheery fellow who now joked about his ignorance and inability to study. He lived in a tiny terraced house with his fiancée, who had also dropped out of higher education. According to his father, Adrian's disturbed behaviour was the culmination of three generations of unhappiness. However, it seemed more immediate, for in the first part of the study his mother had blamed her attempted suicides entirely on this only child, and told me that she had 'detested him' when he was little. By now, Adrian had managed to exert some control over his three addictions of gambling, drink, and cigarettes. He had been through the worst, was neither flippant nor depressed, but working and aiming to improve himself. What he needed, and what he had organized for himself, was a healing mental peace in his own home.

Adrian Lambert's father:

I'd rather expected Adrian's intelligence to help him understand his mother and her problems, and he did try, until he went bitter, and he still can't forgive. To an outsider, the life my wife led was pretty unforgivable; I have the most enormous amount of tolerance, which bordered on stupidity. The basic cause was that there were so many men in her life, mainly because, poor girl, she was too damn' good-looking. Adrian couldn't take it. It was he who eventually said 'You can't stay here and have that fellow; it's got to be Dad or him.' 'Well, you can't tell me what to do,' she said, and off she went. He has been desperately unhappy. I know that fathers and sons don't often get to talk to each other very deeply, but I have managed to talk to him on a couple of occasions.

He used to have so much imagination as a child, I gloried in his humour and his wit. When he was very young he had read and written a lot, but in his first weeks at the secondary school a most dreadful English teacher made him look a fool in front of the class, and he never wrote another thing; stopped absolutely, even reading for pleasure. I was appalled, because his imagination still shone through.

Adrian Lambert *(highly gifted, aged 22, a milkman):*

My dad cherished the way that I dealt with English; he loved the stories I wrote. I still love writing, though, and I do when I can get round to it. The teachers at my comprehensive were very supportive and encouraging. It was much more than I deserved. They tried everything, even ringing me up at home. I really let them down and I still feel guilty. I was amazed to pass my A-levels, because I hadn't turned up for weeks, so I decided to take them again to improve my marks. I went to see the headmaster, but he treated it as a joke. I didn't blame him. That knocked me back, so that's how I ended up on the dole for the best part of a year. It was terrible and I reckoned that anything was going to be better than that.

Then I enrolled at the Polytechnic, and left after a year by mutual consent. I'd picked the wrong course, History of Art, Design, and Film, and I couldn't draw a stick man, or name ten painters or one designer – I'd never even heard of Turner then. The only thing I knew was ten films that John Wayne had starred in, and what Captain Kirk did in *Star Trek*. I met my fiancée there, so it did do something for me, but not education-wise. Then I decided to earn some money. I was very, very lucky to get this job as a milkman. I'd go into the Job Centre and they'd say, 'You've had no experience,' and also I was competing with cheap

16-year-olds. Fortunately, I knew someone who recommended me – and it's not temporary. I've enjoyed the job a lot. It's a physical release. I can run everywhere, and the faster I go, the faster I'm done. I've got the after-noons free to myself, though I'm zonked out by eight – I'm up at half-three in the morning. I must have a good memory, because this is only my sixth week and I can remember most of the people in over 400 houses.

My mother had left on several occasions when I was a child. I suppose I stored it inside, which is what gave me all the trouble and guilt later on. I used to get very intense bouts of anger. It ended up once in my taking a few tablets, tranquillizers, and booze, or I'd zoom off on my motorbike as fast as it could go. I used to get a terrible feeling of desper-ation. I always thought of myself as very mature at school, and yet I acted very immaturely, but I have eventually developed through the trauma, learnt through experience. It's a pretty weird situation: I'm driving a milk-float round and worrying about what time I'm going to get finished today. How can that be so structured and so definite on this planet, and yet on all the other millions of planets, you've got a simple little amoeba floating around in space? It's such an imbalance. I get so wound up with all the thoughts and theories. It's very much easier to get back to today, driving the milk-float around, and trying to get finished by 12 o'clock. So I concentrate on that.

'Ostriches'

Of the eight gifted young people who said their giftedness was an insuper-able barrier to making relationships, all but one were male. Their loneli-ness could be terrible, and by the time of the follow-up the outlook for its ultimate relief seemed bleak. Like academic ostriches, they had sometimes buried their head in their studies, thinking that the rest of the world could no longer see them.

Sigmund Freud was the first to describe the workings of psychological defences, which these gifted ostriches were hiding behind. These protective emotional strategies are formed when people are up against an anxiety-provoking situation and unconsciously avoid seeing it. Some may simply 'repress' it, appearing to be quite unaware of any criticism; others 'project' the problem on to someone or something else, as in, 'It's not my fault I was late, the traffic was very heavy.' Some bend over backwards to deny any difficulty, like the girl with the limp who wears red stockings, or, in Shakespeare's words, 'the lady [who] doth protest too much'. Although in fact defences are cover-ups for insecurity, they can be decidedly aggressive, in the sense of 'I'll hit you before you hit me'. This, of course, often provokes an angry return, which can send the spiral of relationships spinning downward, the other person's sharp reaction simply convincing the self-defender of the need to keep the barriers up.

The favoured psychological defence of the intellectually gifted is to hide behind a façade of scholarship, so opting out of the normal cut and thrust of learning how to make relationships. Yet, of course, the gifted need relationships as much as any one else. Nor do the carefully devised defences serve to put an end to unhappiness, because the defender is retreating further into isolation, even more disabled by the presented psychological wall itself from reaching out for reassurance, and maybe angrily preventing anyone from offering it. Children in hiding from the threatening world, mingling less and less with others, develop poor feelings towards themselves and others.

For some of the highly gifted young people in the sample, the psychological defence systems they had built against anxiety had started in early childhood. Over the years, their withdrawal behind those barriers had gone to extremes, cutting them off from emotional contact with others. Six young men had gone so far as almost to sever any intimacy with other people – a process which they all blamed on being gifted.

Ian Nicholson's mother told me, 'You'll find him interesting.' Indeed I did, and also gentle, thoughtful and sincere. At 20, Ian was a slim, tall, slightly stooping young man in an old-fashioned dark suit with a plain tie, studying classics at Oxford. He had started to set up his strong psychological barriers against the rest of the world as a very small child. His difficulties in communication, he said, were because he was so intellectual, but he also was aware that he hid behind long words and concepts which his listener might not be able to understand. His brilliance, he thought, was a barrier to any friendship, and although he claimed not to care much about being without a single friend in the world, he seemed distressed while he was talking about it. To protect his sensitivity, his life had become all work and no play. The excellence of his academic work seemed to be his only means of making himself feel worthwhile.

Ian Nicholson's mother:

He's never had a friend, and can go for days without speaking to another soul. His teachers used to say he was a loner. He never even told them when his father died – nobody in the class knew. I've known other boys make friendly advances to him, but he doesn't respond. He's had parents who've loved him, who've been interested in him, and been prepared to spend as much time with him as he wanted. Now he's staying on to do his D.Phil. Another three years at Oxford's just putting off the evil day of coming into the world and having to fight for a living. If he can get a job as a don, I believe that he'll stay in those quarters for the rest of his life.

Ian Nicholson *(highly gifted, aged 20, studying for a D.Phil.):*

The only school activity I was involved in was the Christian Union. I also worked in the school library for six months as an assistant. I had a really good time then.

Even at Oxford I'm conscious that I'm brighter than most people. I also work harder than most, and I tend to keep to myself more than most people. But I work incredibly slowly. At times, it's taken me three hours to read an article, and I wonder where all the time's gone. Having Christian beliefs, where the majority of people do not, and because those matter to me very much, I'm in a radically different set-up from most of the people about me. I was very disappointed that I was not accepted to become a clergyman. My bishop said that although there was the positive factor that I can relate to people and be sensitive to their feelings, the negative factor was that I am very independent and tend to work on my own, and wasn't in a position to cope with a group of people. Obviously, though, I had thought that I could. I suppose that having taken on an enormous workload has meant that I've not had much time to see people. The trouble is that the things which I value seem to be in decline – classics, the Church, railways, the countryside. But then, perhaps I've always had work as a let-out.

The nasty crop of acne which Martin Glaskin was enduring cannot have helped him in his unkind world. He said he did have a friend once. His intense reserve was off-putting to anyone who would have liked to get to know him, and he lacked some basic social graces – such as offering me coffee during the three hours of the freezing morning we were together. Like him, his father was an academic scientist, and of firm views, especially about the roles of males and females. His mother was a house-wife, who always waited for her husband to speak first.

Sadly, each of Martin's academic successes, such as his first-class degree, turned to dust in his hands, so that he needed to go on for more. At 21, and in the first year of his PhD, he was worried that he would not be able to keep up the pace. He found it impossible to envisage the future, and could not even muster some youthful optimism. Even at school he had worked very comprehensively, reading around the subject, writing notes to summarize it over and over again, until he understood the concept behind it: 'I never wanted to know my teachers, I just wanted the instruction.' Now, he had moved even further into isolated study, cutting down on his feelings towards other people, and sliding closer and closer towards the stereotype of the backroom scientist; he peered down microscopes by day and returned alone to his room at night. Yet he never took any steps to alleviate the pain of his sorrow; I felt he was almost wallowing in it, sinking himself deeper and deeper into the mire.

Martin Glaskin *(highly gifted, aged 21, studying for a PhD):*

I feel alienated; maybe I'm too sensitive. If people like me I don't understand why, though I don't usually notice other people's reactions, and anyway, nobody's ever told me anything about myself. I give up very easily in social life, probably because I never concentrate on what people say. I just watch them talking. I know I'm selfish and negative, and a bit of a snob as well. I may be 21, but I don't think I've grown up yet. Getting depressed holds you back. I spend my time on my own really. It's getting worse, and I don't always know that I'm going to come out of it. It's especially bad because I'm not in an environment where I'm forced into contact with people, so I have to go out to find them. If I'm thrown together with somebody I get on with them all right, like I might go out to the pub, unless of course I'm feeling depressed. It's quite a while since I felt angry. I feel disillusioned, and I've given up wondering why I'm here, because it just depresses me.

Just Good Friends

In direct contrast to those sad youths, the majority of the gifted young people had entirely normal relationships with friends of both sexes. Few, however were as gifted as Jeremy Kramer, who seemed to have perfect control over his emotional relationships, as indeed he had over his study habits (see pp. 83–4). He was tall, very attractive, and it was for lack of neither opportunity nor know-how that he had made the decision that, until his studies were more advanced, he would avoid emotional ties with girls.

Jeremy Kramer *(highly gifted, aged 20, studying medicine):*

I made a conscious decision to give up girlfriends – I suppose I've never met one who is quite irresistible. I get all I need in life from my friends of both sexes – apart from physical pleasure, of course. But it's almost as if the only extra thing that a girlfriend could give me is sex. My best friend is a girl, and if I'm worried about something I'll go to her and we'll sort it out – she knows me down to a tee. Any girlfriend's going to get pissed off about the time I spend with her; and it only creates problems. If I do mess around with girls, I make it plain where I stand, and it's worked well for me.

Measured ability, no matter how high, did not affect the majority of the sample in their ability to have good relationships. It was more a matter of outlook: 'I've got some life in me, always something to talk about, and being a lively sort of person, I get along with a lot of people.' What did make a significant difference was respect for others – difficult for some, who saw their giftedness as making them somehow superior. One highly gifted youth, studying physics at Cambridge, spoke for many who, like him, have friends of many kinds and abilities: 'I give my full attention to people, and take them seriously most of the time. But I've got academic integrity, not putting up with second best. I want friends who will stand up to me in conversation, pick me up when I'm being stupid, not put up with idiocy; friends that are stimulating.'

However, the gifted could not always keep to the standard of discourse they would have preferred: 'Small-talk is very boring, and sometimes I don't make the effort.' It could become tiresome, for example, in a mixed-ability school, where being friendly and open to one's classmates was simply not satisfying, at least not all the time, and so some did try to find older friends. Even at the selective girls' grammar school, Justine Williams (gifted, aged 17, at school) said:

I definitely don't like the company of people younger than myself, not even if it's by just a year, because they're going through something that I've already done – been there, done that. At school, in all the corners, everybody, morning after morning, tells you about what they did the night before, and sometimes it gets so boring. It's hard to look interested. Hopefully, university might be different.

Love hit the gifted as it hits other young people. As one bright girl said, 'I thought I'd never fall in love because I couldn't imagine anybody ever liking me, and if they did they'd have bad taste, so I wouldn't like them. But I've overcome that. Also, I just think he's gorgeous. I'm not sure. I think I love him. This is the best yet.'

EXCEPTIONAL SENSITIVITY

It is not easy to live with exceptional sensitivity. The super-sensitivity of many gifted children means that not only may they take modest criticism terribly to heart, but they can also react to a wider range of subtleties. This super-sensitivity can be either encouraged or blunted by ridicule, and for some less robust personalities it can turn inwards from a world which they find too painful to bear. However, it may be that it is a high level of innate sensitivity in infants which itself enables giftedness to develop.

In the first part of the study, even for the youngest children, the higher their IQs the more they said they could see life through another's eyes – the more they could empathize. In the follow-up, the results were less distinct, although the young people's feelings of sensitivity, particularly with regard to other people, still had a positive relationship with IQ scores. Yet, whatever their intellect, that empathy was not available to everyone. Many had not developed enough maturity and self-awareness to feel at ease with other people and still remain whole, so they changed with the prevailing wind; a 17-year-old saying, for example, 'Sometimes I will play the part people expect. I don't really know the real me, I'm not sure.'

It was for some a difficult part of themselves to cope with. Being highly sensitive and passionate, even at 17 David Baker needed to give vent to his emotions. His parents said that he would 'rant' for over two hours – in his articulate way – and cry openly when things upset him, such as a play on television. His prickly, uncomfortable relationship with his mixed-ability school was not eased by his 'arty' style of dressing, for which he was sneered at with some local derogative terms for homosexual – and the barbs stung sharply.

David Baker *(gifted, aged 17, at school):*

I think more deeply than a lot of people, and I feel more than they do. It's as though I had a depth of feeling that has to be used up, though I wish it wasn't like that, because I feel too strongly over people and things. Sometimes I cry or feel incredibly happy over just one thing.

I'm far too sensitive, because it results in depression which is generally self-pity and a waste of time. Loneliness brings on really deep depression almost immediately, even though there might be people all around me, and even while I'm talking to somebody. Half the time when I'm sad I'm enjoying it. It's genuine, though. I lose the will to do things, but I don't get depressed out of laziness, it's just that it doesn't seem to matter any longer. Perhaps it's a desperate need for a rest, because when I'm ready, somebody can say something that can pull me right out of it and make me very, very happy, and very active and animated quickly.

Anger is easier; it generally comes out. At home I can shout and scream, and cry and cry, and really just get it out. Then I'm tired. But life carries on, and I've not changed anything. I just say, 'Sorry,' and I'm annoyed with myself for getting angry.

Sometimes I can feel with people, even without speaking to them, thinking how they think. But I feel very, very different to the people who sit in the school common room. I'll come in after I've had so much fun looking at things, sketching and talking, and they'll say, 'Oh, he must be drunk.' Well, that's partly our school, and it's because I'm so much happier than them, and they don't seem to be able to visualize happiness through thinking and friendship very much. While people grow up, it's essential that sexes are mixed. Essential. It's so sickening listening to the attitudes of boys who are in an all-boys environment. They're so narrow-minded. A lot of my friends are girls, and I find that a bit worrying. You question your identity as a male if you fit in with females. One of my teachers calls me 'a decadent, namby-pamby boy'.

I usually laugh it off as a joke, being labelled 'queer', but it's also an insult, and because I've not fitted in sexually sometimes. I'm not prepared to get off with girls just because it's the done thing. You should be what you are, and I do find some gay men incredibly attractive; not that I'm wildly mad about them sexually. I think they're so sweet and loving and they've got so much, though some of them are degenerate. Gay women are butch and absolutely great. But sometimes two men making love turns my stomach up and I realize it's not natural. It's not something that appeals to me. It's always a good thing if you can find love and it doesn't matter about male or female.

Social giftedness, in the sense of being able to take another's perspective, was measured with children between the ages of 3 and 6. They were asked to think up what someone else would like as a birthday present, and given a range of toys to choose from. The intellectually gifted did in fact make the most correct choices, confirmed by the other child. However, other studies of young gifted children have shown that, although they score higher than average on the theoretical understanding of moral reasoning, as measured by tests, their playground behaviour was not necessarily on a par. It was rather more, 'Let's share: I'll go first' (Abroms, 1985).

Those in this sample who said they used empathy consciously and frequently in their daily lives were most often the intellectually gifted. Some used it in their studying, though only for the arts subjects. For example, in English:

I'm very empathetic, so that when I read a really good novel, I experience it as though I were there. So whatever I've read about, I've experienced. I care very much about almost everyone I meet, even people on a bus. It's very strange. I've always thought that was why I could comfort people. At school, girls came to me with their problems. Maybe it was because I had a very happy outlook, because I had a basically happy life.

And in history:

I'm pretty good at empathizing. You have to do that to exist in harmony with people around you. To understand someone, you've got to see things from their point of view. That's why I'm so good at history; I empathize with times past and also with the people from them. And you've got to do it then with a restricted amount of information, because you're never going to have as much information as you do about a person who's standing there.

Quite a few used the ability to help others:

When I'm helping someone, the quality I have is in not saying, 'Well, if I were you I'd do this,' it's because I *am* them, so I'm thinking exactly the same way that they think. It's different for every person, so I'd give different advice in the same situation. That's why it always seems to work.

This positive use of her exceptional sensitivity, in the form of empathy, had provided one girl with a way to make relationships and keep her serenity in a mixed-ability school. Suzanne Murphy, with an IQ over the top of the scale, was beautiful, with a pale, clear complexion, and a gentle but firm demeanour. She was working to full capacity and radiated happiness, which she distributed generously to all who needed it.

Suzanne Murphy *(highly gifted, aged 16, at school)*:

Everybody comes to me with their problems and I help them sort them out; in fact, I'm a bit like an agony aunt at school. I'm a believing Christian, so I try to put other people first. I try to understand things from their point of view to be able to comfort them, and if I'm truly patient I always can. Often, I can identify so closely with people who are in trouble that it really upsets me, even moves me to tears sometimes.

I work hard for things I feel strongly about. For example, a lot of my friends smoke and I won't tolerate that. I've managed to persuade my choirmaster to cut down from twenty to two or three a day. And if people start smoking, I'll just walk away and they know why. I do get angry at times, but then I try to look at myself and ask why I'm feeling so angry, and what can I do about it. Am I just being impatient or silly? It calms me down. When I was younger, all I could see was what was happening to me, and I used to feel – 'poor little me'; but now I can look at how other people feel, and try to take that into consideration. If people really tried, they could get on.

BOREDOM

Boredom drains energy, detracting from the ability to cope, and certainly from the ability to strive. Most children experience some boredom at school, as in everyday life, some just filling in time: 'In lessons, I draw, write a bit, think, and daydream a bit.' Being bored is after all a state of mind, which can be felt by some in situations which are exciting to others. But it can become developed in early childhood to the extent that the habit of expecting boredom stays through life and lowers achievement.

The intellectually gifted can have special problems of boredom because of the speed of their learning; that is, in coping with the 'three times' problem of teaching repetition. (See p. 123.) But the results from the first part of the study showed that it is unlikely to be a major difficulty for them, unless either they are unhappy because of home circumstances, or the school is too rigid to accept them for what they are. In that first survey, only six parents from the 210 families said their children were constantly bored at school, and those children spanned the ability range. Not one of the children complained of it specifically. In fact, as they were growing up, the young people complained far more about boredom at home than at school: 'I'm often left in the house bored stiff with only my Mum and Dad for company.'

Looking back, most of the young people felt that any childhood boredom at school had eased off: 'The further back I remember school, the more boredom I remember, because I was enjoying fewer subjects then.' Others expressed longing for their earlier simpler lives: 'When I was younger I used to be very happy sitting down with a book. Now, I haven't time to do that, so there's more potential for being bored.' But the boredom they described was well within the normal range, even for those who had it badly: 'I get bored at school, I get bored at home, and I get bored in the holidays because since we moved to the country there's nothing to do.'

In general, it was difficult to conclude that these gifted young people were more or less bored than others of their age. But far more high achievers reported the feeling of 'let-down' which can come to everyone at the end of hard work completed, with the release of tension and the sudden vacuum of time – a well-known aspect of stress in the business world. It came to many in the sample who had worked hard for a project or after examinations, and it was sometimes seen in terms of boredom. It was described by many:

The harder I work, the more bored I get when I stop, if you know what I mean. Like after exams, I've worked like mad, and I'll go straight down to the pub, put down a couple, and think what the hell am I going to do now? I can't seem to strike a balance between working too much, then not having enough to do and getting bored.

That let-down which masqueraded as boredom could also come in a more extended way to those at university, particularly those who had been heavily tutored, devoting so much of their young lives to getting there:

At school I was occupied, then I had my homework to do, so I didn't get a chance to be bored. Now, when I can't think of anything I want to do, I walk around Oxford for hours feeling bored. It also happens to me frequently during the holidays. That's when I tend to be lazy. But if I was forced to do something, told to 'Go and do that, now!', the feeling might leave me again.

LEADERSHIP AND MORALITY

Gifted children are sometimes described as the leaders of the future (Sisk and Rosselli, 1990). That is why they are said to need special education, to help them acquire the understanding and skills needed for those later roles. In America there are leadership courses, though Europeans, several times bitten, are shy of the idea that any children should be trained to lead. From earliest childhood, the gifted leader is supposed to show enthusiasm, easy communication, problem-solving skills, humour, self-control, and conscientiousness, as well as very high intelligence.

There is also a frighteningly implicit assumption that children of exceptional intellect are somehow morally superior, and therefore better suited to be leaders – although history has never supported that belief. In fact, some intelligence tests, such as the standard Stanford–Binet, present questions with a built-in moral code. For example, 'What ought you to say when someone asks your opinion about a person you don't know very well?', to which the answer is that you do not gossip; or 'Which girl is prettier?', where one is pictured as wild and one is preppy neat; or 'Give two reasons why children should obey their parents': the alternative choice of disobedience is clearly not imaginable. It can sometimes be better for a child not to obey parents, such as in a criminal family, or when being sexually abused by a parent. Child abuse carers are actively teaching children that they have the right to say no. You know the answer you are supposed to pick, and if you want the mark you play the game; your taste is irrelevant.

There is, however, the alternative myth about gifted children – that they are morally more fragile, so that if they are frustrated by an inadequate education they will surely fall prey to delinquency. This argument does not hold water because the relative number of delinquent gifted children is no greater than in the rest of the population, and the likelihood of all gifted children receiving a totally fulfilling education is not high.

When I asked the whole follow-up sample about their religious beliefs, two-thirds told me that they prayed in private, but they often explained that their idea of God was more of a general life spirit than a 'sentient being' who listened in. Many said they did it as a good-luck device, which could do no harm. Although religious beliefs in my sample were not related to intelligence, whether they were believers or atheists the gifted were often more intense in their choice. Those of nearer average intellectual ability were far more likely to push such questions aside as beyond them and accept, at least overtly, what they were expected to believe.

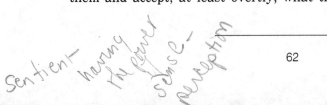

Sentient – having the power of sense – perception

However, the ability to think and act independently of the crowd is an aspect of leadership which several of the intellectually gifted in my sample were aiming for quite consciously. Those young people spent time in deep and critical consideration of the ideas they had been given, and they worked independently and honestly towards living by their own principles, to a greater extent than the non-gifted. But in doing so, many had discovered that it brought them relationship problems – they felt they could see things so clearly, which others could not.

Andy Spurgeon *(highly gifted, aged 17, at school):*

The outlook of really bright people is never going to be the general view. Just by virtue of being brighter, they're operating on a different level, more interested in what's going on around them. I'm different because I think more than other boys my age, who tend to take things at face value, views which are strengthened by the establishment, and school in particular. It's important to me to be honest, and if asked, I'll always say what I think or what I feel – and quite often when not asked! But more importantly, I'm honest to myself, I know what I can do, what my limitations and my abilities are, and what I feel within myself. And if I were to suppress what I am in order to be part of the group, I wouldn't feel happy with myself.

It is said that you can't put an old head on young shoulders, but someone must have done it for Quentin Cooke. He was a round, beaming teenager, with the manner of a bank manager who knew what was best for you. However, it did not seem to me to be his advanced moral thinking which had denied him friends, but rather his general lack of tolerance.

Quentin Cooke *(highly gifted, aged 19, at school):*

I often feel that I have a more mature outlook from most people my age. It sounds a terribly high-minded attitude to take, and some people pretend not to understand me, because if they did, then I'd explode all their myths about their petty little values. Sometimes it seems that the only way that everybody agrees is when they all disagree with me.

He certainly stuck to his guns, whether from moral and physical courage, or from a defensive inflexibility born of fear. His mother described what would happen:

He was always morally two years ahead of any of his peers. Where they were still hitting each other for fun, Quentin had worked out that this was silly. He used to try and reason with them, but they didn't know what he was talking about. So while they were hitting him, he was busily pointing out the reasons why they shouldn't.

Danny Smith had a very different personality, lively and laughing a good deal. But although less dogmatic, he had similar social problems because of his principled moral outlook. As he spoke, he seemed to be trying out ideas with me, not only to see how I reacted, but how it sounded to his own ears.

Danny Smith *(gifted, aged 17, at school):*

I don't think I'm any better or any worse than other people, and I don't like to blow my own trumpet, but – you're lowering my barriers of modesty here – I'm a devout humanist, and I don't think many other people are. If people would be nicer to each other, the world would be a much happier place. People have got a lot within them, but they just won't show it. I try and bring it out, you see, and that lays me open because boys like to make out that they're big, hard, and tough. If you're more gentle in your feelings, you're more vulnerable. I'm quite willing to accept it, because I'm trying to show them there's a better way – you don't need to be horrible to people. But I have very few friends at school, and at times no friends at all. I'm trying to be honest with myself. That's a big thing of mine. Everybody's unique and personal, though sometimes it's very hard to see where they're coming from.

P.S. Danny has since gone on to study psychology at university.

There is no evidence that morality and IQ are related. Indeed, neither extremely high scores on a paper-and-pencil test of morality nor a high IQ score will serve to keep an individual on the straight and narrow, although all children become somewhat better at aligning their moral reasoning and social behaviour as they grow up. In spite of my closeness with these young people, I would not be prepared to hazard a guess at which of them, of any ability, were on the way to leadership. The lessons of history show that it is something which results from the interplay of circumstances and constitution. Poignantly, there were no differences in outlook across the sample when asked whether they thought they could help in any way to change the world. Most felt helpless.

Chapter 4
Inside Gifted Minds

The highest intellects, like the tops of mountains,
are the first to catch and to reflect the dawn.

THOMAS MACAULAY IN *SIR J. MACKINTOSH'S HISTORY OF THE REVOLUTION,*
JULY 1835

The major difference between the very highly intelligent and others is in the way they deal with information, usually from an early age. They can often take an overview of the best way for them to work (metacognition), and so can marshal their intellectual forces with greater flexibility and speed to be at their most effective. This is particularly advantageous for flying through both exams at school and projects in adult life, but it can cause frustration when the learning environment is inadequate for its exercise and development. Some gifted children, though, may need assistance to function at their best because circumstances detract from both their energy and positive attitudes to learning.

TYPES OF THINKING

All babies have to organize their mental experiences in memory, in order to cope with them. But it may be that gifted infants, whose supersensitivity intensifies their awareness, have to manage an exceptional amount of incoming information. They would then need an appropriately more complex or advanced system of mental organization than their baby age peers in order to reach the highest levels of thought and performance of which they are capable.

The process starts for everyone with the accumulation of 'bits' of unconnected experience, and as the mental collection expands, it is sorted into more manageable 'chunks' of connected knowledge. With growing expertise and associations between the chunks, knowledge is further clustered into wider relationships, which are stored in memory as 'schemas'. These active bundles can then be used as a whole for reference, without each bit or chunk having to be considered separately.

Schemas

This is how individual accumulations of knowledge are stored, in schemas, varying from general ideas abstracted from experience, to specific memories. The more intricate the degree of understanding required, such as of a mathematical concept, the further it has to be classified into more and more detailed arrangements. Schemas filter and guide the way children and adults see and think, affecting decisions, and are thus the blueprints for action.

For the most efficient learning, schemas must stay flexible, so that new experiences can be fitted in and the old learning adapted to them. This is the active way in which understanding grows (Piaget, 1971). But this intellectual processing is not confined within children's heads, because they live in a social world and are involved with the people around. Each child interprets experience through the framework of the way he or she lives at home, within his or her culture (Nisbet and Shucksmith, 1986; Vygotsky, 1990). A flexible outlook enables information to be used creatively in a wide variety of places and problems. It also helps in working with others, in such basic ways as children coping with differences between teachers and their methods.

However, schemas which were once useful can become too rigid to be changed by new learning. Young children, for example, usually understand women in terms of their mothers who care for them. But should the child's schemas in this respect become rigid, either for lack of any alternative experience in a strictly divided society, or from fear of change, they may continue to see women's role as stereotyped in those ways. Another example of an emotional schema is one of obedience, which may be useful in some early childhood situations. But if it is prevented from developing, and becomes fixed, personal development may become so limited that thinking a situation through and making one's own decisions is not really an option. This happens to young children who must earn by working, maybe as indentured labour, as they are in many parts of the world.

How well new situations can be smoothly interpreted and integrated in successful learning depends not only on a set of flexible, accessible schemas, but also on a solid and growing knowledge base. Should either be limited, learning is less easy. This can happen when a child from a home which has a low level of school-type learning starts school and where the teaching does not take this into consideration and make allowances, so that lessons are set too far from his or her understanding and may not be properly absorbed. Exactly the same kind of thing can happen when a highly achieving gifted child jumps a year or two in school and so misses a vital part of the coursework. It was one of the reasons why several of the undoubtedly gifted young people in this study had not achieved their expected results in the school-leaving exams.

Strategies

The next stage in the organization of mental operations is the formation of strategies. These are active sequences of schemas aimed at a goal, and the more efficient their design, the more effective the effort to reach it. The most valuable and sophisticated strategy for all mental purposes is metacognition. This is the overall awareness of one's intellectual assets, such as concentration and memory, as well as how they work best, which enables them to be used most productively. The study showed that the intellectually gifted had a high degree of such awareness, and were often able to function nearer their best for more time than the others. The brightest could sometimes describe in detail how they managed their mental learning resources, and what they did to improve their learning strategies. The most successful examinees also knew about the importance of involving the whole self – intellect, emotion, and body – in their learning.

All children ought to but rarely do acquire the level of insight of this gifted mathematics student at university:

> The secret of my learning is that I've got to understand what I'm doing. For me, there are two approaches to work. If it's a subject that bores me or a problem I find difficult to understand, I know I have to plough through it, referring to notes and back, just learning by heart. But if it's something I enjoy, like maths, I just sit back, look for the important points, and I can do it.

Good strategies, like the schemas they are made of, must stay flexible and open to changing circumstances. Competent planning for learning involves choosing from different possible strategies, and perhaps even rehearsing them mentally to see how these feel for a particular task. Indeed, the highest level of planning starts out in a broad and generalized way, but has a variety of sub-plans available to be tried out. The most frequent strategy used by the successful young people in this study was to look for the principles in their work first, and then fill in the details appropriately. To do that calls for the confidence to take an authoritative overview of both the subject under consideration and one's own mental approach. Such a gifted flexible learner, studying medicine, told me, 'I'm a great believer in trying to find a rule that makes things work. I can very often remember the principles first time through. I certainly avoid learning things by rote.'

In fact, once mental strategies have been found useful, people often find it quicker and less mentally energy-consuming to stick to well-entrenched pathways of thinking. A typical example is using tired stock responses in conversation, instead of really considering what has been said. Many people find this useful at times, because they can follow their own trains of thought while responding politely. The intellectually gifted, who are much better at following more than one idea at the same time, may be tempted to use it too much, getting into bad conversational habits which distance them from other people – possibly the root of the absent-minded professor syndrome.

Not all the outstanding young people used their mental capacities efficiently. To different degrees, about a dozen had allowed their study habits to become rigid, and relied heavily on their exceptional memories in a relatively superficial and unthinking way. Samantha Goldman was well aware of doing it, and it did give her the school-leaving results that she wanted at the time, the highest in the sample. But her poor metacognition, that is her lack of awareness of how best to use her power-ful mind, showed up when she had to survive on her own at university and find things out for herself.

Samantha Goldman *(highly gifted, aged 20, studying science at univer-sity):*

People say I'm weird because I will think of something which will remind me of something else, then my mind will go racing along the new train of thought. I'll arrive at an observation which has got no relevance to anything that anyone else can see. It's a handicap when

spurious —
not
genuine
pretended

I'm trying to learn, because, say I'm looking something up in an index, I'll be triggered into finding something else to look up, but then I won't get back to the original thing for hours. I still have to rely on my memory.

As Samantha had demonstrated, though a learning strategy may be inflexible and inefficient, such as too much reliance on memory, with enough effort it can produce good achievement in exams. Rote-learning, memorizing pages of information, is still common in schools, especially in developing countries. It is not only inefficient in the long term, but boring. Its attraction is that it appears to take less effort, certainly for the teacher. It also offers an immature, spurious emotional security, in that the pupil does not have to make his or her own learning decisions, but only reproduces what an authority such as a teacher or textbook writer has said. In the anxious run-up to exams, even the most sophisticated thinkers in this study sometimes abandoned their valuable, higher-level strategies for a frenzied, indiscriminate search through their notes.

The effects of hiding from his emotional self in the false security of such rigid learning strategies had become a longer-term problem for Raymond Grey (highly gifted, aged 20, studying physics at university). His anxious personality and natural reserve had been clear at our first meeting when he was only 10 years old, and it appeared to have been reinforced by unrelieved academic pressure at school. No one there had ever helped him develop feelings of competence in himself, or the skills to use his extremely high potential in a flexible and productive way. As a science specialist, he had been advised to drop all the arts subjects, and so had developed little insight into or love of the more creative aspects of life. His responses to my wider questions about how he saw life were often simple and immature, though commenting on his experience of being advanced two years at school he said, 'It's not a good idea, no.' Even at university, Raymond was despondent about what he felt was missing from his life, so much so that he was considering dropping out before his finals. Nor had his study methods improved: 'I don't read textbooks: I'm not very good with them. My notes are so vast, 50 pages of dense writing. I go through them again and again, just writing down occasional sentences. I learn all those, and then go through problem sheets and exam papers.'

Alternately, the gifted are sometimes faced with the temptation of frenetic mental activity, which may not appear to be to any productive purpose. It seems to happen when the emotional part of a person becomes either disregarded or actually crippled, as though it were irrelevant to the individual's thinking and creativity, almost as though someone has become just a brain physically supported by the rest of the body. Such a person can enter a maze of ideas, developing theories and sub-theories which have no useful function other than intellectual exercise. William Sidis, the American genius who supposedly had one of the highest IQs ever measured, found himself trapped by such mental convolutions. His upbringing had led him to believe that he was only valued for his intellect, compounded by the devastation of his peace of mind through his fame for being brilliant. His relatively little productive work has not stood the test of time (Wallace, 1986).

This emotional inhibition can be seen in many good school learners as they go through life, keen to show how much they know by answering other people's questions, as on quiz shows, rather than creating ideas. Some devise exquisite intellectual manoeuvres, especially on computers, in the way one lonely, 14-year-old, gifted boy described:

> I learned to program when I was 8. Now, I'm working out a formula to translate into computer language. It's quite a simple program, finding elements in Pascal's triangle. But the thing that made it a lot more complicated was that I wanted to do it for very large numbers, so it required a different method of storage from the ones the computer actually provides for you. At the moment, I'm working on a version of Manic Minor, a computer game on a large scale with 50 different screens. I invented a card game once called Seven Card Wiggle and typed the rules for that, which I don't think I'll ever finish because there are about 7,000.

The 'Figaro Gift'

In Rossini's opera *The Barber of Seville*, Figaro the barber describes in an aria his successful efforts to attend to the demands of his many customers at once – obviously a gifted man, though he found it difficult. He was working at the intuitive end of the thinking spectrum, of which the opposite dimension is analytical thinking. At each extreme, information is processed differently, although most intellectual activity uses an amalgam of both kinds along the spectrum, along with all the varieties of schemas and strategies that are available (Schofield and Ashman, 1987):

- Analytical thinking (successive processing) uses information in a time sequence. One thought must follow another, each link in the chain of reasoning being dependent on the last. It is slow because, although it uses only a limited amount of information, the thinker has to keep it all in mind while working with it. It can also produce large errors, because a contradicting detail or a missing link can break the thread of an argument. An example might be planning a journey by working out a bus route with connections quite accurately, but without considering the train service, which is direct.

• Intuitive thinking (simultaneous processing) is when all the parts and relationships between the elements are worked with together; the city's whole transport system as well as alternative possibilities. This includes planning and decision-making, and implies the ability to overview one's own thinking – metacognition. Truly intuitive thinking works like perception, in the sense that 'A picture is worth a thousand words'. It is fast and impressionistic, without the person being conscious of all the details of what is going on. In processing information simultaneously, there is no limit to the amount that can be called upon. Indeed, it demands a bird's-eye view of all the ideas on the subject that could be relevant, including one's own feelings about it. Luria, the Russian psychologist, suggested (1984) that it is a powerful sign of intellectual maturity in children, because it is more like the mental processing of adults.

In the first phase of this research, all the children had been asked whether they could follow and cope with two or more things at once – that is, whether they could process them simultaneously. Of those with an IQ of more than 141, 43 per cent said they could – almost twice the proportion claimed by those with IQs of between 97 and 140 (24 per cent). Ten years later, when they were asked the same question, the results were much the same. The higher the IQ of the young people, the more likely they were to say that they were able not only to give attention to more than one thing at a time but to process them together. However, this was sometimes frustrating for them when listening to several people, as they could not physically answer them all at the same time.

Almost all the young people of average ability had found it extremely difficult to take an overview of their learning processes, and none had been given any help from their teachers in attempting it. Many of the more average ability young people described it like this unskilled worker: 'I used to read a book, close it, then try to write the stuff down. Then I'd open it up to see if I was right, and invariably find I was wrong. On the odd occasion, I spoke into a tape but I found it did me no good at all. I'd go off by myself, working up in my bedroom shut off from the television, but I still wasn't very good at revising, so I used to walk out of the room and forget it.'

Not only did the youngsters of very high IQ appear to be distinctly better at simultaneous processing than the others, but in the whole sample, significantly more of the girls (86 per cent) claimed this Figaro gift than the boys (66 per cent). This ability of females to do many things at once has been recognized in many studies, and is probably partly learned. Among these young people, for example, the education of the brightest boys was often in selective, academic, single-sex schools, which usually have a more funnelled, achievement-orientated approach to learning. The education which the bright girls received was much less specialized, enabling them to range more broadly. In the same way, children from homes which encourage intellectual growth and experiment would be expected to be better at processing ideas together than children from poor or rigid cultural backgrounds.

The ability to work in several areas at once is useful in both intellectual and practical ways.

Sarah Mortimer (highly gifted, aged 20, studying computer systems engineering at university):

I often do two things at once. Right now I'm building a synthesizer, so I've got piles of components and bits of things to stick to this piece of board. Unfortunately, as I haven't got them all, it's a bit difficult trying to imagine where they're going. I've brought it home to do, so I do it while I watch television. I like to have something on in the background, because it's a boring job; the first component in is much like the eightieth component in.

The efficiency of how one uses available mental resources shows up best in a novel situation. That is where the gifted are most likely to shine in their capacity to combine a speedy overview and go on to form an effective strategy, as well as in the ability to monitor their own performance. Indeed, the American psychologist Robert Sternberg (1986) suggested that the main difference between the intellectually gifted and other children is in the way each gets hold of and carries out a new task. The adult-like planning competencies of the gifted are often noticed by teachers and parents, and are probably the major reason for their greater speed in problem-solving. But this exceptional facility may not work for all kinds of planning. It is important for adults to understand how an individual learns and thinks, so that in an educational situation, each learner can work in a style which best suits him or her. It is not that a teacher has to adapt to each pupil's personal style, which would be impossible in a classroom, but that each pupil should have enough freedom to learn to some extent in their own way.

Speed of Thinking

Some psychologists, such as Hans Eysenck (1985), have said that the level of intelligence can be measured by its speed, either by electro-encephalographic traces of brain action, or from how quickly people can discriminate between similar test signals. It is indeed true that a high proportion of these gifted young people could think very rapidly.

Sarah Mortimer was a highly gifted girl who could not only process many ideas at once (above), but had also taken full advantage of her ability to think at speed. She knew her learning style and the subject area in which she worked best, was fortunate in finding herself in all the right places at the right times, and made the most of every opportunity. She lived in an intellectual home, where there were many books, a few choice antiques, musical instruments, audio-tapes, and records. Her parents listed their hobbies as walking and reading. In the average home I was often welcomed with, 'Make yourself comfortable,' and, 'Would you like a cup of tea?,' but in Sarah's home I sipped my dry sherry and enjoyed a hail of questions and suggestions about the research.

As well as having highly intelligent, supportive parents, she went to a school where her brilliance and hard work were recognized and handsomely provided for. At university, she was the youngest as well as one of the most outstanding students, enjoying many happy relationships. She was excited there by the fresh rush of ideas and insights, coping with them smoothly, brilliantly, and swiftly. There was a powerful brain at work behind the big specs, under the carroty hair.

Sarah Mortimer (highly gifted, aged 20, studying computer systems engineering at university):

At school, because I was the only one doing further maths, it meant that I went at my own speed, so I would say to my teacher, 'I think I know this well enough now,' and we would move on. We were streamed for the other subjects, but at university it's mixed ability, everybody in one class. There are 25 of us on our course, and we're spread out across the whole ability range. Those who want to work quickly can get on and then take more free time than others. But I'd really prefer to be in a group where everybody wants to work quickly.

I like working quickly. You don't sit next to Sarah unless you want the answer before you've started the problem! I sit there, and the question will be written on the board, and before the lecturer's finished the question, I've started writing. And while everybody else is writing down the first formula, still wondering what to do, I'll say, 'Finished!' But that speed only works for logic and maths because it's numbers and figures and symbols. Something I could do symbolically in a couple of minutes might take me upwards of half an hour to explain to somebody else. Anything where I've got to express my own ideas and explain why something happens, or write an essay, takes a lot longer, because you've really got to stop and think.

There's a work gear and there's a social gear, and I'm almost two different people. It's not difficult to switch, though, because it's very rare to be working hard and then suddenly socialize, so there's always a gap between the two. But if I've been working intensely, like during an exam, when I'm really hyped up, it's quite hard coming down and getting back to everybody else's speed. My thoughts tend to come in big chunks rather than little bits, which means there's a danger of skipping steps – I might have a mistake glaring at me, and not notice it because I've been just too quick. But I find it very hard to stop to think in the middle of a flow. I'd much rather get it down, then go back and check through every step. In an exam, I'll whiz through the paper, spending about two-thirds of the time writing, and the other third going through, checking my answers and often changing things. It's a case of, does it feel right and does it make sense?

The intellectually speedy mind not only showed itself in studying, but in all other aspects of everyday life. As one bright boy said: 'The kids at my school, you knew what they're going to say. So you could get far ahead of them, and just think about anything while you were waiting.'

Andy Spurgeon (*highly gifted, aged 17, at school*), provided more details of the everyday problem:

Oh yes, gosh yes! I not only have to wait while other people understand what I explain to them, but I also have to wait while people explain to me what I've already understood. In an argument or a discussion I'm very fast, and people find that a bit jarring sometimes, so I try to slow myself down occasionally, just to make it a bit easier for them. I always hone my ideas down to a very precise form, and I do get impatient if other people don't get that precision. And it's not for lack of words, I've got a fairly wide vocabularly. The worst thing is when people start saying something, and you understand what they want to say immediately, but they persist because they've got to get that bit out, and you have to come back again when they've finished.

I'm very pleased with my mental abilities really. I'm glad that I can do things. I like being able to sit back and ignore lectures and then do the work. I know now that I do understand things faster than other people. I can grasp things faster, and as a result, I'm usually idling when they're working hard. But it's got that I idle more and they work harder, so eventually they will begin to find the work easier than I do.

Those who were in command of their faculties enjoyed using them, and in doing so seemed to be spurred on to even greater mental agility. None of the speedy ones found it such a handicap in their dealings with other people that it got in the way of good relationships. However, conversing with the mentally quickest of these young people, I found it better to use crisp, short questions rather than lose the last few words in the enthusiastic responses of my listeners, who could not wait for the question mark. It was exhilarating and kept me on my mental toes. Even though they had to be patient with other people at times, it certainly could not be said that their speedy thinking acted as a barrier between the gifted and others.

HOW THE HIGH ACHIEVERS STUDIED

Most research on learning and thinking is carried out in an experimental way, albeit sometimes in classroom settings. Such studies are concerned with how children interact with an exceptionally ordered physical world that follows clear rules. But this is not always in evidence in the normal classroom, and certainly not at home. Such experimental designs are supposed to keep the measurement 'pure', to avoid the influence of the child's personality and social environment. But it is also very much easier for the researcher to carry out experiments which are largely controllable than to study the endless complexity of natural interactions between people.

Mental skills, however, are part of the whole child in his or her life circumstances. They are demonstrated in each one's cognitive style – the way each person approaches experiences, whether emotional or intellectual, practical or academic – one's personal manner of learning. Cognitive style includes personal preferences for the learning set-up, such as working alone or with others, learning by hearing or by reading, choice of subject area, persistence, and the rhythm and length of concentration. It also includes the way that such aspects of learning are used together; that is, with the preferred mental strategies.

Cognitive style can be explained in terms of the relative use of the two sides of the brain, each of which has different ways of operating. The left hemisphere (opposite the right hand) is considered to work in a careful, ordered way, tackling problems analytically (successive processing), while the right hemisphere takes an all-over, more picture-like view (simultaneous processing). Given enough time, students have been found to reach equally deep levels of learning via many different styles, though the more creative aspects of putting that learning into action call for both sides of the brain to be used.

The high achievers in this sample often had a good grasp of metacognition – knowing how they learned – and the ability to use it in ways which suited them. They were often able to describe their cognitive style explicitly, and say how it could affect their results. In that way they were able to harness the mental power they were born with in hard work that was well aimed and coordinated, although very few had been taught how to do it. They were also much more keenly aware of different possible approaches to the work than the less successful students, who had to use more energy to cope in a more rigid way with less information.

It was succinctly explained by Sarah Mortimer (highly gifted, aged 20, studying computer systems engineering at university):

Everyone knows which is the best way for themselves to work. Children have got to choose their own way, otherwise they're not going to do their best, and it may be difficult for them to express themselves in a way which doesn't fit their style. I would have liked the teachers to know what we thought. It would have been nice for us to have been able to say, 'Look, I don't like the way it's done. Is there nothing we can do to change it?'

Learning Style and IQ

It was clear from this study (as well as those of countless others) that the young people's IQ scores, measured in 1974, had provided a reliable and regular indicator of future academic success. Therefore, after investigations with other methods, and in full recognition of the influences of the environment on it, the IQ score was chosen as a basic and certainly reliable measure of intellectual ability. The whole sample was sorted into three groups for comparison: high IQ (140–70), above average IQ (120–39), and average IQ (92–119). (See Table 4.1.)

Table 4.1 *The IQ Groups*

IQ group	IQ range	% of sample
High	140–70	44
Above average	120–39	31
Average	92–119	25

Although all the young people had answered the questions about their mental processes quite independently and privately in their own homes, many of their responses were closely associated with those of others in their IQ group. Statistical analysis showed some associations to be highly significant (1 per cent), so that this relationship was extremely unlikely to have arisen by chance. In line with their IQs, the young people described very different styles of approach to their study.

Concentration and IQ

Concentration is greatly affected by emotion. All children experience potentially stressful events, such as the arrival of a new step-parent, family rows, going to hospital, or moving house. Sometimes those moments of heightened emotion, though they need be no more than people expressing differing points of view, can remain vivid throughout life. But each person reacts differently, depending on temperament and circumstances. Although intellectual growth has even been found to peak in certain situations of mental discord, this is far more usually detrimental. The energy required for a child to keep 'afloat', when disturbed and unhappy, makes it particularly difficult to focus on learning – to concentrate. If this happens early in life, it can put a brake on the formation of good study habits, and a child who has failed to learn them is then handicapped in learning. This is an important reason why nearly all children from emotionally disturbed backgrounds so often fail to develop their full potentials. Instead, a child may exercise his or her talents by becoming streetwise instead of school-wise.

Sometimes the high IQ young people in my study had indeed been ground down by their circumstances, and in their distress they were learning in a much less efficient and productive way than they could have been. The twelve young people who had had a very high measured level of emotional maladjustment in the first survey had all achieved at a much lower level in school than would have been expected from their IQ scores. This was pinpointed in their lessened abilities both to concentrate and to take an overview of the subject matter to be learned. That is, they relied on successive mental processing rather than on exercising their simultaneous processing abilities. Of the well adjusted, 33 per cent said they would usually try to see the whole picture in their studies, compared with only 9 per cent of the least well adjusted.

It was difficult for Helen Sergeant whom I had noted as nervous even when she was 10 years old. Now, although she had a new father (whose name she had not taken), her family was not happy and she had tried to distance herself from them emotionally. In addition, her home was so cold and dank that it chilled even on a warm, summer day. There were packages and parcels all over the house, smelling strongly of damp paper, the bare boards on the bathroom floor were stained, and the badly cracked lavatory had no seat. Because her circumstances were psychologically very painful, she had had to use energy to keep herself mentally steady. She had also partly cut herself off from that pain by escaping into daydreams, but this route had become so tempting and frequent that it was threatening her progress. As a further defence against anxiety, and without the necessary free energy to think around her subjects of study, she had become excessively self-controlled, relying on highly structured successive processing. She was probably the most assiduous worker in the whole sample, though sadly not the most efficient.

Helen Sergeant *(gifted, aged 17, at school):*

I can't just do it in my head. I always feel sleepy the minute I've got to do some work, so I drift off, and realize that I've wasted ten or fifteen minutes. Sometimes I slip into bed for a while where it's warm. I find myself daydreaming, and it gets to be a habit, even during exams where there's terrific pressure, and it can't do my marks any good. When I study I make brief notes on cards, with dates and facts in different coloured pens to emphasize different points. I also record on tape – I read my notes into it, and then listen to it. I read through my notes several times, and the textbooks, to see how they differ. I can't be bothered to think it through, so I try to memorize as much as possible. I write down what I can remember, maybe two or three times, basically learning it off by heart. I then write myself a short point-test on it, and then maybe I do a timed essay. The only thing that gets me through is determination, I suppose.

It was different for most of the high academic achievers, however. They seemed to recognize and use their own optimum rhythm of concentration and relaxation as an integrated part of their study methods. In her crisp way, Sarah Mortimer (highly gifted, aged 20, studying computer systems engineering at university) knew her personal best style of working quite specifically:

I like to work half an hour hard, then take quarter of an hour break – in fits and starts, because that's how I think. When the natural flow stops, I take a break and then come back, and it starts to go again. Probably I don't get through any more work than other people in the same physical time; they may even take less time, because I have to stop quite often. It causes chaos if I'm trying to work on a group project.

The higher the IQ of the young person, the more able they seemed to be at controlling their mental focusing, to use it to prime advantage. While some said their normal span was only a few minutes with constant breaks, others claimed many hours of unbroken concentration. Others described how they could adapt to whatever the circumstances called for, altering the length and depth of concentration appropriately: 'I usually take breaks about every ten minutes. Once, though, I worked from four o'clock when I got home, till half-past one in the morning, and then had my break for tea. I concentrated totally. It was just something that had to be done.'

For most of the young people, of all abilities, their longest concentration span came at times of deep involvement in what they were doing, such as in exams: 'motivated by fear, enveloped in it'. This showed that the potential for deep concentration was present in most of them, but was not always used at other times. The successful students seemed better able to call upon it: 'In music, when you're practising, you simply have to learn to concentrate intensely.' That involvement was clearly described by Sarah Mortimer:

I love what I'm doing; I could do college work till it came out of my ears. I've really enjoyed computer programming and never notice the time when I'm tapping it in, running it, finding a bug, changing something, running it again. I'm just staring at this little screen and watching things run by, and I tend to work all the way through until I suddenly think, 'Gosh, it feels as though I've been here a while.' Sometimes it's twice as long as I thought it was. I sometimes talk like that too – once I get going, you can't turn me off!

But whatever the rhythm or the reason for concentrating, overall, the higher the young person's IQ, the longer the span they were able to manage. The relationship between IQ and length of time concentrated is very close indeed (see Table 4.2).

Table 4.2 *Q: What's the Longest You Have Ever Concentrated?*

Mean IQ	Concentration (hours)
144	4 or more
138	3
131	2
124	1

Many had their longest spells of concentration in the activities they chose to do outside school. At 16, Derek Girling (highly gifted, working for an electricity company, aged 23) longed for a car, but his parents had said no. However, his mother told me that on returning from her work one day, she found a battered wreck in front of the house with Derek underneath it poring over an instruction manual. His mechanical skills had come entirely from such reading, since there was no one who could tell him what to do. He took nearly a year to put that one right, then sold it at a handsome profit, afterwards going on to other cars. He loved it: 'I've spent spells under the car of four or five hours at a time without coming up for air.'

Andy Spurgeon *(highly gifted, aged 17, at school)* found that his exceptional ability to concentrate had unexpected effects:

My concentration span is at its longest when I play music, like the length of Mozart's Piano Concerto Number 21, because then I can completely lose myself. I'm sure I could go longer, but it's difficult to say how long your concentration lasts, and how much you're actually just playing by memory without having to concentrate too much on it. I used to stay on after school to play the piano. Once, I got so carried away that by the time I'd reached the front door there were enough alarm bells going to wake the dead. I was in a quandary then whether to stay and wait for the caretakers to come and shout at me for not leaving – although really they should have cleared me out – but in the end, I climbed out a window and ran away.

Most of the highly able had taken their lifelong ease in concentrating for granted, though the assumption that it was always available caused some problems when extra mental discipline was needed for higher-level study.

Gina Emerson *(highly gifted, aged 19, studying English at university):*

This last term at Cambridge, I've found concentration incredibly difficult. It's very irritating, because I'm not used to it. I sit in the library for three hours and I think I'm working, but I know that I'm not. I read the things we're told to read, but I don't get inspired and write impassioned essays, which everybody else seems to be doing. It gets vaguer and vaguer and less and less controlled as I go on, and I find I have to discipline myself more than I used to. I feel much less intelligent than I was about ten years ago. Even in concerts now I don't concentrate for a second together on the music, because I'm thinking about other things, like what I'm going to say to the person next to me when it finishes. I have too many things in my mind at once. I'm always thinking a bit about what I'm going to do tomorrow and why I didn't do the washing-up tonight. But reading novels, I do really get carried away and then I'm shocked that it's 2 in the morning.

Redundancy Control

The ability to concentrate is influenced both by the amount of distraction around and by how much one can resist its intrusion – 'redundancy control'. Background noises like traffic or soft music can be used to absorb emotional responses, leaving the mind free, though they have to be carefully controlled: too much, and they compete with what one is trying to do. The most successful achievers appeared to be better able to adjust their learning environments for prime effectiveness, using the type of redundancy control which suited them. The academically less successful, though, appeared to be less aware both of the variety of options and of what would best suit them.

Many successful students chose music to blanket intruding, unexpected noises: 'It blocks out all other sound, and I start associating music with work; certain pieces even with particular exams.' Others went for silence. Sometimes, paradoxically, exam anxiety itself can take up energy and so impede study, but the highest achievers had their own ways of controlling that form of redundancy too. Richard Neville (highly gifted, aged 19, studying physics at university) purposely transferred the skills he had sharpened in chess to checkmate his anxiety:

> Chess has helped me practise concentrating and not getting flustered. If your opponent hits you with a good move, there's no good falling apart. It's the same with a question that you can't do. In exams, I'll go out for five minutes if necessary – shut my eyes, count to ten, take deep breaths. The next day, there's another three-hour exam, and my friends around me get very exhausted, very tired, and very strung up about it, but I don't.

The 'three times' problem described on p. 123 was not an uncommon feature of the gifted learner, involving very sophisticated skills for controlling redundant repetition from the teacher.

Competition and IQ

Competition is a way of finding out and defining one's own capabilities, but the comparison must be meaningful or it is a waste of time and effort. Self-validation, or assessing one's own progress, is not the same as seeking the approval of authority. It involves commitment to the experience, and can promote independence of action and a sense of competence, of power in oneself. That is different from neurotic competitiveness, where the thrill of winning is all, and the experience itself means little. Very young mathematicians seem particularly keen on competition with themselves. They may spend more time than other gifted children on their own, practising calculations and thinking about their mathematical interest (Radford, 1990).

From early childhood, many of the potentially high achievers in this sample had been described by their parents as competitive, comparing themselves with both their own previous performances and those of others. In the first interviews with me, they had far more frequently chosen a high-status occupation for themselves in the future than the others (72 per cent compared with 40 per cent). Nor did they leave it to chance. They often went to great lengths to do their best, taking time and effort over the learning and practice needed to get a skill right in their own eyes, yet often expressing less than total satisfaction with the results. The high-IQ group had the highest aims of all, sometimes accompanied by an urge to perfection. Their combination of high ability, motivation to succeed, and a capacity for hard work proved to be an excellent recipe for success in reaching their goals.

Jeremy Kramer was a young man who typified a gifted mind learning at its best. His mother said he was such a keen learner that he had even demanded more teaching in nursery school. As he grew up, he had consciously devised a self-challenging style of approach to his work along with an excellent repertoire of learning strategies which suited his personality.

Jeremy Kramer *(highly gifted, aged 20, studying medicine):*

When I was younger, I thrived on competition with friends, but now I do it for myself. I always set myself an aim, and have to achieve it. Even during the day, I'll find my own little challenges. Like, I can just go down for a game of snooker, not because it's nice and relaxing, but sometimes it's, 'Right, I'm going to beat this guy, and I'm going to really go for it, get the best score I've ever done.'

I've got exams in three or four weeks, and I'm being quite honest when I say that I haven't opened a book all year. I like to feel the pressure, to build up some anxiety, so I know that if I don't start now, I'm definitely going to fail. It's the challenge of doing that. I'm fully dedicated to working at this point, and only at this point. For my first-year exams, I only started revising two days before. My method is to cram for a couple of weeks, doing 24 hours a day, and not sleep for a few nights. I'm a totally different person when it gets to that stage. Everything seems to go in at that point, so I must be able to absorb the stuff.

I can do this last-minute stuff because I understand the principles, so I understand the subject before I even start working for it. If I were totally lost, then I'd really start worrying. A lot of students sit in their room with a book and slog away at details, but if you test them on the principles, like something that they're supposed to deduce, then they fall down. That's something that I can get right and they won't. I'm only learning the details at the last minute, and I find that a lot of them stay with me. Even now, I remember a lot of last year's work, which I'd only learnt in a few days, where other people I know have forgotten it.

It's important for me to spend a very large period of time each day on my own, thinking and sorting out what I've been doing. I need that thinking time to be productive. Even if it's 3 o'clock in the morning when I get to bed, although I might be very tired, I'll probably stay up another two hours just thinking.

Memory and IQ

Anyone who has studied for exams knows that the most valuable mental asset is a good memory. Indeed, for the highly achieving young people in this study, it seemed to be the most powerful weapon in their academic armoury because so much school-level examination success is based on the ability to reproduce material in the few hours allowed, rather than to think it through. The relationship between memory and IQ had been seen in the first survey, when the parents of the high-IQ children described them as having exceptionally good memories nearly three times as often (35 per cent) as the parents of all the other children (13 per cent). And that was still the picture in the follow-up: the correlations between IQ, memory, and examination success were close and statistically highly significant. The higher the young person's IQ score, the more likely he or she was to claim an excellent memory – and the better the examination results.

For a high proportion of those in the top 1 per cent of the IQ range the facility of memory came very easily, and at that level of intelligence it showed in the arts and the sciences, as described by two highly gifted girls at Cambridge University. One, who was studying English, said: 'I never worked as hard as other people because I never had to. It's terribly easy for me to remember things short term, like revising for my O-levels the night before. If I read things through, shut my eyes, and repeated my notes to myself, it would be there for the exam the next day.' The other, a scientist, said: 'I remember pretty well from class, so for my A-levels I didn't open my school-notes once. But the morning of my physics A-level,

I got up at 5 o'clock, and revised the whole syllabus. It took me two and a bit hours. But it was only a multiple-choice question paper, so you don't have to know anything very well if you know the principles.'

The relationship between memory and IQ was especially close for those who said they remembered facts best, although the high-IQ group did not all have identical types of memory (see Table 4.3).

Table 4.3 *Type of Memory*

IQ group	Good (%)	Facts (%)	People (%)	General (%)
High	84	46	8	45
Above average	66	23	15	62
Average	57	17	14	69
Mean IQ		143	131	132

Girls particularly made much use of their visual memory, and a few even said they had a true photographic memory, such as the gifted 16-year-old who said:

I'm able to picture it, wherever it was. Things like poems and diagrams, I can remember where the bits stick out: once I've drawn a diagram a couple of times, then that's enough, I picture it in my mind. I never put a bookmark in; I always remember what page I'm on. I can sometimes remember enough from the page to take it with me into the exam and read it off; it comes back to me which side the page is on, what colour the ink's in. But I remember better the things I want to remember than those I have to. I'm always forgetting things I have to do and things I should have done.

Others had auditory memories:

I never write when I'm revising, I recite, like for learning muscles and muscle attachments. I'll read it through, then cover it up, and say it over out loud. If it's a subject I find easy, it will go in with a couple of reading throughs. Almost all my A-level revision was just a matter of reading through my notes two or three times, though every now and again, I would need to write down things like a physics derivation.

Or like the brilliant musician who remembered by touch:

I'm a very tactile person – certainly when I'm memorizing music; I can't memorize away from the keyboard. I've got to physically feel and hear what I'm doing, whereas there are some people who can sit on a train from Edinburgh to London and have a piece learned and go away and play it. It's all visual memory; they actually see the music then – actually see the page as they're playing it. I always hear it and feel it.

Most of the young people had only vague (if any) memories of my visit to them ten or more years ago. Four boys, though, remembered it in uncanny detail, and each one had left school with all A grades. Richard Neville (highly gifted, aged 19, studying physics at university) was one. 'Oh, I remember,' he said, 'it was March 1975.' How did he remember? 'Oh, I just remembered, because I remember things.' On checking, he was absolutely correct. He continued:

I can remember when you gave me your last interview when I was 11, and I can tell you virtually everything that went on then, like some of the tests you gave me. One of them, the only one I got wrong, was the string of beads. You got me to do a bearing test, and I stood up with my hands like this, and worked it out, east, west, south, and a few other questions. That's just the way I learn academically, with things that have happened to me, rather than from a book. I can remember vivid things in my childhood, and the words that were spoken to me then. I do it by making relationships, almost like a rhyme, but in pictures. But I haven't got a real photographic memory of books, so I might have difficulties in recalling facts and formulas – which can be a handicap.

But the highest academic achievements were clearly gained by those who said their memories were best for facts. Simon Powell (highly gifted, aged 20, studying mathematics at university):

I can't remember what I was doing yesterday. But machine code, I could remember all of about 60-odd totally abstract numbers all in hexidecimal, which is nought to nine, A, B, C, D, E, F – that's to base 16

– and I could remember pairs of those as operational, and the whole lot, dead easy. I do have a good memory like that, but I was terribly upset when I had to ask a girl what her name was, and I'd known her for a year.

Textbooks are really boring. I prefer my notes, because when I'm revising, they remind me of what we did in the lesson; little things that the teacher said explaining it to you. It helps me remember a bit better when I read a factual text, to go through the first sentence or first line of each paragraph of a section. Then I go back to the beginning and read it again, skimming across the pages and picking out names, places, dates, classification of ideas. Then I will read it through in its entirety, and be able to think about it properly. If I remember something in an exam I will use it, but I never struggle to remember something because that never works, and I just end up getting panicky and blocked.

MOTIVATION TO SUCCEED

Assuming that there is enough intelligence and competence in learning to do the work, most differences in school achievement can be attributed to the pupil's motivation – the strength and direction of the effort made to acquire the learning. Yet how is it that some are motivated in one area of schoolwork, but avoid any effort in the others? Psychological theorists have produced different concepts of motivation, such as 'need for achievement' which can be distinguished from 'fear of failure', all kinds being affected by 'test anxiety' or 'effort avoidance'. It would be simplistic to say that motivation is just the result of reward and punishment, or even of more sophisticated conditioning by parents and teachers. People's behaviour depends not just on how they are treated, but also on how they perceive and react to the situation.

Tony Stewart, for example, was not gifted, but was a youth of well above average ability. He was the first generation to pull himself up from the poverty trap which had kept his family as labourers in Ireland. However, he was not concerned to pick up the middle-class mores that his school offered: his criteria for success were not theirs of academic achievements or money, but simply a job with a future. Almost all his friends were out of work and with little prospects of improvement. Some of them, he said, were very depressed about their situations. He wanted, above all, to be valued for his personal qualities, for himself.

Tony Stewart *(above average, aged 20, a trainee car mechanic):*

My grandparents were only educated till they were 11 or 12 years old, and then they had to go out in the fields to dig. There was no education for them, nor for my parents, who had to leave school at about 14 to earn money to eat. Just a continuing process. My mother was quite bright academically, but there was no way she could carry on in further education because she had to get out and work. She would've liked to pick some up later, except for having so many in the family. My father came over to England, from Ireland, when he was 17 and worked in tunnels. Academic qualifications are not what really matter, but the type of person you are; how other people respect you and such.

In their concern with children's education, by far the most frequent question parents and teachers ask of psychologists is, 'How can I motivate them to learn?' There are some answers available, and they can often work, though putting them into practice calls for patience and understanding.

In general, motivation and the accompanying increase in level of work are encouraged by giving children a feeling of individual competence and a goal to aim for, even examinations. But too much adult pressure and control can actually undermine good motivation, because constantly being obliged to depend on someone else's decisions conveys feelings of incompetence to a child, an idea referred to as 'locus of control' (Stipek and Weisz, 1981). This means that if pupils see control as located with the teacher or some other authority, they will be less involved and motivated in their own learning than if they feel more in charge of it themselves. So much experimental research in schools has shown that motivation and achievement levels go up when children are encouraged to take more control over their own classroom activities that it is interesting to wonder why teachers put it into action so little. It also helps poorly motivated youngsters to improve their urge to learn when they are encouraged to help others; for instance, getting unsuccessful adolescents to take on the role of tutors to younger children.

The best kind of motivation is intrinsic – the kind which is generated by interest or relevance, and fired by children's belief in their own effectiveness. That energizing kind of assurance in one's ability to tackle a task comes best from positive personal experiences, especially from feedback that children have received on how well they did. Some of it they can see for themselves, but if other people's responses are to be effective, they must always be genuine, whether good or bad. Sincerity is the key. False praise, such as telling children they have done well when they know they have not, will not enhance their intrinsic motivation. Although a 'Well done' for following easy instructions may be pleasant on the ear and vaguely encouraging, it is not deeply meaningful. In neither case do the children feel in charge of what they are doing. Particularly undermining feedback would include telling a child he or she was just lucky in getting the answer right. Whether lucky or not, this certainly would not enhance anyone's feelings of competence.

However, the situation is not entirely controllable by adults, as children can interpret feedback in different ways, depending on the psychological context and the child's personality. Telling one child he or she is doing badly may be interpreted as an excuse to stop work – 'It's not worth the effort' – though for another, the response may be an increase in motivation – 'I'll prove them wrong!' Paradoxically, too much praise, particularly in a system of close supervision, may tell a child simply that he or she is doing the bidding of the teacher, rather than personally exploring the area of study and so developing competence. This can undermine intrinsic motivation, because it becomes psychologically impossible for the child to feel in control of his or her own progress in learning.

All children, whatever their ability, want to feel effective and engaged by challenge, which must include a risk of failure. The highly able need challenge at least as much as any others. Experimental work has shown that if children are given a superficial reward, such as money or sweets, they are far more likely to choose the easiest ways of succeeding, whereas if they are enjoying the activity for itself, they choose harder tasks, usually just above the level of previous success. No child can reasonably be expected to work hard in all areas of the curriculum, since individual interests are influenced by many things. But when children are interested in what they are doing, they have a natural tendency to take on challenges that exercise and expand their limits of competence.

The advantage of looking back at the lives of individuals who have made outstanding achievements is that one can detect the broader influences on their progress, which might be missed by using more limiting methods of psychological testing or experimentation. There are always powerful motivating reasons why people have taken the paths which have led to their eventual success. Without those reasons, little would have been achieved. For all high achievers, the most important influence in their lives has almost always been exceptional support and encouragement from their parents. There were plenty of incentives for learning from an early age, and any success was warmly acknowledged and rewarded. Also, their teachers often praised readily and appropriately, which was particularly effective where pupil and teacher liked each other. As they grew up, the motivation of some may have been spurred by curiosity, while for others it was the desire for glory, fame, or riches.

In America, Professor Benjamin Bloom and his team (1985) spent four years attempting to get a retrospective picture of the process of exceptionally high-level achievement. They interviewed, mostly by telephone, 120 men and women under 35 years old, who had reached world-class levels of accomplishment in particular fields – pianists, sculptors, research mathematicians, Olympic swimmers, and tennis champions. Respondents told them that no matter what their initial gifts, they had not reached high levels of achievement without a long and intensive process of encouragement, nurturance, education, and training. Very few of the successful had been regarded early on as prodigies, so that predictions made in their childhoods would have failed, not least because of their unknown ability at that point to stick out the years of hard work ahead of them.

The parents of these high achievers said they were keen for the children to do their best at all times, and provided the role models with their own behaviour. Many of the parents were obvious perfectionists, setting high standards for the successful completion of a task. They worked on the maxim that if something is worth doing, it is worth doing well. Work was always completed before play – one did not idle in those homes. They checked their children's homework, and household chores were shared by all members of the family. Although these strictures may sound right – touching the guilt in all of us – it is hard to know what the effect of similar parental behaviour would be on children who did not 'make it', as there were no comparison groups of families in Bloom's study, nor the detail of ups and downs that could have been discovered by a more intimate style of investigation.

Yet the question remains – why did these youngsters stick at it at all? Why did they work continuously at one type of activity for well over a dozen years and not rebel against their parents' designs for them? As young children, they said they had enjoyed playing at their particular interest, like the piano or swimming, taking a great deal of pleasure from their learning. It was as that initial enthusiasm waned that their parents had stepped in. They had taken the children to lessons and made sure they practised every day, rewarding them regularly with smiles, gold stars, or even chocolate bars. And the children had often formed deep relationships with their teachers. Practice became a routine habit like cleaning teeth, which in the end produced the shining feelings of competence and mastery. The high achievers described a lifelong interest in and emotional commitment to their particular field, a desire to gain outstanding attainment in it, and a willingness to put in the great amounts of time and effort needed to reach their very high levels of achievement. However, the young people did not always remember that when they had flagged in their enthusiasm it was their parents who had kept them going.

Parental Pressure

In general, the higher the parents' occupational group in my study, the higher their child's IQ. This was true in relation to both parents' levels of education too, but especially for the father's. Higher-level parental occupation and education were also directly related to increased pressure on the young person to be academically successful, with the expectation that this would happen.

Fortunately, most of the high-flyers seemed to have minds which coordinated well with those of their parents, allowing them an easy and fruitful growing up. The rated estimate of pressure in a family (see Table 4.4) was drawn from a mixture of objective measures, such as what the parents said they had done (for example, choosing a school because of its academic results) and of my own impression. There were homes in which the pressure to succeed was almost palpable.

Table 4.4 *Pressure to Achieve*

IQ group	Strong pressure (%)
High	64
Above average	28
Average	21

Self-motivation

It was not just pressure from home that moved the high-IQ pupils to direct their energies into study and to do as well as they did. They were much harder on themselves than were their parents. Significantly more of them than of the other IQ groups described themselves as lazy (see Table 4.5).

Table 4.5 *Perceived Laziness*

IQ group	Parents say lazy (%)	Subjects say lazy (%)
High	6.8	20.3
Above average	13.2	9.4
Average	14.3	00.0

This finding was unexpected and emerged spontaneously as the young people described themselves. There were two possible reasons for the gifted to have such feelings about their own efforts. Firstly, it is probable that they could well see the way things should be done, but when it was not within their power to fulfil those aims, they may have blamed themselves for their 'laziness'. Secondly, it may have been not a genuine laziness (as most of us understand it) but a form of 'guilt' for finding work so easy, when others had to struggle. This attitude was typical: 'I could have gone in for anything if I'd done the work. The fact is that I did no work and still got seven [Scottish] Highers, so I can sit back and say, yes, I was totally and utterly lazy.'

A few of the gifted young people were particularly hard on themselves, such as Vijay Patel, a tall, gentle youth. Both his Asian parents were cultured, sophisticated scientists. He and his sister, also a scientist, had written a novel which they hoped to publish, and his four A grades had secured him a place at Cambridge. His mother, though, said that she and his father had been somewhat disappointed by their son's results, explaining that he did not do his best in exams because he was so nervous. Vijay and his parents agreed that he should have worked harder, and he rebuked himself for inefficiency because he had followed some tracks in his learning which proved to be dead ends. He was even appreciative of the trouble that one of his teachers had taken in marking his work down to make him strive harder, but had the satisfaction of knowing that 'They all said about me that I was self-motivated.'

In this study, there was a distinct relationship between academic potential and the drive to realize it from both parents and the highly able children. Both generations seemed to be aware of what the children were capable of academically. As a significant proportion of the highly able in this study were in selective academic schools, it can be assumed that they were also given much encouragement there to do well at their exams. Thus, not only did those who were successful have the required innate ability, they also often had an educational environment from both home and school which promoted its fulfilment. Perhaps most importantly, they normally worked in harmony with their circumstances.

But harmony was not given to all, and heavy pressure does not always come from parents to children. It was the lack of balance between the pressure Brian Hancock put on himself, and the total absence of it from his parents, that caused him emotional problems. They had both left school at 15 and harboured few ambitions for their son. His dedication to work seemed self-generated, though he was well supported by his school, where he had been totally focused on his career, driving himself beyond most young people's endurance and eventually achieving A grades in five science A-level exams. His latest move was consciously to modify his northern accent to a southern one, the better to achieve his career goals. His one creative indulgence was playing the clarinet in the university band.

David Hancock *(gifted, aged 21, studying medicine):*

When I was at school, it wasn't that I wanted to be working all the time. I always made a point of not working in the dinner-hour, because I felt you should have a break in the middle of the day, but sometimes I used to think then that there must be something more useful I could be doing. So being bored in lunch-hours was my own fault: I could have worked if I'd wanted to. I don't see any reason why I shouldn't be able to get into a position where I get high up in research and find a new vaccine, maybe for AIDS or rabies. I like to think that in my time I will do a bit of good as a doctor.

Chapter 5
The Flowering of Talent

*To believe in your own thought, to believe
that what is true for you in your private heart
is true for all men, – that is genius.*

RALPH WALDO EMERSON, *PRUDENCE*

Talented creativity starts very early in life, sometimes in the cradle, and yet in order to reach mature flowering it needs the means and the encouragement. The creative spirit can be inhibited by an educational environment which is too information-based, analytical, and inflexible, and also by restrictions on the emotional development of children so that they become too fearful of others' opinions to express themselves in their own ways.

CREATIVITY

Creativity is involved in many, if not most, everyday decisions and activities, and although it is one of the most sought-after features of mental life it is perhaps the most intangible – the electricity of the intellect. It is a sensitive way of using knowledge for searching out problems, finding solutions, and communicating results. No special mental skills are necessary to be creative, other than those to which we already have access. Creative artists of any sort use the same two ways of knowing as everyone else – feeling and reasoning. Feeling suggests the direction, and what you feel to be right can be as valid as a consciously learned technique. Reason supervises decisions, checking that the impetus from feeling is workable.

Although one form of knowing may be dominant – physically, mentally, and spiritually – harmony in their use is crucial to the expression of talent. The ability to coordinate them develops with experience, but it is moulded through innate sensitivity. Talented creativity is a fragile flower.

Though the production of a creative work is controlled by the two forms of knowing, the key state of mind is open flexibility. An artist has to be able to lift emotional repression and relax mental structures to get to the deep and sometimes irrational feelings from which the work springs. It calls for a strong tolerance of anxiety, because these feelings can be very disturbing in their ambiguous and conflicting meanings. There is also considerable pull between openness and control, between the need to keep the mind open to new information while being aware of inner experiences. It demands the ability to hold a complex mixture of ideas in the mind at the same time, to play with them, and to work methodically to resolve them into a new form. Indeed, creativity can be seen as a resolution of conflicts, in which the creative individual is able to see the extremes and manipulate them into a working unity. In fact, creative people often prefer complexity – for example, asymmetrical designs rather than simple, geometrical ones – perhaps so as to impose their personal style of order.

A talented student of the violin in my study obviously had the reasoned knowledge to play her instrument, and she described how she also used her feelings to make the production of a score her own: 'Playing music is a very individual thing; the way you feel it and interpret it, and the way you express it in the instrument you play. I experience what I play; I feel very emotional, very compassionate towards the music. It's just a wonderful sensation.'

Creative behaviour is not distinct from the kind of intelligence measured by tests, but can be thought of rather as intelligence in action. But to be truly effective, as distinct from a flash in the pan, all aspects of creativity need an above-average level of intellectual ability. Many studies have settled on a figure of about IQ 120 as a minimum basis for producing lasting creative work, for bringing ideas into a form in which they can be identified as worthwhile, although a high IQ alone could never be used to predict a creative bent.

Certainly, without a good input of intelligence, creative behaviour is so rare as to be a wonder. It is occasionally seen in mentally retarded individuals who can draw or play music extraordinarily well, though experts say they merely reproduce variations of what they perceive, rather than working imaginatively (Howe, 1989). The exceptions are the brilliant, mature drawings by some autistic children; for example, a 9-year-old girl called Nadia who drew horses (Selfe, 1983), or Stephen Wiltshire, who draws buildings (Wiltshire, 1987). One theory is that, being autistic, the children do not use the normal, verbal mental route to reason through their productions, and so they are free of the inhibition of reason, although this does not explain their technical skills.

Research over many years into the lives of successful creative people has shown that they are indeed intelligent, and also intellectual, in that they not only produce art, but like to think about the problems and issues in their field. A major intellectual aspect of creative work is in the focusing on ambiguity and feelings, changing them into symbolic form such as words or musical notes, which the artist usually enjoys. This intellectual aspect of the arts was explained by Anna Markland (her real name), a highly talented pianist (aged 20, studying music at university):

> There's a difference between music as a subject and music as a practical thing, and the two don't always meet. There were quite a few people at [music] school who were excellent performers but death on the academic side. The two must be combined, because if you don't know how music is actually put together and how it ticks, then what chance can you have of communicating something to an audience? You've got to actually know what it's all about. Thank God I'm doing a music degree.

Even though similar learning experiences give rise to the acquiring of information and the flexing of creative ability, creative ideas must contain the seeds of change, of fresh ways of looking at things. However, the combination of knowledge, flexibility, talent, and intellect is still not enough for the truly creative person. The ability to derive a personal and unique understanding of experiences, then arrive at and stick to one's own conclusions, takes great independence of mind, as well as courage. To be creative is the reverse of being passive and contented: it means being dissatisfied with the status quo and in its fulfilment, and may at an extreme involve rejection of one's own original style of life. The individual must have a personal grasp of distinct values, beliefs, and ideas of self, and an awareness of opportunity – all of which are needed to provide structure for that person's particular sensitivity and perceptions of the world (Perkins, 1981).

All studies of fine artists, writers, etc. have shown them to have had a lifelong tendency to develop unique viewpoints, with enough strength of character to withstand social disapproval as they go on to define themselves in their work. But being creative is not the same as being pointlessly deviant. Real creativity is original and relevant to real life, even though it may take time for it to be seen as such. It also requires long-term effort, or the gifts may lie fallow and unproductive, even in the most potentially rewarding circumstances of the right place and at the right time. In a large American study (Goertzel *et al.*, 1978), many artists said they had chosen that way of life because they felt clear about the way they wanted to express their feelings, as well as a strong need to put something right. They said they were sensitive to the way others thought and worked, but often had to work without the understanding of those around them, at times even in an atmosphere of distinct disapproval.

Babies show aesthetic preferences as soon as they can physically begin to select from the environment, which is soon after birth, reaching a reasonably permanent stage of reliability at about 8 months old. Newborn babies show clear tastes for, say, green over red, or different foods. By their first or second year, potentially creative children can already be seen to behave somewhat like creative adults. They are enthusiastic in the time and effort they put into their chosen activities, with an uncensored openness to their experiences. There are two major differences, though, between the child and the adult who is creative. Firstly, what is novel in the child's experience is not necessarily so to adults, which means that the child is much more tied to the here and now, with a limited knowledge base from which to work. Secondly, the child has not acquired the technical skills to carry out his or her dreams. Because of these two handicaps, children's work is not exactly like that of adults, even given such genius as Mozart's or Picasso's. Such work is, however, prodigious for a child (Radford, 1990).

Jean Piaget, the great Swiss psychologist, emphasized that early childhood is the most creative period in life in terms of curiosity, candidness, and openness – until society squeezes these into conformity. Understandably, parents usually teach their children school-type skills like numbers and letters, to encourage school success, and so the natural creative interests of the child are not always recognized. How then can a child remain both school-clever and creatively productive? Keeping track of a toddler's interests in a diary will provide a lead for parents as to which direction development should be encouraged in, while still leaving the child feeling free to explore. Many other methods are outlined in my book *Bright as a Button* (Freeman, 1991).

Going It Alone

Laurence Bidston (his real name), a tense, thin youth with a strong Liverpool accent, had chosen to follow his star of creative artist as a fashion designer, with precious little to back him up. Yet at the age of 21, in just a year, he already had some national recognition, and occupied a whole floor over a shoe shop in the centre of the city, displaying his chunky, simple clothes. He had shown immense courage. His father said that Laurence sometimes went to the big stores selling his wares with apparent confidence, but once outside again, he'd head for the nearest lavatory to be sick.

Laurence's parents were easy-going, warm-hearted people. They lived in a poor area on the outskirts of the city and had put up their home as security for a loan to give their son a start in his business; his huge debts did not bother them in the slightest. At our first meeting in 1974, they told me that even as a newborn baby he 'hated to be swaddled', while as a toddler he was 'determined in all he did, with a memory like an elephant, and an adult sense of humour, which didn't always go down well with other adults'. At 11, he only had one friend, an 18-year-old boy. His parents had hoped he would become a doctor, with which he had agreed at that time. But he was also 'a bit clumsy', and had fine motor problems which showed in his difficulties with handwriting; this was interesting in view of the fine, detailed work this very sensitive, creative young man had chosen.

Laurence's father:

He wanted to be a fashion designer from about the age of 15. When he'd finished school he asked us, 'Will you allow me a year off to see what I can do?' He'd already started selling clothes on a second-hand stall. Mother taught him some basic stitch-work and I taught him a little bit about pattern cutting, and now *Vogue* [the fashion magazine] has called him a top young British designer. He showed great tenacity and he works extremely hard. I don't think anyone could have made him work as hard at any subject he didn't want to do. He wants to get rid of his overdraft so he can give us our deeds back.

Laurence Bidston (*highly talented, aged 21, fashion designer*):

Design is something you've got to have an eye for. Most of the people that come out of the poly here in Liverpool – the stuff they do is rubbish. Well, I was scared of having my talent diminished by having to conform with what teachers wanted me to do, because that was what had happened in art at school. It was the cutting technique that I needed to know, so I got a book on pattern-cutting, and taught myself to cut and sew the basics – arm, body, back, etc. Now I can build blocks for cutting out, and I can alter it to whatever I want.

I took some stuff to a shop in London, they bought it, and in about three months it was in *Harpers* and *Vogue*. So then I was just caught up in it. Every six months, I do a collection. I go to the library and get the names of about twenty million fabric manufacturers, then phone or write to them, get the samples, and choose. I get really paranoid waiting for the reactions to a collection, and if I get slagged off I can get really depressed, because it catches my self-doubts about the work I'm doing. If I'd gone to a very good fashion school, I would at least have a degree to back me up, but I keep saying to myself, 'They're wrong, I'm right.'

I started off really idealistic, head in the clouds about designing. Then I had some real setbacks because there was nobody to tell me about the pitfalls. On one occasion, I could have made 15,000 quid, and I didn't, because I didn't know about the production line, so the delivery was late, it wasn't accepted, and I was left with all the goods. I've learned by experience, and it's improving with each season as I get more professional. I think I'll try for the mass market soon.

My parents were very good, and when I got all this good press they said 'You must go on.' When they see me in all the magazines, my Mum can say, 'Oh yeah, those are our Laurence's clothes in them magazines.' I think they'd have been happier if they hadn't had to put the house up for security, but I think they've got faith in my ability to pay this overdraft off. Making money enables me to buy books, to buy materials so I can do some art, things like that. If I'm good enough, I'll probably have to go to Italy, and I have this dream that I'll go out to New York as well. Right now, it's quite a good act; for the last four months, I've had a flat. But I never have any spare time; I just go to bed when the day ends.

P.S. Laurence worked abroad for two years, and returned to run his own establishment in Liverpool. He is thriving and becoming known.

INSIGHT

Taking further my analogy of creativity as the electricity of intellect, insightful thinking is a spark which appears to short-circuit reason in a flash of illumination. It is an ephemeral, satisfying joy with a magical quality (Bastick, 1982). It is part of all aspects of life, an experience common to everyone, no matter what their level of intelligence. In its various guises, it may take the form of just an everyday hunch offering a clue for making a decision, or it may be a deep, 'Eureka' experience. That vital spark often comes at times of relaxation, during easy, familiar action, in the same way that (tradition has it) Newton observed the falling apple while musing, Archimedes was taking a bath, James Watt was watching the kettle boil, and Poincaré, the great mathematician, was getting on a bus. Millions of other insights have been responsible for practically every innovative human creation to date. Even Poincaré said that logic alone could create nothing new, nor lead to anything but tautology.

To be insightful is to be human. The computer, though it is a powerful tool used to analyse the most complex data, cannot ask even the simplest meaningful question by itself. Insight is basic to all levels of learning, and the most effective teaching constantly seeks to develop it. Yet the thinking styles required for school learning and everyday life are different. School problems normally demand responses from the analytical, sequential end of the thinking spectrum to cope, for example, with calculations which have specific structures and answers – not the end from which creative ideas come. Everyday matters require far more of the intuitive, flexible end, with sensitive and free use of feelings. Life concerns are rarely so clear-cut that everyday problems have only one right solution; sometimes several seem equally possible. Your choice, though, like whom you marry or where you choose to live, can change your life. In fact, just identifying the cause of the concern, let alone the solution, is usually difficult, because it is part and parcel of the way you live. Everyday problems are very persistent, too; one decision sometimes only seems to pave the way for the next set of problems. One cannot just close the textbook and go away. Furthermore, solving a life problem is one thing, but convincing people of the rightness of the solution is another.

At times, the brightest youngsters in my study caused some consternation in their school-class with their flashes of insight, especially the gifted mathematicians, who vaulted the recognized stages of computation. Although it is often a valuable exercise for such pupils to have to retrace their calculations in a more careful way, too much back-tracking can also act as an impediment to the creative aspects of their thinking. Understandably, teachers have some anxiety in knowing how to help their high-flyers balance the desire to soar with the need to check their working, as the following two boys found:

Simon Powell *(highly gifted, aged 20, studying mathematics at university):*

> They thought I was only of average ability when we first moved to Scotland, so they put me in the bottom maths class to start with. But my parents complained. Then they moved me up and I immediately went to the top of that class. They were surprised because in maths I used to miss out the working, just write down the answer. One of the masters tried to stop me doing that, tried to make me more methodical, so I stopped making quite as many silly mistakes. Even now at university, I can do a maths question and get everything right, except the addition of two and two. I like to work with concepts, and I just go at too fast a rate. Where I make silly mistakes, other people make conceptual mistakes.

It was not only in mathematics but in the arts too that a gifted young person would have a flash of insight, but fail to describe the reasoning behind it, leaving the listener wondering how he had reached that point.

David Baker *(gifted, aged 17, at school):*

> The English teacher sometimes only understands what I mean three hours after – and by that time I can't remember what we were talking about. Once, I suddenly turned on the banks because they were investing in all the evil countries. That's evil invested in evil, which all seemed very relevant to *The Duchess of Malfi*. But the teacher didn't understand at all why suddenly I'd gone on to banks. I had to explain that Barclays was investing in South Africa and Lloyds in Argentina and then she understood.

Insight springs from the heady stir of past and present experience, and because intuitive thinking involves the whole self, both emotion and intellect make up reactions to the mix of familiar and unfamiliar. Mild anxiety may build up before the 'flash', but after it happens and one knows the rightness of the insight, that confidence releases the tension. People have described it subjectively, but it can also be measured by changes in skin response, heart-rate and respiration. It produces a feeling of satisfaction if not euphoria.

There was joy on the face of Sarah Mortimer (highly gifted, aged 20, studying computer systems engineering at university) when she described one of her big mathematical insights: 'Last term, suddenly in the middle of one lecture, I understood the whole point of the course. It suddenly made sense, and everybody else was still sitting there in a haze, wondering what was going on. I'd grasped the concept and that was it. I was away. I could do the rest of it.' The confidence which comes from insight also acts as a psychological reward to continue using the intuitive way of thinking, so that the more it is practised, the better it becomes. However, in a threatening situation like examinations, too much anxiety most often inhibits intuition.

Like any other pupils, the gifted need the enjoyable stimulation of variety and the excitement that can come from the juxtaposition of ideas. That is why when lessons are too easy, as can happen in a mixed-ability classroom, the gifted lose what the other pupils may be getting from it – the satisfaction of tackling and resolving problems. To compensate, they may deliberately stir things up, either in their own minds or among others in the classroom, just to taste the spice of stimulation. Without that, schoolwork becomes just a rather boring matter of taking in and reproducing what the teacher says, and the flame of discovery burns low. The answer, of course, is to provide the gifted with education appropriate to their needs. One highly gifted boy's mother considered this the reason for her son's early disturbed behaviour: 'From when he started school until the age of 8 he used to cry and scream and have tantrums, because he wasn't being [mentally] used up, though he was teacher's pet.'

THE ART MEDIUM

What makes one child chose the medium of paint and another that of words or sound to channel their stream of creative energy? Do the arts of painting and writing flow from the same source or have they different springs? Both my own and others' research have shown that general artistic ability does indeed come from the same broad source, but the form the surge takes is to a large extent directed by circumstances.

As soon as babies first open their eyes their senses have begun to be directed, and as they develop, what they learn to perceive becomes their personal truth. Small children accept what they are aware of as normal.

This was how young Catherine Goumas had come to take up the violin. Her mother, a violin teacher, describes below how she had given her the musical expertise to get to a prestigious music college. It is very likely that there are millions of children like Catherine and her sister, who could be helped to enjoy a very much higher level of aesthetic awareness and the pleasure of practising it, with the right teaching.

The family lived in a bleak farmhouse, high in the northern hills. The night I went to see them was pitch-dark and well below freezing. Inside the farmhouse it was not much warmer than outside. We huddled around the only heat – a low open fire in a very small grate – though curtains held up with bamboo poles over the doors kept out some of the wind. Only the kitchen and that little room were heated. Just once, Mr Goumas came in from working outdoors, clad only in a sweater and slacks, carrying four small, welcome, pieces of wood, which he put on the fire. He seemed a pleasant if gruff man, but when his wife asked if we could have some more, he replied firmly, 'No, there isn't any more wood.'

Mr Goumas's own farm childhood had been very hard – penny-pinching and windows nailed open all year round – and he had learned to be careful. His wife said that every penny he earned went into the bank – and stayed there. It was only now, when his teenage daughters were performing to applause, that he was beginning to take some pride in them. Catherine was very happy with her mother's choice for her as a violinist, though she did let slip: 'Sometimes, I felt it was all music, and I really wanted to try something else as well, but I was never given that opportunity.'

Catherine Goumas's mother:

> Jacqueline du Pré's mother did precisely the same with her as I did. She sang with her, and tapped rhythms out, frequently and regularly. This is how music starts, and any child, I reckon, could have done what mine have done, if they'd started in the same way.
>
> Cathy was always on my knee when I was teaching the piano, so she soaked up a lot of music. I usually have serious music on the radio at the same time every day. Both girls came in for musical bombardment one way or another. I teach a lot of bright children and I reckon that if I can catch them early enough, and with parental help, they do exceedingly well. The average child I teach, say from the age of 5, can get into the [specialist] music school in five years.
>
> It was that early music training that got Cathy into the music school, because she was able to sing well in tune. She had a good ear. She

could recognize rhythms. She could distinguish high and low notes, intervals, etc. It's the oral side that's very important at an early age, not the practical side, which is a skill only developed over many years – unless, like Yehudi Menuhin, they start off with it. Then, when they're 18, they don't know what on earth to do and they have to start all over again because it doesn't come naturally any more: he had a terrible problem in his teens. As you know, somebody with a gift for something doesn't think about it, he just does it, and then if somebody else says, 'How on earth do you do it?' it can sometimes kill it for them stone dead. They stop doing it because they start to think about it.

There are very few people who are tone deaf. It's simply that that part of the brain hasn't been encouraged at a young age. The difference between the bright children I've taught and the ones that aren't bright is that they find it easy, and so they just charge ahead. They're doing all the right balances and everything naturally, whereas with the other ones, you're continually saying, 'Balances . . . gently raise this, lower that.'

We did get a colossal grant for their education, but we still have to pay out a lot of money, and that has hurt my husband. It's very hard on somebody who's been trained only to save. He has refused at times and I've had to take out a loan, or work extra hours and pay for instruments myself. I've really been the main support of the girls. What most people fear for musical children, except the few that have so much confidence, is insecurity. She's not good enough to be a soloist, and it's a case of where the opportunities come. My whole reason for teaching them music was because it was the one thing I *could* teach them. I know that if a child is good at one thing, even if they're stupid at everything else, they feel they've got a place in the world.

It was a similar story for David Baker but in quite another direction. His architect father had shared with his son something of his own love of nineteenth-century art, to which David had directed his exceptionally high ability.

David Baker *(gifted, aged 17, at school):*

I like Manchester a lot, going sketching and looking at it. Sometimes I go into the City Art Gallery or the Whitworth Gallery and look round for inspiration. I really get a kick out of looking at things like the Pre-Raphaelite paintings – Janie Morris is just incredible, and William Morris – Andy Warhol too, and other artists, they really move me.

My painting does a lot for me. Compared with my peers, it's the best – that's what the teacher said. My art work is original; I'm well into Fauvism; I like colour and I know I have got an ability. I do get a big kick at having spent my time creatively and developed a skill. I'm aware of beauty all the time. Just walking down the road sometimes, looking out of my window, and there's so much here at home – you don't really have to look very far to be moved artistically in here. Just look at the flowers, or the graphics on the record player, not that they're very good, but look at that carving. I'm not wild about the television – I think I'd take that away.

But there are, of course, genuine differences between the technical production of the arts. The world-famous guitarist Segovia once said that he could never have become so skilled if he had not had a strong thumbnail. And though poetry once demanded some fine motor skill for writing, the age of writing machines has alleviated some of those problems – on which hangs the following tale.

When I first met Mary Owen (highly gifted, aged 17, at school), she was 9½ years old. She played the recorder, loved reading, had a mature way with words and was about to take her national bronze medal for writing poetry. At that time, she wanted to be a musician, and described herself as 'somewhat aloof' from her classmates' world of pop culture. Her great love was 'a quite authentic Victorian dolls' house' that her father had made for her. However, her mother said Mary had problems at school, for which the headmistress had suggested remedial help.

The next time I met Mary was in the presence of Princess Anne, who was handing her her prize as winner of a National Poetry Competition. Mary was the outright winner from approximately 35,000 entries, chosen quite independently by each of the four judges, of which I was one. But I had not recognized her name. She came up to me and asked if I was the Dr Freeman who had done all that research with gifted children. 'Well,' she said, 'I was one of your subjects, and you are coming round to see me soon for the follow-up!'

Mary had also won other poetry prizes in her young life, including the national Poetry Society prize. Here is one of her prize-winning poems, which she wrote at 15:

Sea Swan

Swan flew heavy
over the sea
clapped white wings in the wind:
snake-neck straight.

Snow swan
settled pressing on the water
    watching the faces
of young girls less white than his feathers.
    Grey against grey,
the sea and sky met dull as morning
upon Wales.

Low in the tide,
    two islands
echoed with hollow bird-cries:
January-bare.

Night-dark, in the hills
Fann swims among the reeds
neck gold-banded.
Present in dreams;
she calls to her mate.

And at Moonset
two swans dawn on the water,
ringed in blue-gold;
part of someone's madness.

Like the swan on our sea,
they unfurl their wings to fly,
    leaving only a ripple on still water.

Mary's background was typically Liverpool – mixed and somewhat exotic: one set of great-grandparents were black, possibly from the West Indies, one grandmother she thinks was Jewish, one grandfather was Scots, and the other was from Liverpool. Mary had jet-black hair, long, thick eyelashes, a fair skin, and a lively twinkle in her eyes. The family had moved up a couple of social classes. One of her grandparents had been in service (a maid), one was a bus driver, one a docker, and one did very little. However, their children, Mary's parents, had both had higher education in art colleges, and were now art lecturers. Their home held a wide variety of books, including philosophy, poetry, and biographies of painters. Mary had an unusually broad understanding of politics, her mind ranging far out of her own surroundings.

At the follow-up, it was clear that Mary's early talent and sensitivity had remained intensely verbal. 'Writing poetry,' she said, 'has changed the way I experience life.' However, just as Laurence Bidston, a 'clumsy' child (described above), had moved into the technically precise work of making clothes, Sarah had a similarly intriguing problem in view of her brilliance with writing. Her mother described it:

She's always had terrible difficulty with handwriting. When she was younger, she could cope by writing slowly, but by the time she was 15, under pressure, it was so bad you just couldn't read it. She also finds drawing and painting very difficult. Now, she types up a lot of her stuff.

At junior school, her needlework was a disaster, and we had to go there lots of times about it. They thought she was being difficult, but she just couldn't cope. She used to come home shaking, really distressed because she couldn't manage needles. The school sent her to the child guidance clinic, and they said her IQ was at gifted level, but the gap between her intelligence and her fine coordination was absolutely awful.

At first, for her, school was total panic and despair. She didn't want to go, so I used to make her, though I used to feel awful coming away. It was a nightmare, so in the end we took her out of junior school and tutored her at home for a couple of terms, until she went to the comprehensive school. At first, she did well there, but then at the end of the second year they began teasing her. She wrote well and her essays were read out, and she knew a lot of things that they didn't know – odd things that made her feel that she was a swot. It wasn't helped by her being a very late developer physically as well; she looked babyish and young. Then we moved, so she was entitled to go to the girls' grammar school [selective], where she could grow up a little bit more slowly, and she's been happier than she's ever been in her life.

The teachers say she's really exciting to teach because she'll stand up and argue and give ideas. The sort of thing she'll do just for her own pleasure is like when she wrote a critical essay on Tennessee Williams. When she only got a C for her English Literature O-level, the teacher wrote in her report that she'd probably written right out of the topic and gone on to something quite different, which was a bit too sophisticated for that level. Winning the Poetry Prize has let her realize that other people had actually seen that she could do it. I don't think she'll ever stop writing, which is nice.

P.S. Mary went to university to study English and History, but she found it boring, she said, because it was too easy. She became very thin and dropped out after only a year. She then took a secretarial course and has had several jobs, but has not written a word of poetry for 5 years.

MUSICAL TALENT

Music is the most popular of all the arts, and is important in the lives of most of the world's people – and it also had a special place in this research. All twelve children who were at a specialist music school in the first study had agreed to be included in the follow-up (7 per cent of the whole), and their progression in the intervening years had frequently been particularly interesting. They had often found the competition fierce, and carving a route through to success had always demanded of them exceptional determination and discipline, as well as an enthusiasm and dedication from their teachers, far beyond that of normal teaching. This keenness was not unique to the musicians, however. As a student actor said: 'I'd never send a sensitive child to a stage school – no way. I've seen people who were really talented come out of that place who did not have the killer instinct, and left within twelve months. But since the stage is such a competitive industry, perhaps that's the way it should be.'

At the specialist music school, pupils studied the full academic syllabus as well as their instruments, and consequently the overall workload was very heavy. Several had found it so difficult to integrate their academic and musical work that they had given up the struggle with one. But for most, in spite of the intense pressure, the love of music and joy of playing were quite enough to keep them hard at work.

Deborah Lewis *(musically talented, aged 19, at music college);*

We were there to work. If you didn't do your homework properly because you said you had a rehearsal till quite late on at night – that was no excuse. And if you didn't get to a rehearsal on time because you were doing your homework, or because you had a lesson, that was still no excuse. Even in the time when it was getting close to A-levels, you could have rehearsals till half-eight at night, on top of a full day at school.

Can you imagine having to go home and start your homework about half-nine, especially if you're tired? At A-level time especially, I was still at school till about eight o'clock in the evening. Then you'd be expected to come home to four hours of practice, homework on top of that, and it was often twelve or one o'clock before I was in bed. I was never able to rest. A lot of people skipped games, thinking that the two hours was a waste of time and they'd much rather practise, which made the headmaster worried about his pupils not getting enough fresh air and exercise. You had to feel sorry for the boarders. Some had been there since they were only seven, maybe because their parents wanted them to be musical whiz kids.

The standard of competition is so very, very high, and not winning can be so wounding when you're young. You've got to go in with the attitude that if you don't play well on the day it doesn't matter, it's no indication of your talent. But when you're up there playing, you can control your nerves because you're putting your whole self into the music.

Most local education authorities in Britain have a system in which musical instruments can be rented at nominal cost, and music teachers will come to the school to give free lessons if there are sufficient pupils there. It inspired many a young musician, as Deborah went on to explain:

I got my first oboe lessons from the Salford Music Centre; they helped me choose an instrument. Anybody could go free, if you were willing to learn. It's on Saturday mornings, and there's all sorts of wind bands and orchestras, and once you get to a certain standard, you can play in them. It makes it all good fun. The oboe is very difficult to start with because it doesn't make a particularly nice sound, but I plugged away at it and I really liked it in the end; in fact it's my whole life now.

The Home Support System

As concert pianists go, Anna Markland's background was far from promising, and yet she had won the most prestigious all-instrument, national competition in Britain, the BBC's Young Musician of the Year, before millions of television viewers. Both her sets of grandparents had come over from Ireland to live in the poorest, toughest part of Liverpool. Her father described his family as 'factory hands', but (and this is where detailed questioning pays) her great-grandparents on her mother's side had both been concert performers, her grandmother having 'got her music degree, her cap and gown, at 14 from Trinity College Dublin'. The maternal talent seemed to have entirely skipped two generations. Anna also had an uncle who drove a motor-bike in the Wall-of-Death, sometimes running a fairground booth, or at times simply dug ditches.

Anna's parents now lived in a tiny house in the middle of a large, featureless, pre-war council estate outside Liverpool. It must have been designed to look pretty on the drawing board, without any idea that its inhabitants would own cars, so that there was a dark, icy walk of more than a hundred yards from the road to reach the front door. Once opened, however, it revealed a gleaming, magnificent, full-size grand piano, which filled about a third of the entire downstairs area. Anna, now studying music at Oxford, had made the cultural jump to her present status as a nationally known figure with great assurance. She loved her parents, who had given her all the support they could, and visited them often.

Anna Markland (highly talented, aged 20, studying music at university):

When I was 10 years old, my music teacher arranged for an audition for the music school: great fun for about two-and-a-half hours. They told me how I should be playing the violin, as opposed to how I was playing the violin – and they took me in to study the piano!

I thought there was too much emphasis on music there, music, music, music all the time, when people should have been going pot-holing, or playing sports. A lot of talented young musicians lose out on that. A lot of them also suffer from an adverse amount of competition, especially string players. They get so anxious, going round in kid gloves all day to protect their fingers. Maybe I shouldn't be playing hockey now, but I've never come to any harm, and I'm careful and look after my hands.

I use as many differing emotions as I can get hold of in my playing, and I gained from the experience of the BBC competition and all its ramifications with other people, like jealousy. It's useful being a pianist: whenever I'm feeling fed up, I just go and hit hell out of that piano for two hours. But during a concert I don't feel moved because I'm concentrating on communicating; it comes afterwards. The emotions are somehow inbuilt in a piece. Take the Liszt sonata I'm doing at the moment. I've thought out a particular theme for it and whilst I'm practising I'm thinking, – 'yes, he's meeting her, he's taking her out to dinner for the first time'. But then when I'm playing it for real, I'll play the whole thing through from beginning to end, trying to play it the way I think Liszt would have wanted me to.

I like to put in between four and six hours' practice a day, though there's only room in my academic timetable for about three. But I'm basically a very lazy person, and anyway, there's more to life than doing academic work and music. I can concentrate quite easily, but when I've finished maybe four or five hours of solid, concentrated practice, I'm completely exhausted.

I'm very lucky to have an audience to play to, with, let's face it, national recognition. I've found something that I'm good at; it's marvellous, and I'm just incredibly happy. From the mercenary point of view, it is nice to be able to go out and buy what you want; I get professional fees now. I get days when I think – 'God, wouldn't it be lovely to take the musical world by storm – I'm going to be a performer.'

'John's singing in a concert on Friday,' Mrs Asgard said. 'Wouldn't you like to come so that you could then say you'd heard him sing before he was famous?' She was a woman of passion, with absolute faith in her family, and had devoted her life to their achievements. John, a large, easy-going fellow, took it all in his stride, and agreed with her that because he was so clever, he didn't have to exert himself academically; and consequently he had not done well in his school exams.

John Asgard's mother:

John definitely has a presence – a sort of aura. It was definitely proven by the time he was 2½ that he was musically gifted. My husband proved it inasmuch as he tested him. First of all by the fact that he went to the piano and would sit there for over an hour, which is good at that age; concentrate and sit there. Not plonk, plonk, plonking, or banging, but picking out little notes, not definite tunes, but obviously a tune was in his mind. It was even obvious to me, who's tone deaf.

When he was between 3½ and 4, and hadn't yet started school, he used to carry around a small book about musical instruments; he'd point to the violin and say that he wanted one. We had a violin on the top of the wardrobe, which someone had given to us. One day when I was cleaning upstairs, I got it down for him, and he was absolutely thrilled trying to get tunes out of it. My husband felt that we ought to try and encourage this, and to that end, we asked a local violin teacher, but she refused to teach him, saying that he was much too young. We were at our wits' end because it was getting increasingly obvious that he wanted it very much and was obviously able to do something. So I phoned up the School of Music and asked them could they recommend a violin teacher who would take on a very young child. They did, and he started having lessons just before he was 6.

Even though he passed the audition for the music school at 6 years old, the Education Authority said they wouldn't pay till a year later. So he had to wait. I'd like to say that Mozart was composing at 4, but if he'd have come under our Local Education Authority he wouldn't have been acknowledged. It was a desperate thing for us to pay for these private lessons at the time, and also to get him to his lessons. We didn't have a car, and I had to take him on a bus and a train, and I had two other young children. But we managed, and he went on from strength to strength. That year, after he'd been refused entrance into the Music School, he entered various competitions and just wiped the board at all the local festivals. Eventually, he started there at 7.

John Asgard *(talented singer, aged 19, at music college):*

I gave up the violin when I was 12 because I hadn't progressed as well as I could have done, but it did give me a good background knowledge of working in orchestras and learning different sorts of music. Since then I've been singing, though I took up the double bass whilst my voice was breaking. You've got to wait for your voice to develop fully before you can really get anywhere, but whilst it's settling down, you can always work on repertoire and languages. I'd like to end up in either Italy or America, if I can get to the right standard as an opera singer.

STIFLED CREATIVITY

Both the creative and academic aspects of intelligence are promoted by the same general environmental influences – encouragement, example, and educational facilities. But at their highest levels, the emotional aspects of those influences may diverge, and even be contradictory. Because creativity draws on emotional and personality factors, it needs emotional freedom to flower, whereas successful academic achievement is more dependent on emotional control, as well as educational input.

Conformity and repression are the enemies of creative activity, but they are excellent for promoting high achievement in school exams, especially in science. The intense absorption of information that had been expected of many of the intellectually gifted pupils in this study sometimes left them feeling creatively and emotionally squeezed dry. Those university-door-opening A grades demanded such single-minded determination that leisure activities were squashed by study, which sapped the young people's time and inclination for anything else. Even their critical thinking was dimmed; some saying wearily that it was simply easier for them to stick to getting through a hard day's travel, school, and homework, without spending precious energy considering alternative points of view.

When you are gifted across the board, how can you be expected to know yourself so well in your early teens that you can choose which side of the educational chasm to climb? The problem is that almost all higher education students are selected on the basis of their school academic results, with the inbuilt expectation that somehow the brightest will be creative in their work when they get as far as research, whether in science or the arts. Several young people in this study who had been placed in that dilemma at school had made the wrong choice; they had then either to try to put this right, or to continue on the wrong track. Fortunately, though, many did survive the selection system with both creative and academic traits intact.

In high achiever Donald Purdey's home, there wasn't a book to be seen, and all he had known from his school was an indigestible diet of learning, more and more information. But now, at university, his emotional shell was starting to crack with the new growth of his long-stifled creative urge.

Donald Purdey *(highly gifted, aged 21, studying engineering at university):*

The school I went to was so far away, I couldn't take part in extra-curricular activities. Anyway, it was a real sweatshop, so I didn't really enjoy it very much. I couldn't go to the local comprehensive because it's not very good; it hasn't even got a sixth form. Round here, you usually just finished school at 16 and go into an apprenticeship, but my school was all geared towards university, so I was swept along in the tide. The trouble was that Oxford and Cambridge were the be-all and end-all, and I didn't make it.

Sometimes I feel disadvantaged in that I crammed a lot of science, but didn't develop myself culturally. I've never read novels or anything like that, and I've never bought a book in my life, even at university, though I intend to try and catch up on it. With having to do all that work, I was quite happy to be rail-roaded, and I didn't think a lot or question things. That's how I came to try LSD. I was just intrigued to know what it was like, because life is about feelings that you get out of doing something – pleasures and experiences. But it was hallucinogenic, horrible.

My dad's a painter and decorator, but he just puts up the paper that somebody else has chosen; I'd like to work out what would suit the room best, and maybe one day even design a house. One guiding reason for doing engineering at university was that I was sponsored. To have done another course would have been stretching things financially, and my dad wasn't too keen on giving the parental contribution.

I've been working with steam turbines. The way it was taught at university, you didn't have to be anywhere near one, but you do really have to learn its notes to know how it is running. It's through my analogies of where I feel it fits into the real world that I can see an application for all the maths I learned straight off. It is exciting to design. If I'm designing something that needs thinking out, and I suddenly realize that I'm getting there, I can't get it out of my mind. It's always there from morning to night. I just can't switch off it. I did it at work on one of my own designs; I haven't read it in a book, I'd worked it out all by myself. I was concentrating on it all day, and time goes so quickly then.

Science or the Arts?

Gifted youngsters do have a tendency to throw themselves into their chosen activities with such force that alternatives are left bobbing in the backwash. At school in Britain, they are often obliged to choose in their early teens between studying arts and science. In my study, the idea was found to be popular, especially among parents, that if you chose sciences you could always pick up on the arts, almost as hobbies, but that if you went for arts subjects, sciences would remain a mystery to you for ever. When earning a living was felt to be the most important goal of education, parents saw science as pre-eminent: 51 per cent considered science more important in education, only 8 per cent thought the arts were more important, and the rest made no choice.

An unskilled father voiced many parents' feelings: 'There's not really that much call for music or arts. Then again, some people do get a lot of pleasure out of art, but what you go to school for is learning, to get a job at the end of it, to get you out of the house.' And a gifted girl reasoned: 'There are a lot of jobs which are general, but jobs which are for scientists you couldn't get if you were an artist.'

Quite apart from the heavy academic workload which the high achievers in all subjects had to face, many of those who opted only for science had the additional distress of feeling aesthetically isolated and unfulfilled; their anticipated self-generating understanding of the arts had not, after all materialized.

Raymond Grey *(highly gifted, aged 21, studying physics at university):*

I'm really an arts person, but I am also very good at sciences and that's what I chose at 15. But the timetable at school was so rigid you couldn't mix subjects, and it was a mistake. Taking science restricted me in a way that I didn't think it would. In the end I just never got the chance to try anything else, and that was when I began really to hate and detest what I was doing. They said that you couldn't possibly get through your A-levels if you were doing a subject that you didn't like. I didn't believe them, and I was right. I got all As. Trouble was, I failed my Oxford interview when they discovered I wasn't very interested in physics. They nailed me when they started asking questions about reading around the subject, and I hadn't done any. But I'm still studying physics. I do like music, not that I'm ever moved to tears or anything, but it often stirs me. I'd like to spend more time with it one day.

It could happen the other way too. No matter how much a talented and enthusiastic child wanted it, and no matter how carefully it was con- sidered, to enter a specialist school and devote one's life to the study of an art was sometimes the wrong decision. An ex-music school pupil had, quite simply, made the wrong choice. He said:

I came to the conclusion that I preferred the sciences, which is why I left. It's a totally different type of person that likes music from one that likes science. A musician knows things will happen, but he's not both- ered why. He knows that playing his violin is going to make a certain sound, because he's holding his fingers that way. Whereas for a scientist, that wouldn't be enough; he wants to know why it's doing that. He'd learn all about nodes and wavelengths, and lengthening the strings. Musicians aren't worried about the wave form in there; they're just happy with it as it is.

Another, a girl, said wistfully, 'I went there to do music, I know, but I have a creative tendency and I would have enjoyed some alternatives, like fashion design, or textiles.'

The Cost of High Academic Achievement

At times, academic research can be hard, unproductive work. But then a revelation which was quite unexpected can light up a whole new area. This happened in the follow-up study with responses to the question, 'What gives you the greatest pleasure?' It had been designed simply as a pleasant way of rounding off an interview of many hours. Table 5.1 shows how the whole sample answered.

Table 5.1 *Q: What Gives You the Greatest Pleasure?*

Response	%
Relationships	37
Achievement	24
A mixture of things	23
Creative/aesthetic activities	7
Nature	5
Physical activities	4

Using all the collected data from the whole long study, a statistical comparison was made between those who chose achievement as their greatest pleasure – the Achievers – and those who found their greatest pleasure in creative activity – the Creatives. (The procedure was adjusted for the proportions of the 41 Achievers and 11 Creatives. Indeed, it was striking how small a proportion of the 169 young people found their major satisfaction in creativity.) The results, tested below, provided a clear picture of two kinds of young person in terms of their outlooks, personalities, and scholastic success, all at high (1 per cent) levels of significance. Overall, the Creatives came from homes which gave them more aesthetic example and support, whereas the achievers came from homes where academic success, especially in science, took precedence over artistic appreciation.

- *IQ*: The most important finding was that there was virtually no difference between the general intelligence of the Achievers and the Creatives. Both were at gifted level. The non-gifted had been less specific in their answers and so did not enter these categories.
- *Gender*: Most of the Achievers (93 per cent) were boys, and most of the Creatives (73 per cent) were girls.
- *Examinations*: Although the Creatives had taken a wider range of subjects than the Achievers, they were considerably less successful in terms of grades.
- *Parental attitudes*: The Achievers had usually grown up in families that had greatly encouraged them in their schoolwork from an early age, though their creative urges were more often curbed.
- *Culture*: The general ambience and décor of the Creatives' homes were more carefully considered, and there was a wider range of books around than in those of the Achievers. But the biggest cultural difference was in the quality of music. The Creatives had a much more serious level of music at home, and were far more likely to sit and listen as a family, almost never using it merely as background.
- *Emotion*: The results of a test of emotional adjustment (Stott, 1976) which had been given to the children in 1974 was looked at in terms of their present behaviour. Even then, the potential Achievers had been significantly much more troubled with emotion and relationship problems, and it still proved to be so. Ten years earlier the Achievers' group had scored by far the highest hostility rating to the whole sample, 33 per cent scoring above average on the nationally standardized test. But of the Creatives at that time, 91 per cent did not manage a single score on the hostility rating. It was a similar picture with relationships – the Achievers then had scored the highest peer-maladaptiveness rating of any grouping, while the Creatives scored nil.

In the follow-up the Achievers described themselves as significantly more often experiencing depression at times, and had much more difficulty with friendships than the Creatives. Although both groups had the same high intelligence, the Achievers saw their giftedness as a social handicap, an aspect of themselves which other people did not like (63 per cent) and on which they blamed their lack of friends. This was not so for the Creatives (9 per cent), who largely disregarded their gifts. The differences were clearly in each one's self-concept, and not in actual ability. The Creatives in this comparison also felt themselves to be empathetic twice as frequently as the Achievers.

Achievement does imply some competition, if only with oneself. It could be that the competitive element in the ambition to achieve runs counter to forming close relationships, especially with people of one's own age. Far more of the Achievers (17 per cent) said that they only had friends older than themselves, which was entirely untrue for the Creatives, almost all of whom had friends of all ages. The Creatives were much more communicative; twice as many Creatives (40 per cent) as Achievers (20 per cent) described themselves as talking a lot. To me, the Creatives were also livelier and much more fun to be with.

The Creatives were far more likely to be unhappy with their schools (36 per cent compared with 10 per cent), and many more of them (19 per cent compared with 5 per cent) had serious problems there. But they also had livelier, more individual attitudes to school, far more (55 per cent compared with 24 per cent) suggesting at least four ways in which they thought it could be changed for the better. It looked as though either the creatively inclined had much greater difficulty in fitting in with the system – or the system was not flexible enough to cope with them.

One creative boy explained:

One of my great grudges against the school is that they only like people who conform – 'Do your collar up,' kind of thing. Well, I'm a bit different from the other people. They all tend to sit down and do work, and I don't. I'm a bit more extrovert, and they don't like that; I like to have a bit of a joke with the teachers – I don't go too far, I don't think, though my hairstyle tends to provoke some 'mention'.

Their discomfort in the system also showed in the Creatives' greater dissatisfaction with their careers advice, because they more often wanted to tread an unconventional path. The vast majority (82 per cent) were unhappy about what they had been given, compared with the Achievers (43 per cent), who usually went on to conventional courses at university, and so had far fewer vocational problems.

Though the Achievers actually had a greater variety of spare-time pursuits than the Creatives, fewer of those, such as team sport, could be termed creative. They also showed less involvement and perseverance in their chosen activities than the Creatives, and they tended to opt out and relax more into TV, 76 per cent of Achievers choosing mainly light TV, compared with 54 per cent of the Creatives. In childhood, though, the Achievers appeared to have enjoyed the same creative satisfaction as the rest of the sample, but as they reached the peak of intense study at 18, and certainly by the age of 20, few reported it, unlike most of the whole sample, for whom there seemed to be little change.

The big pleasure for all the gifted teenagers was language. It showed in their floods of words in answers to my questions, though one boy admitted he talked in such torrents because it was expected of him as a 'gifted youth'. It also showed in a great deal of private poetry, and in reading; 'Balance is what I aim for. I do a little bit of drawing, and sometimes I write poetry. I'm deeply moved by poetry because it's very intense – far more so than novels. Poets work best when they're depressed, and that's when I've written some of my best stuff. In the summer, when I've not got much else to do, I read about two library books a day. My own, I read over and over again.'

Most of the Achievers, however, were well aware of their probable loss of creative satisfaction in choosing to go all out for high examination success, and some had made considerable efforts to harmonize the academic and creative sides of their lives. Many of the most ardent Achievers, however, had some difficulty in answering the questions which called for a touch of imagination, such as how they would spend unlimited money. The Creatives, though, took a more enthusiastic view of such a windfall.

Danny Smith (gifted, aged 17, at school):

I'd build a commune. It would be huge, really massive, and take millions of pounds to build, and the people in it would be totally good. There's a few people like that around, like me, you know, people who think like I think. It could be in a huge, secluded house, with really nice places around it, with lakes. Then you don't need anything else, it would be just like Utopia within twenty-foot stone walls with an electrified fence on the top. It would be great. I spent the whole of Sunday afternoon planning it when I should have been doing my homework.

Chapter 6
Schooldays

And gladly wolde he lerne, and gladly teche.
GEOFFREY CHAUCER, PROLOGUE TO *THE CANTERBURY TALES*

Gifted children's experiences of school are different because they often have their own ways of learning, which may be at greater speed and depth. They can also see school life differently, being more keenly aware, and would appreciate more say in the way their education is conducted. For them especially, schools are often places with limited vision, and they very much appreciate good, honest, enthusiastic teachers, even if not necessarily brimming with knowledge. However, in common with others of their age, the gifted sometimes have concerns other than school study.

THE BRITISH EDUCATION SYSTEM

Schools in Britain range from large, highly organized, all-comer comprehensives to small private ones; from those with 95 per cent ethnic minority pupils to others where none has ever been seen. While in some state schools the teaching of one foreign language is the maximum, others offer alternatives such as Urdu, and some private schools oblige 7-year-olds to learn Latin. Although there is a similarly widely varied situation in other countries such as the USA or Australia, there is much less variety in more centrally organized ones such as France or those in Eastern Europe. To complicate matters further, when seeking pupils' views on school, each reacts in a further variety of ways to the same provision. But it is only by asking those on the receiving end how they feel about their education that it is possible to see where they find it irritating and useless or satisfying and valuable, especially with such an articulate group as this sample of bright, sensitive young people. They attended a great variety of schools and their sincere accounts provide valuable feedback for those who will heed them.

There is no getting away from politics in education. Perhaps the greatest difference in outlook between the two major educationally influential countries, the United States and Britain, is that in the former education is presented as a vehicle for opportunity in life and there are always chances to keep going in spite of any breaks from it. In Britain, however, children have to jump through state examination hoops at particular times, or face heavy psychological and financial disincentives from re-entering the educational system. This more black-and-white view adds some pressure to completing the course at the appropriate time. In addition, centuries of continuous educational selection, whether by wealth or by ability, and of deference to those who have passed the barriers have left their mark on a society where élitism can still sometimes masquerade as high quality. The details of the British system and the sample's academic performance in it are described in Appendix I.

SCHOOL EXPERIENCES

A normal classroom is a fairly structured place, activities focusing on the content of the lesson, which is designed so that the pupil's performance is correctable and thus improvable by the teacher. There is usually a dominant concern with information, which provides a problem for pupils who are also interested in ideas for their own sakes, and the connected social problem of how to adapt while remaining intellectually alive and thus different. In fact, it is virtually impossible to show intellectually gifted behaviour without distinguishing oneself from one's school-fellows. Occasionally, pupils' efforts at serious thinking around the syllabus were treated as flippancy, but even more so were attempts at creative work. This was even true at some rather rigid primary schools, as graphically described by Adrian Lambert (highly gifted, aged 22, a milkman):

In junior school we were told to write a book, to take a week, and I filled about three books in a day. But it wasn't what the teacher wanted, so, to make sure that everybody else was more diligent, she read it out, then ripped it up in front of everybody, with some of my funny poems too, which everybody else appreciated. She'd rip them up to general amusement. If I'd say anything that the teacher didn't have knowledge of, I'd be seen as a real smart alec, and she wouldn't ask me again.

The gifted may thus find themselves intellectually isolated, and need the frame of reference which is to be found in the company of people like themselves; as a highly gifted girl said with feeling: 'If I have a child like me, I would definitely send him or her to a school where I knew they catered only for clever children. I would pay fees, and go without things myself to give my children that. Or at least, a school which had quite a lot of clever children, because then you get some sort of companionship, people to talk to of your own ability.'

Some children cope with their dilemma by behaving stupidly in class; for instance, shouting out silly answers to show how 'normal' they are. Others may become overly conformist, divert attention to someone who is an even more determined scholar, or become the class clown. One highly gifted girl explained: 'If I'm not in competition with people the same level, I get very lazy. Even with only moderate ability differences, I just feel superior, and so bored when we go over things so often.'

There is also sometimes a 'work-restriction' norm among pupils, which is more common where school education is not highly valued but it can even operate at selective schools. There seems to be a strange classroom lore that it is acceptable to come top of the class as long as you are not seen to work for it – as though achievement were predestined and to work hard is interfering with nature. At some schools, it can mean that a child who wants to achieve high marks may have to study in secret to avoid the disapproval of schoolmates.

Unfortunately, although they are usually unaware of it, many teachers (even those who teach the gifted) direct the class to work at around its average level. Unifying the class in this way makes teaching easier, but can cause difficulty for a gifted child in a predominately average-ability school. A student teacher in my sample noted: 'From having been a pupil and having attempted to be a teacher, I see that the middle-ability band gets by far the most tuition, the top stream gets bored, and doesn't get stretched enough, while the bottom stream haven't got a clue what's going on.'

Many bright youngsters felt sympathy for the teacher in what they saw as the impossible task of teaching them in mixed-ability classes: 'It's just asking too much of one teacher to be able to cope with the diversity of abilities every single lesson.' Some felt a little guilty: 'It's not that I want to dominate people of a lower ability, but it's too hard for the poor teacher, having to teach at all ability levels.'

Some teachers coped with this problem by making 'assistant' teachers of the more advanced children, using them to instruct the slower ones. But for the brightest, who did not seem to enjoy the teaching, it really meant that they were marking time till the rest caught up. It was described quite spontaneously by several in the sample, as by Quentin Cooke (highly gifted, aged 14, at school):

When I was about 6 or 7, we were divided by age and I was very, very far ahead of most others. Often, when the teacher got so overworked with children not understanding, she used to send them to me to try and explain it. Well, I felt partly flattered and partly annoyed, because it just took up my time when I could be doing something else; it was so unbelievably easy that I didn't benefit from doing it all over again. And some of my 'pupils' were resentful, too, but I could take that.

The 'Three Times' Problem

In a normal classroom, the teacher usually says the same thing three times. First as an introduction – 'This is what I am going to tell you'; again to boost it – 'Now I am telling it to you'; and then to summarize and make sure – 'That is what I have just told you.' But the gifted remember it the first time round, so in order to avoid the tedium of the repetition, they often devise a special technique. They teach themselves only to listen consciously on the first occasion and switch off for the following two. This demands a very high level of mental skill, which takes some practice to perfect.

Highly gifted Caroline Hardman described how it was for her:

In the lectures, I listen to everything the first time, but when they start going over and over the same thing, I use my automatic switch-off button. It started at school, where lessons were more or less handed to you on a plate. You can tell by the tone of the voice when it's coming again; it becomes a knack after sitting through hours and hours of lessons and lectures, especially when you keep having the same teacher. And it's the way they say, '*Now*, then,' and I think, 'Right, I've got five minutes to myself now.' It can be really boring when lecturers say the same thing four times. We had one who asked, 'Now has anybody got any questions?,' and nobody said a word. So he said, 'You've taken so long with nobody saying something that obviously none of you can understand it, so I'll go through it again.'

The danger is that before it has reached a state of reliability, the switch-off may go on too long and cause the child to miss some explanations first time round; and the missing parts may be vital – perhaps a brick in the foundation of knowledge on which future learning has to be built. And it can get to be a bad, lazy habit. It becomes easier to slip into a dreamland of one's own than to adjust one's mind to new information. The learning of the gifted can seem erratic because of it; they seem to learn some things well – whatever they have listened to – then have gaps – where they have switched off. With bits missing they can grasp the wrong conclusions, which nevertheless they may hold firmly.

Even in selective education, the 'three times' problem still holds true for those of the very highest ability, because there is always some difference of ability between members of a class. A highly gifted boy explained: 'Even in our rarefied maths set, there were one or two people who found it intensely difficult, so the teacher would sometimes have to go back over certain points several times. I'd cut off, but I didn't lose track of what was happening; I would switch back in again when we got on to a new area.'

TYPES OF SCHOOL

To make a basis for comparison, to see how the young people of different IQ scores had fared in their school careers, the sample was sorted into three IQ groups of high, above average, and average (see Table 4.1, p. 77). It was immediately clear that the pupils with the highest IQs, and thus the most academic potential, were not distributed evenly throughout the different kinds of schools. They were far more likely to go to selective (either private or state) single-sex schools, while the lower IQ pupils were more likely to go to mixed-ability comprehensives (see Table 6.1).

Considering both the potential academic ability of their pupils and their high level of examination orientation, it was really not surprising that the selective schools produced an overall higher level of examination success than the other schools.

Table 6.1 *IQ and Type of School*

Mean IQ	Type of school
153	Selective
143	Private
134	Grammar
128	Comprehensive
127	Secondary modern

Selective Schools

When they could, parents of gifted children often chose a school where classes were selected by ability, and although the majority of children at such schools had won scholarships to them, some were paid for by their parents. Several families had even moved house to an area where there were still grammar schools. A mother of a highly gifted boy explained:

Up to the age of 11, he was standing out like a sore thumb. He used to come home from school and say 'I won't put my hand up any more and answer questions.' Now in this school, because they select, at last he's one of the lads, and it's such a relief. There's so much there that he enjoys. If he had to change school and go back into mixed ability, he would try to smother his talent again.

To some extent, the young people's attitudes towards selective education reflected their own experiences, though a few would have liked an even greater degree of selective teaching than they had actually known, as a highly gifted boy explained:

Even at this school I didn't learn any new maths for about eighteen months because there was no streaming at all, and maths is one of those subjects where some people can grasp it and others can't. Now that I'm in the top maths set, I can state that having me in the same class as some of the people who are now in lower sets didn't help them, and it just held me back. I would have something worked out, conquered, and be ready to move on to something else, but I would have to keep on battering at it for three weeks because somebody else needed to take longer over it. What a boring year!

Indeed, there was little intellectual democracy among the gifted in this sample. Of the young high-IQ group, the great majority (80 per cent) preferred to be taught in classes that were pre-selected by ability. The only exceptions they would consider were subjects that were not examinable. One outstanding girl, from a highly selective school, even described how she found some of her fellow students in her computer class at university to be slow. She spoke without a glimmer of humour: 'It's mixed ability – everybody in one class.' However, going down the IQ scale, the other two groups saw selective education as significantly less attractive (61 per cent and 41 per cent), though few were as firmly against it as one average IQ boy, who said: 'It's a task to catch up with the others when you're doing your best and everybody seems to be getting away from you. The bright ones should tell you things, doing good for the people that aren't so bright.'

A substantial minority, mostly boys, thrived on the challenge of school pressure, hard learning, and the cut and thrust of keen competition. For them, a typical comment would be:

> I like feeling a part of a big establishment, with uniform and Founder's Day and that sort of thing. Also it's a hive of academic activity, it's very stimulating. It's very competitive, which I need to work to my full potential. If there's an A to be got, then I want to get it. Exams are a challenge, and I would have liked to have been accelerated at school, again probably as a challenge.

But a mother said: 'It's a stress reaction, which shows physically. In the final year I had to go into school and say, "For God's sake, stop him working. I don't care whether he goes to Cambridge or whether he doesn't." His form master thought it was a rather odd attitude, but I felt that it was more important that he survived as a human being.'

That high pressure was also described in heart-felt terms by pupils who saw the school as abusing their potential for academic achievement – 'a cog in the school wheel'. Justine, aged 15 and at an all-girls' grammar school, spoke of her school's restricted outlook:

> The style of teaching is uninspirational, uninteresting. The teacher talks and you take it down; homework is essays and more writing. They don't

look for new ways to interest the class. They themselves are bored, and of course, so are we. I'd like to be taught in a way that is more relevant to the actual world outside, to involve more personal experiences both on the teacher's side and on mine. I'm trying to fight boredom and frustration, just to get through my exams with good marks. I expect the teachers think I'm very lazy, but I don't actually know what they think because they don't really speak to me.

Pupils were often expected to take in information and reproduce it on demand, which left them feeling intellectually unexercised. Many would have liked an easing off from examination pressure and some concern for their own values and interests. As Justine added: 'There was no time to explore anything else outside your syllabus. I would have liked to have done things like computing, and more languages, to have explored more areas. The school didn't focus enough on the individual; it didn't bring out enough of what you've got to offer.'

Indeed, the most successful examinees of all, normally from the selective schools, showed a lack of broad concern for their subject area and a failure to read around what they were studying. Maybe their natural curiosity had been sated because of the heavy spoon-feeding in learning they had received, because a large amount of material has to be taken in very quickly in order to attain high marks in examinations. One father spoke sadly of his highly successful daughter, now at university: 'The disappointing thing to me is her lack of desire to find out for herself. She lacks the questing mind of a good scientist.'

But a teacher's enthusiasm for the subject could be inspiring, and when it happened, the fortunate gifted pupils responded with delight, like Ruth Huxley:

We had a wonderful teacher once. She made you sit back and think. It was her own enthusiasm, but she didn't so much inspire you as make you inspire yourself. She didn't sit there behind her desk like the big defensive mechanism, she'd sit on top of it. You couldn't ignore her. She'd never give just one side of an argument, she told you the whole lot then said 'Right, tell me what you think.' There was lots of debating in the lessons, lots of creative English rather than textbook English, like improvisation drama.

Not all the high-level achievers were as intellectually curious (or perhaps as fortunate in their teachers), although they had an extraordinary thirst for information. And contrary to what is often described as a characteristic of the gifted, they did not often enjoy finding things out for themselves. The effort of searching in libraries and museums was often described as too time-consuming and tedious, and some even preferred predigested information in note form, straight from the teacher's mouth.

In fact, over a third of the sample said they had never even been given the opportunity to learn through finding out via project work in the secondary school. But the examination high-flyers who had tried it often made such comments as: 'Project work can give you a lot of satisfaction, but it is a lot of work, and it does take up a great deal of time. I really do prefer to work in class.' Others felt even more strongly: 'God, what a waste! I could have done so much other stuff while I've been doing the work for this project. I want an exam to work for at the end.' When they reached university, however, it often hit such students how ill prepared they had been for the independent study they were then faced with. Several had to reconsider their ideas: 'More project work in schools would have prepared me for the sort of thing I'm having to do at university. Now I know what it's all about, I do wish we'd done more.'

But how the pupils felt about project-type work and what they learned from it seemed to be largely a matter of how it was given and supervised. For the more thoughtful, such as Philip Bessant (highly gifted, aged 20, studying science at university), it was an intellectual challenge:

Time is so limited in school lessons. Project work gives you a chance to do a lot more in depth on a subject that interests you. I can't say my projects were always successful, though, because I misconceived them. It would have helped to have worked more with the teacher first, to sort out the priorities of the problem. But it taught me how to plan better, and even more how to look through an idea, and what possibilities I'd have to research into and beyond it. It also built up my confidence to go out and find the information for yourself. If there'd been more of this at school, it would have been better.

Comprehensive Schools

The major benefit described by the gifted comprehensive school pupils was social – that it had been a good thing to learn to mix and make friends with all kinds of people. Mary Owen (highly gifted, aged 17), the poet, disagreed with her mother, who thought she had been unhappy at the comprehensive school. Mary's view was:

I've experienced both, and I really preferred the comprehensive system, although the teaching was very patchy because the teacher had to flit across various intelligences. You did need some discipline there too, because otherwise nothing would have got across at all. I can see that it's much easier with some selection. When I came to the grammar school, I found it quite amazing that most of the girls were studious and interested in the work, and they were all so well behaved.

The major debit many described was their belief that they could have done a lot better academically at a more selective school. A university student said:

At my comprehensive there was absolutely nothing, not even the occasional ten-minute talk. I'd have liked some debating, say at an informal inter-school level. At Cambridge, I've seen that people from other schools have been more stretched. They've completed the syllabus a lot earlier than we did, and they were also taught much better how to tackle exams. Then they've done extra preparatory study for the university course, which has helped them considerably. I didn't get any of that.

Another debit in some comprehensive schools was the real lack of resources, including teachers and teaching. This sometimes led to some remoteness between staff and pupils: 'Half the time, they don't seem to know who I am.' Poor facilities are, of course, a considerable drain on the learning energy of all pupils, but it was particularly poignant for those who had the ability to fly through the syllabus and go on to higher-level creative thinking to be obliged to set their brilliant minds to the treadmill of copying by hand for hours. It is a terrible waste and a disgrace.

Fortunately for Geraldine Christy, unlike most of her schoolmates, she had an intellect that would see her through the material handicaps of her comprehensive school. The range of the ten subjects she was studying in depth, however, would make the mouths of many children at selective schools water, because there the syllabus is often more exam-orientated and restricted. Hers included chemistry, physics, electronics, craft, design and technology, music, English language and literature, Welsh language and literature, and mathematics. She was the youngest in her class, yet had been top in every subject since she started at the school.

Geraldine Christy *(highly gifted, aged 16, at school):*

We haven't got enough textbooks to go round, so you have to copy about 50 per cent on to your files. I don't learn from it, because I don't read as I write. We do get photocopied stuff in English, but they've been told they've overspent, so the English teachers pay for it out of their own pockets. I was going to buy the books, but the teacher said it's not worth it because you have to have a new one every term. We've got plenty of technical equipment, though, like electronics and computers, because the school's been chosen by the Manpower Services Commission for this new scheme, Technical Vocational something. It's in English and maths that we're short of textbooks and stuff.

There are teachers that take our books in regularly and mark them, but there are some who have that many classes they don't have time to do it. The maths department – they can't hardly take our books in at all. In the sixth form, you might go nearly a year without teachers seeing your book. I'm glad we're streamed, though, because we can all go at the right pace instead of having to wait for other people. Even so, I think that if I worked hard it would cause embarrassment to some of my classmates, because I could really do better than I'm doing.

Of the six high-IQ young people who had experienced both selective and mixed-ability schools and their learning cultures, concerns were put most clearly in this account:

Andy Spurgeon *(highly gifted, aged 17, at school):*

I had to leave the private [selective] school for money reasons and come to the comprehensive. It's been a very educating experience. There, I'd been in an intellectual environment, where everyone was very outgoing with their talents. But at the comprehensive, I started to understand some of those people who were less intelligent than myself and who weren't going to have as many job opportunities and qualifications.

But in order to stay sane, I had to make myself an average person within the school. So I refused to be in any sports teams or school productions, and I even held back on the academic side. But since I've been in the sixth form, which is a much more enlightened, smaller group, I've been able to do more things, and they've started to accept me. One of the bad things that comes out of holding back on the reins is that I've found it very, very difficult to let go again. I do the minimum of work, because I was already at the top, and the force that goes behind the working kid is usually the competition, not the teacher. I would have been an abominable person if I'd stayed at the other school, but I certainly would have had better exam results.

Harmony

Yet there were a few gifted young people from poor homes in this study for whom the comprehensive system had been the only one which could have helped them to develop their potential. Children who would have found it difficult to cope with the middle-classness of a grammar school, and who could have been crushed by the snobbery in some private schools, could find their way academically with teachers who spoke with the same accent, along with their friends, and with support from home. Whenever there are cutbacks in education, such culturally delicate youngsters are bound to be affected.

George Booth is such a youth, who had no alternative resources but his hard work and his brains. Miles of drab, low-quality council housing surrounded his house on the outskirts of Hull. Of about twenty of the local shops, only one was open, and that was heavily defended with metal grilles. The boards covering the windows of the others were heavily daubed with graffiti. The area was surrounded by chemical industries – fat chimneys and black, spiky towers topped by the everlasing flames of burning fumes.

George lived there with his widowed mother, who glowed with love for her children. He was tall, handsome, at the top of the IQ scale, and doing very well indeed in spite of being blind in one eye. He was at the local comprehensive school, in a mixed-ability class of his own age. The teachers there cared for him, giving him the kind of feedback and encouragement that some youngsters at expensive schools have never known, and it was there that he had learned to have ambitions to be an accountant or lawyer.

It was a situation, however, which highlighted some of the problems of gifted working-class youth, fighting for a place in the professional world. Both George's parents had left school at 14, and the family income had to be supplemented by welfare benefits. But George's most obvious problem was that he was not articulate, and what he did say had a heavy local accent. There was no smooth flow of words to beguile the ear of a prospective tutor or employer outside the region. He was accustomed neither to talking to the full extent of his vocabulary nor to reading. There were no books in the house and the only newspaper he ever saw was a tabloid, the *Star*. But he was fighting hard to overcome his disadvantages. The one paradoxical advantage he did have, though, in not being from an educationally aware home was that he was quite free of the hang-ups of being labelled gifted. Nobody had made him feel different. He was very happy at home, and with his neighbours and teachers, and was at one with his world. When someone is in such harmony, good things come out of it.

George Booth *(highly gifted, aged 17, at school):*

I give other people in the class help, and they prefer getting it off me, instead of them running to a teacher. Sometimes they'll ask questions in class that I wouldn't, so I just listen, and sometimes it helps me. I get on all right with my mates, and just leave the ones I don't like. I don't care what they think, but I don't think I'm any different from them. If my work's good I feel proud, and if it's bad it's my own fault. I can't blame it on anyone else. They don't tell me I'm a bright lad, but I know that if I've got an exam question, if the teachers give just a hint, I'd be able to give the answer straight off.

You don't feel confident if you come from a poor background, like going for a high-up job when there's someone else there from a higher family. You'd always feel he'd had the upper hand. That's what I'm working so hard at school for, to show them. I've joined the rugby team, and I play of an evening three times a week. If we get beat, and I know we could have won it, I'll come home and explain the whole story to my Mum. I keep telling her till I calm down. I think she's seen it all before.

TEACHING THE HIGHLY ABLE

The essence of teaching is in communication, and I am presenting a plea here for a genuine meeting of minds – the exciting minds of teacher and pupil. Education for the gifted is not just a matter of dispensing ever more refined pearls of wisdom, nor of fitting pupils for high-flying careers. As with all children, it has a profound and echoing psychological impact on their feelings about themselves. Like other children, the highly able need teaching of a sufficient quality to promote their development – intellectually, emotionally, and spiritually. Successful teaching for learning helps children to a sense of control over both the learning situation and themselves, and there is ample research evidence to show that this involves guidance by the teacher. And the gifted children want it too.

Significantly more of those with the highest IQs (87 per cent), compared with all the others (68 per cent), much preferred to work along with a teacher, whether to listen, or better still as someone off whom to bounce their ideas. The gifted had a high regard for teachers who were willing to listen as well as talk. It was put succinctly by creative David Baker (gifted, aged 17, at school): 'I talk a lot, and so I talk to the teacher about what I think, and what's going on, what I've read and seen on the news, what's happening in life in the world about us, and the actual theory that he's teaching us. It's much more fun than talking to my peer group, because teachers know so much.'

The value of different approaches to teaching is clear to most pupils, and the bright, perceptive young people in this sample were extremely concerned about the way they were taught, the curriculum they were obliged to follow, and the way the school was managed. Dominating their concerns was the wish that teachers should be sensitive to their needs, so that they could work better together. Of all the sample, only 76 per cent felt they had enough personal communication with their teachers, nearly a quarter saying they felt relatively unknown. A constant cry echoed through the interviews – for pupils to be treated as real people, not lumped together as a class. At times, they said, their grades seemed to matter more than they did. Some would have preferred smaller classes so that relationships could develop more easily. They felt it was too tempting to coast along in the crowd and would do less than their best. Just a few, though, did not want a close relationship with teachers at all.

Those who teach the gifted should have a high teaching calibre, though not necessarily specialist knowledge. Expertise in sheer teaching skills was very much appreciated by the brightest in my study. The gifted did not ask for nor expect super-teachers, but wanted honest, competent individuals, who would do the job to the best of their ability, so that respect could flow in both directions. One outstanding boy at a comprehensive school described such a situation: 'The teacher couldn't keep up with me, though she knew most of the stuff. But it was OK. She knew the syllabus, and had an idea of what was expected, so she kept pushing me and could tell me what to do.'

The best communication in the classroom must be two-way, so that teachers can also learn from their pupils: 'Teachers forget that no matter how young the kids are, they are thinking for themselves all the time.'

Pupils have a good idea of what works best for them, and they have a right to know and a right to ask. Flexibility is really necessary, so that the teacher can understand which things he'd taught well and which things needed going over again. Once in a while they should ask us how we think they're doing, and that way you'd get some positive results out of it.' However, it did sometimes seem that many of the young people had expected high effort and commitment from their teachers, without being prepared to make the same contribution themselves.

A recurrent theme from students was that honesty and two-way communication with teachers was particularly valuable to the gifted, as Samantha Goldman (highly gifted, aged 20, studying science at university) described:

> I was the physics teacher's first A-level pupil, so she was always testing the water, saying, 'Tell me, if I teach you this in a different way, would you understand it better?' She was very flexible and tapped into me. It was good fun. When I wanted to take astronomy, at first the school said no, but I asked again and again, and eventually the teacher and I learnt it between ourselves, and that's how I came to study it at university.

This implied a willingness to be seen to be human, as Robert, a highly gifted 15-year-old, said:

> When a teacher can make a nice atmosphere to work in, one who can take the odd joke in a lesson, you produce better work. You've got the option to try and tell them what you think is wrong with their teaching style, and why they're not coming across as well as they might, and why their ideas are not being picked up.

The young people hoped for respect for their abilities too, as 17-year-old Dominic, a gifted student in a highly selective school, pointed out:

> Class-time is so short and valuable, and writing is something that you can do at home, so the good teachers use it to do something else. We're interested in other things than the straight syllabus, so the best kind of teacher is willing to go into side matters. One of our best teachers very rarely gets round to doing any of the syllabus – we spend all the lesson talking. He's so interesting, I'll remember all the stuff from class, and then if I don't get any time to do revision, which is often the case, I remember it from the first time.

Poor Communication

Poor teaching is poor communication based on poor judgement of what is
appropriate for the children. For example, what may be poor teaching for
the less able, such as loose structuring of the lesson, could actually be of
benefit to the highly able. But so much of the poor teaching which these
bright young people had experienced was from teachers' carelessness, and
was relevant to all pupils. Those who wanted to learn had suffered
unnecessary intellectual frustration.

This in-depth study has discovered a novel and quite unexpected aspect
of teaching gifted children – they were sometimes taught less conscien-
tiously than other pupils. Just because they were so good at learning (and
often well behaved), some teachers clearly felt free to leave the classroom
during lessons. A gifted grammar school girl said: 'Most of the girls are
pretty conscientious, so a lot of teachers just write exercises on the board,
then go out and wander back in twenty minutes.'

Such teacher behaviour always took place in the selective schools, most
notably in mathematics. None of the average-ability pupils reported it.
The gifted young people felt they were being short-changed, rather than
seeing it as a tribute to their competence in learning. It was a penalty of
high ability and they were obliged to use their ingenuity to get round it,
as it sometimes endangered their progress. Three of the sample had
resorted to finding extra teaching: 'One of our maths teachers didn't
always turn up and she had charge of our examinations. We presented a
complaint from the whole class, but of course the school didn't do anything.
So we had to go to night-school to get through.'

Others just managed with what was to hand, like Rachel Wallace
(highly gifted, aged 19, studying mathematics at university):

You have no possible way of protesting about it, because most schools
wouldn't trust the child. We had one maths teacher who would come
into the lesson and say, 'Well, I expect you know what to do,' and drift
out again ten minutes later – never said a word – and there were only
four of us in that A-level class. One of my friends was very helpful; he
used to teach me while the teacher was in the staff-room.

This straightforward neglect of the brightest seemed to be mostly in
mathematics and physics, and most usually with teachers in academic
schools, whom pupils would describe as 'having good, very good qualifi-

cations, but incompetent at teaching.' Andy Spurgeon (highly gifted, aged 17, at school) was not alone in saying:

> There are certain teachers that everyone in the whole school knows are very bad. The head of the maths department is a brilliant mathematician with all sorts of awards and prizes for doing maths – but he can't teach. There are kids who are going to fail because of his teaching. Last year, they had to have another maths teacher in to teach his class at the last minute, but they still keep him on.

Some teachers combined the two deficiencies. Nicholas Fawcett (highly gifted, aged 21 and long out of work) said: 'My physics teacher was one of the most intelligent men I've ever met. He'd got his PhD and really should have been in a university. But I couldn't understand him. He would come in, go through this, that and the other, set a problem for you, and then disappear to do whatever he did – most of the class failed.'

The more academic the school, the less likely it seemed that the pupils had any communication, much less a relationship, with its principal. The head was often a remote figure who did not know their names, and whose instructions were either announced to the assembled school or came through the medium of a less exalted member of staff. This same person would be assessing their chances for university or a job, often filling in their reports for applications. Sometimes a single interview was the only one-to-one meeting between pupil and headteacher.

Some felt they might have been better off without that contact, though, such as imaginative Danny Smith (gifted, aged 17, at school):

> I don't like the headmaster. Once, he suspended me – on a Friday, and told me to come back in on the Monday. He called me into his study and said, 'Smith, you look like a bloody cockatoo! It's going to go down in your report that you've been suspended.' Pathetic. I didn't do anything; just turned up with my hair still in pink spikes on Monday. Nothing happened.

Feedback from Teachers

Nearly a quarter of all the young people in the sample felt that they had received far too little direct, one-to-one feedback from their teachers on their work. Teacher 'comment' was usually a mark at the end of a written piece of work, with an occasional cryptic remark; but sometimes not even that, only a tick to signify that the work had been seen to be done. However gifted, pupils felt the need to be told when they were on the right or wrong tracks, and to feel that someone cared about their progress. David Baker (gifted, aged 17, at school) had mixed feelings about it: 'My last maths teacher wouldn't let us know what we got in our tests. Fortunately, I didn't want to know, because in maths at that time I wasn't doing too well. But I don't know how they expected us to learn from that.'

Several pupils only found out how well they were doing from information filtered through parent–teacher evenings. One girl was distressed that 'The art teacher told my parents that my work was terrible. I wish he had told it to me to my face, because it came as a shock; I'd thought I was quite good.'

Perhaps giving praise is not part of the British culture. It seemed to be in very short supply in the classrooms. Teachers were not forthcoming in telling pupils directly that they were very bright. The messages they gave were more subtle, such as nuances of speech, and maybe, if pupils were lucky, a 'Very good' beside a high mark. Yet most of the gifted did get the message that they had been recognized as such and that the teachers' expectations of them were high in some way. It was pithily put by Andy Spurgeon: 'They write things in my report like, "His loud and flamboyant personality is perhaps justified in his results" – they never say, "Well done." We once had a mixed parents–teachers–pupils evening, though, which was very interesting and very useful.'

Some had to find out in other ways, though. Gina Emerson (highly gifted, age 19, studying English at university) felt it was all pointless:

They wouldn't let on if they thought you were intelligent, because they thought it was bad for you. In English I was told it would be a struggle for me to take the exams, and now it's my subject at Cambridge. I used to be marked B, and oceans of red all over my essays; it really discouraged me, so much that I started out doing sciences. Then when I changed schools and had a teacher who used to rave about my essays, I thrived on his encouragement. It's probably a hangover that I still think it's a terrible thing to think highly of your abilities. I'd expected everyone at Cambridge to be brilliant, and that I'd only just slipped through the net, but I am actually very good.

Teachers' Estimation of Pupil Ability

There was no direct questioning of teachers in this follow-up because so many of the young people had by then left school. However, teachers did show how they estimated their highly able pupils in three ways (details are given in Appendix II):

1   By putting them in for public examinations. So as not to waste public money, teachers are obliged to estimate each child's probable success before entering him or her for the free public examinations, and it looked as though they were pretty accurate in their assessments. Even though some of the young people were still not old enough to have had access to all public examinations, there were quite clear relationships between IQ scores and available results. The pupils of higher IQ had been entered for more subjects and achieved significantly better grades than those of lower IQ. Their outstanding successes were apparent in the three areas of: academic level of examination, the numbers of subjects passed, and grades achieved.

It is recognized that those who take science subjects are more likely to reach higher grades, and in this study, the brightest children were more likely to take science or a mixture, rather than the arts – a close reflection of their parents' preferences. Thus, the brightest had a double boost to their marks from both ability and science subjects.

2   By accelerating pupils within the school system. The highly able pupils were more likely to have been accelerated. Of the high-IQ group, 23 per cent were either accelerated or were young for their school-class.

3   By letting pupils know they were seen as bright. The young people were asked how they thought their teachers rated their ability in school. Their answers corresponded well with the IQ measure, and, to a somewhat lesser extent, with results on the Raven's intelligence test.

On the whole, the teachers appeared to be good judges of the examination potential of their pupils and acted on what they found. But in fairness, they were often judging future success on the basis of present success, and (understandably) had much more difficulty in recognizing the gifted when their potential was undeveloped for reasons such as poor presentation, as in spasticity, emotional problems or lack of encouragement from home.

DISCIPLINE IN SCHOOL

Teacher–pupil relationships at all ability levels were beset with problems of discipline – how much, or how little? No one wanted a weak teacher who let students get away with murder, but they made a clear distinction between those who were easy-going and approachable and those who were easy-going and slapdash. Ideally, particularly for the older, brighter pupils, there had to be respect flowing both ways – a bond between pupil and teacher. But this was not always so, in either direction.

Most pupils wanted the teachers to be concerned with their all-round well-being, as well as providing firm direction to see them through the examination hurdles. Teachers who could combine the two, knowing when to pull gently but firmly on the reins, were much appreciated. Sarah Mortimer (highly gifted, aged 20, studying computer systems engineering at university) had benefited from this:

> The teachers who got the best out of me were the ones who knew when to say, 'Look, come on, buckle down. You've not done enough.' But when everybody was working hard, they'd relax the atmosphere and say, 'OK. You've worked really hard, we'll do something a bit different for a while.' They know what's going on and they know what's going to get the best out of everybody. You know where you are with those teachers.

Teachers who could communicate well like that did not have discipline problems, as Jeremy Kramer (highly gifted, aged 20, studying medicine) explained:

> If the teacher was sensitive and could understand people, they didn't need to tell anyone off; everyone was immediately quiet. They under-stood. But I'd be silent as anything if there was an interesting teacher, no matter whether they were firm or not. A teacher that gains respect must give respect.

It was not so much the examination system which the gifted pupils railed against as rigid educational strictures, which they saw as sometimes quite pointless, and also unfair. The adjectives with which the very able described their highly academic schools were often those associated with eating – such as force-feeding or spoon-feeding. One boy put it in drinking terms: 'You can lead a horse to water, but you can't make it drink.' Indeed, the eating disorder of anorexia was described as prevalent at two highly achievement-orientated girls' schools, probably due to their overbearing strictness and lack of good teacher–pupil relationships.

Some, though, loved the firm touch, and had learned to lean on their teachers or parents for work discipline instead of developing their own: 'Some of the best teachers we had were the strictest and most old-fashioned, especially the Latin teachers – heads down and get the work done – but they brought out the results. It's not that I like lessons with a firm teacher, but I work better under one. That's the problem.'

For others, too much strictness in the classroom could be negative, producing tension and detracting from the learning environment, especially for older pupils who were keen to flex their intellectual wings. A gifted schoolgirl found that: 'With a very strict teacher, I become more tense and can't think properly; my train of thought becomes chewed up. There's no two-way communication, just the one way. I might as well not be sitting there.' Several of the brightest teenagers very much resented the old-fashioned discipline which seemed to go with the education provided in the more academic schools: 'On our first day, the headmaster told us, "I'm a traditionalist, and I hope you'll leave here as traditionalists too." '

The gifted had different ways of dealing with unwanted discipline. One or two livened up their days by playing intellectual cat-and-mouse games with their teachers, some of whom handled it brilliantly as in this story from Andy Spurgeon (highly gifted, aged 17, at school):

With a new teacher, I just have so much fun because they don't expect it. I run circles round them and do the most terrible things. I'll give you a juicy example. In the lesson one afternoon, I did a perfect act of the despondent person, completely down and slumping around, and I'm usually very cheerful and bright. The teacher sent me out of the class-room and asked my friend what was the matter, and he said 'I think something is amiss, he's not been right all day.' She came out and asked me, 'What's wrong, Andrew?'

'It's personal.'

'Is it your girlfriend?'

'Yes! She's pregnant,' and I promptly burst into tears and flung myself on her. She wrapped her arms round me and said 'Oh Andrew, oh Andrew. Dear oh dear!'

For the next two weeks, I was smothered in sheets and leaflets about what to do. Then, I just couldn't stand it any longer, because I had to keep a fairly straight face every time I saw her in a lesson, so I told her that it was a false alarm. But she gave me As for all the essays I'd done!

Brief Escapes

About a third of the whole sample (with deep questioning) said that they simply removed themselves from the school premises for a break from the system when they felt they needed it. The proportions were about the same for different intelligence levels, 31.4 per cent taking an occasional lesson off, though 10.1 per cent measured their truancy in days or weeks. Some took the odd day off to catch up with homework or to rest, taking a 'philosophical' approach to school attendance. I had considerable (undeclared) sympathy with them because I had spent all my school life doing the same thing. At least in their early school years, this was not an academic problem to the very brightest, who could intellectually span the missed lessons with ease.

But it could be too much and did catch up with a few, as Adrian Lambert (highly gifted, aged 22, a milkman) found:

I nipped off whenever I wanted to. If you're clever enough, you can cope for years by sitting there and just listening in the lessons. Even for maths A-level, for the first couple of months, if the working out was still on the board when I came in, I could just about scrape through. But when it got to a certain stage, I had to either work or pack it in. So I would just pack it in.

Parents sometimes colluded with their gifted children in this unofficial absence from school. One mother said:

He truanted from school quite a lot, and continued the habit at university. Nobody seemed to have bothered him about it at either place. The Latin teacher at school, whose lessons he always missed, chose to disregard it, possibly because neither of them liked each other. Still, he knew that Jeremy would come out with an A, and of course he did.

Truanting could also be a positive educational experience for the highly able. It was for creative David Baker (gifted, aged 17, at school):

Last year, if I'd worked really hard in the morning, I'd sometimes take afternoons off with a couple of friends, and they'd just mark me absent. We didn't get drunk or play football. We used to write poetry quite a lot, and we'd read to each other. Say, if we'd done *The Wasteland* by T. S. Eliot in the morning, we'd have great fun in the afternoons, spending ages in the park with a bottle of wine, talking about it and eating oranges. We'd also talk about politics and the lumpenproletariat, and things like that.

I was learning more at the time in a different way about life and society, and was beginning to think about things, like injustice and the way human beings were, what people wanted, and why they behaved as they did. Then, towards the end of the summer, everybody had to have a long interview with the deputy head about school attendance and my cavalier attitude to registration had to stop. So, since the summer, I've been there all the time. You could say that I took a new direction in life, and I've even started gardening on a Sunday morning – money-wise, being Seamus Heaney wears thin.

Corporal Punishment

Britain is the only European country that still allows corporal punishment in school, though over forty cases brought by parents claiming assault on their children are pending at the European Court. In 1985, *The Times* in London polled 604 varied parents with children aged between 5 and 16 on corporal punishment. They found that two-thirds approved of it in principle, and more than half in practice on their own children. Two-thirds had received some kind of corporal punishment at school themselves – nine out of ten fathers and half the mothers. In entire accord with those figures, two-thirds of these young people, boys slightly more than girls, were in favour of the short, sharp, physical shock – prescribed for others, usually 'bad boys'. This urge was not, however, based on experience, as less than a quarter of the group had actually been hit by a teacher. Those who had felt it were usually not in favour of it.

Several boys in this sample had been beaten quite strongly by teachers, though they had apparently managed to brush off the assault mentally. But for one sensitive gifted boy, the caning, combined with lack of psychological support from home, had seriously curtailed his potential intellectual and emotional development. He had been diminished by what had happened to him, and was probably functioning at about average ability.

Peter Rhodes was his parents' fourth child, and his mother said he had been by far the most alert at birth. He would walk across the room unaided at 11 months, string a few words together soon after that, and was a very easy child. When I had first seen him at nearly 9 years old, I'd noted what a chatty and lively little boy he was, and how he loved school. There was no cause for concern there.

Then at 13, he had been sent to an old-fashioned, high-status private school. Towards the end of his first year, he was severely beaten with a cane for, he swears, something he did not do. His sentence was five strokes over his clothes, across his lower back and buttocks, causing great weals and fierce pain. He stood up after four strokes and pleaded with the teacher to stop, but the man pushed him down and gave him the final one. Peter said that the teacher who did it was skinny and small, and it seemed to give him satisfaction. Though Peter was proud that he had not cried out, he was terribly shocked. His mother was away at the time, and his father did not want to see the bruises. He blamed Peter, but said graciously, 'You've been punished enough – I shan't punish you any more on top of it.' Like any bruise, the weals lasted physically for only a couple of weeks.

But Peter's hatred grew and grew, both for the man who had done this to him and the system that had allowed it to happen. Should anyone do that to him now, he said, he would give as good as he got, but as a slight 13-year-old, he had been powerless. Things went from bad to worse. He shrugged off the whole idea of school work, eventually leaving the place at 15. He seemed to me to find great difficulty in expressing himself, and obviously was not used to it. His father was a disciplinarian of limited interests, who had risen to some wealth from a poor background. His mother lived very much on the surface of life. She was astonished, for example, that I should expect her to know where her husband had gone to school, saying, 'Well, he was already 25 when I met him.' Of her gifted son's disastrous schooling, she said it was all his fault because, 'He just stopped trying.'

Peter Rhodes *(highly gifted, aged 19, out of work):*

> My parents wouldn't let me go to a comprehensive because it wasn't as respectable as the school they sent me to, though they knew how I hated the place. It was awful. Either you fitted in, or you left, and there was no allowance made for you as a person. The teachers thought I was stupid. We were asked once in a lesson what our IQ was, and I said what mine was, because my parents had had it done – everyone thought I was lying or joking. Even when I did little spurts of work, they'd say,

'How'd you do that? Did you copy it from someone else?' I failed every-thing so I'm going in the army, but my parents would rather I was here where they could control me. My Dad said, 'You've had a very sheltered upbringing, you know.'

Chapter 7
Goodbye to School

No more Latin, no more French,
No more sitting on a cold hard bench.

ANON.

This chapter signals a warning that the academically gifted are not more but *less* likely to receive vocational guidance than other children. Yet a major problem for many bright people is that they can do so many things superbly well. The reasons for taking up particular courses or going to prestigious universities may depend on individual personality and motivation rather than aptitude, which can be wasteful of energy and diminish the outcome of the most gifted.

THE OPTIONS OFFERED

To young children, what they are taught comes from a mysterious source which they do not question. But as they get older and are faced with some choice in their education, it can be bewildering. Without adequate guidance, too many young people pass through the school gates for the last time ignorant of much that would be useful in the world outside. It is especially problematic for those who could turn their outstanding abilities in a variety of directions. Parents and teachers are normally anxious to help, but they rarely have expertise in educational guidance for these special youngsters, and have to fall back on what they themselves are familiar with, so perpetuating what they learned many years ago. However, the wide variety of career routes possible for the gifted can confuse even professionals. As one gifted girl said of a careers officer: 'He came to school and said I could probably do anything!' Another girl was overwhelmed by technology: 'I got a computer printout, which was supposed to select the ideal job. It said "Cut off after 80, 127 remaining." I was supposed to select four. But there wasn't much point when I was suitable in attitude and qualifications for all of them.'

His range of potential excellence had presented Jeremy Kramer with an insoluble dilemma. He was a pupil at a high-pressure academic school, and at the same time attended part-time at a college of music. His school watched him shine in science and expected him to go on to a medical degree, but the college expected him to take a music degree and aim for the concert platform.

Jeremy Kramer (*highly gifted, aged 20, studying medicine*):

> By the time I was 15, I'd finished all the music grades in trumpet, piano, and theory, and the only other thing I could've done was a diploma, but that would have taken too much time from school. I found a terrible difficulty in choosing between music and medicine. I spent hours thinking it over, covering every aspect of why I should or shouldn't have done each one, and came to the conclusion I'd be better off doing medicine. I can do that and still do a lot of music, but I can't do music and any medicine. Also, while I was at music college I saw a lot of really brilliant musicians who didn't manage to find work.

The young people often felt that they were less well informed than they should have been about possible careers because they found their schools very limited in communication with the outside world – 'an ivory tower' or 'a prison camp'. Another simile sometimes offered was of a train which ran on rails and so could not change direction easily or allow variations, such as accommodating to a pupil's late development or change of mind. However, it must be remembered that success in school does not always predict success in real-world settings: the influences of personality and motivation are essential. Werner von Braun, who developed the principles of rocket propulsion, failed in school algebra; Albert Einstein failed the admission exam in science to the Zurich Polytechnic; Picasso could barely read – the list of successful school failures is almost inspiring.

The schools were also widely varied in the choice of subjects they provided. The academically high-powered schools, which catered for the most gifted pupils, were unquestionably also the least flexible. The idea was current (as in the USA: Deslisle, 1985) that gifted and talented young people do not need career advice and development. Many of the highly able youngsters at such schools found that the study area to which they were supposed to devote themselves for years, if not all their lives, was effectively decided by teachers, sometimes without discussion: 'There wasn't any choice – so I didn't need guidance. You take the subjects allocated to you.' These were usually decided on the basis of school marks. Of the whole sample, over a third (33.7 per cent) had not been given a voice in those major life decisions.

When a bright pupil was keen on a particular area of study, school timetables could be considerable hurdles. Although this is true for all pupils, it is a special problem for one who has a real gift in the desired subject area. The alternatives the school offered did not always bear any relationship to the original choice, as for one girl, who said: 'I wanted to do food and nutrition, but the careers teacher said "No," because it wouldn't fit into the timetable – "Why don't you do French?" You see, I'd got a good French mark; so now I'm doing it for university.'

Some of the young people said they were ill informed about what was involved in the subject areas to which they had been directed. This could have been so easily built into preparation for the next stage of schoolwork, and for several this lack had caused extra work, and wasted time and money. Danny Smith, for example (gifted, aged 17, at school), had found himself months into the wrong subjects: 'I didn't get told about what was actually in the courses, just which subjects are usually studied together and which I could choose from. No one ever spoke to me personally about it, never.' Fortunately, being both gifted and a skilled learner, he was able to catch up that wide gap of missing information, pass his school-leaving exams with flying colours, and go on to university.

At times, study areas which were not considered essential, such as language or music to a scientist, were simply cut out of a high-flyer's syllabus, as they were seen to be detracting from 'real' work. Yet the intellectually gifted did not delight in a diet of pure academic study, any more than others. Though most of those in selective education did appreciate the school's academic provision, they also spoke of the need for some mental and physical change.

Only a handful of the whole sample, and almost none of the highly able, had been given any experience of the world of work. One highly gifted boy spoke for many: 'We hardly relate any of the things we're doing to the real world. But something on banking or business, like how to manage your own finances, would be useful.' Nor, of course, can any school assume that all super-intelligent young people will go on to some form of higher education, especially if they have experienced hardship in their social circumstances. It is a difficult problem to help such children overcome the temptations of quick, easy money from low-skilled jobs, and to think of possible greater, long-term psychological and economic satisfaction from putting in more years of study. Adrian Lambert (highly gifted, aged 22, a milkman) had had difficulty in finding work on leaving school, and had a suggestion for both teachers and those who were considering dropping out: 'If you want to be a worker, it's actually better to have left school at 16. The worst thing is to graduate from school but not go on to get a degree. If only they'd taken us out on a bricklayers' course, taught us how to lay a brick wall straight, I could have found work within a day.'

Careers Advice at School

The figures speak for themselves. Just under half (45 per cent) of the young people – of whom two-thirds have a general intelligence in the top 5 per cent of the population – said they did not receive the careers help from school that they felt they needed. More specifically, almost as many (42.6 per cent) said they received no personal, one-to-one careers counselling whatsoever. This aspect of education for the gifted, not only in Britain (Deslisle, 1985), is at best very short-sighted in terms of national needs. In fact, it is a scandalous waste of human resources from any point of view.

Even in my follow-up sample of 169 young people, four students had been directed quite wrongly by their schools, and the majority had been obliged to find their own ways, often by trial and error. It is only necessary to multiply this by the number of school-leavers each year to get an idea of the immense waste of energy and talent in all parts of the world. Each of those four misdirected young people had worked hard in the area they'd been directed to, going on to study it at university. One said: 'Since I got to university, I've changed career. It cost me a wasted year. If I'd had any insight as to what it was like to be an engineer, I'd have started with medicine in the first place.' The underlying reason for so many career problems could be alleviated by good (or even some) educational guidance and counselling. The highly academic schools normally made the assumption that their pupils would go on to university: 'It was just a matter of deciding which one.' Careers advice in such schools was most often a discussion of the best route, usually with the subject teacher – after the area of study had been chosen.

But these gifted students knew that there were other things one could do, even if their teachers did not seem to recognize them: 'There are many different ways of approaching life and a career, other than the professions.' Could this be due to the limited experiences of teachers, of their own schooling and training? This problem of limitations in school outlook is reason alone for requiring teachers to have some form of outside school employment as part of their preparation for teaching. Indeed, the assumption that pupils would go on to university could be a tragic one, as highly gifted Yvonne Barnett found:

> I never should have gone to university, but if you were capable of going, you had no other choice. There wasn't anything I particularly wanted to study, and I would have been better off doing a practical course. I didn't even know about the interesting courses they do at polytechnics; the school didn't tell us because they thought they weren't good enough for us. I just wasted those two years at university before I left.

The quality and quantity of the way the schools perceived their commitment to the post-school lives of their charges varied enormously. On the whole, the academically able were well prepared for examinations, with only a minimal gesture to their wider career concerns, so that many young people, when the cocoon of school days drew to a close, were decidedly on their own. At times, careers guidance was available in theory, but the pupil had to seek it out – not easy if you do not know your problem. Some schools offered an occasional lecture by an outside speaker, others had an evening or two with staff during the final year, and a lucky minority even had some human contact with a careers teacher. But that was rarely more than once, and it almost never took the form of counselling. Too often, especially for the girls, it was advice on how to present themselves at interviews.

Though many bright, ambitious pupils said they did not want help because they had already made up their minds, when I asked them if they had ever been challenged in their choice or had the opportunity to discuss it, they were astounded. Genuine help from school for the rest of their lives seemed to be outside many pupils' frame of reference, being neither given nor expected.

It was not all bad, though; about a dozen had moved on with sound careers advice. There was often a school careers room where students could browse, and a girl studying English at university had an interesting suggestion: 'They had good information laid out, and it was open all the time, but it would have been good if there'd been some standard video tapes on what people do at work. According to all the leaflets I read, it was – study English and be unemployed.' Another girl, trying to get out of the academic rut, said: 'I went through the art box in the careers office and the latest information was from 1973.'

Fewer than ten youngsters (5.9 per cent) had benefited from real contact with the world of industry. One gifted boy found that the experience had redirected his ideas, so that he was very happily at work at university:

I went on a fascinating three-day course on the science of paper. From that, I realized which subjects I'd have to take. Even if I didn't take up paper science, that combination gave me a very good choice – and it was my choice. The careers master at school was very helpful and still is. He's quite open, and we can go back and see him any time we want.

Three schools in this sample had, however, arranged a veritable feast of careers advice. Phillipa Longman (gifted, aged 17, at school) was indeed fortunate:

We've got a careers person, and a careers room, and we have lots of talks – different people coming on different subjects. Most of the sixth form go to the Area Careers Officer too, and we've met representatives from different universities. In the first year in the sixth form, everybody is interviewed by a member of staff, and we have quite a lot of time with her; mine lasted about 25 minutes. She asked us what we wanted to do, and if we'd no idea, she'd give us some. If you wanted information she hadn't got, she'd send away for it.

The more perceptive young people, though, also knew that such matters as self-confidence and personal relationships were as important in their education as the often excellently taught mastery of skills and knowledge. They would have liked some help in developing that side of their overall education. There is a long way for the school counselling services to go in Britain, and a great deal to be learned from countries where it is functioning reasonably well, such as Canada and much of the USA.

In most parts of the world, for want of any other source of advice, most school-leavers turn to their families, and in fact attitudes towards further education are strongly influenced by the parents' own educational experiences and expectations for their children. In this sample, parents' ideas on their children's futures were distinctly biased towards the sciences. For most parents, though, it is impossible to know the wide spread of what is available at present, particularly as many occupations did not exist even a few years ago. So in practice, lawyers often come from lawyer families, and doctors from doctor families or as a result of personal medical experiences, though engineers and accountants tend to make last-minute decisions before opting for the route that seems the most promising.

Moreover, what is taken for granted in some families, like going to university, is unthinkable in others. This is yet another source of haemorrhage of the gifted from areas of life activity in which they would have the opportunity to thrive, from which unrecognized and unyielding adult attitudes bar them. It is often assumed that the gifted have some sort of inbuilt motivation to aim for high achievement, although this study has shown clearly that motivation and aims are highly dependent on personality and social circumstances. Those who do not have an intense urge to use their gifts plus the extra energy it takes to beat the system in which they are growing up, which may be detrimental to their well-being, will find their abilities under-exercised and unsatisfied. It happened to several in this sample alone. Many of these bright young people found that much of their futures had to be organized by themselves: 'Apart from the class careers talk; sending off for the prospectuses, asking heads of departments, and filling in the forms. If I'd lacked motivation, I could easily have ended up not getting in anywhere.'

Even when careers help was available from school, though, it was often described by students as traditional, unimaginative, and gender-biased. A highly gifted girl reported: 'I've just had my first careers interview now at 17. It's a bit late because I haven't specialized, and now I've no idea where I'm going. I was asked, "Have you ever thought of becoming a nurse?" '

If the gifted found the advice narrow in the academic schools, it was often far off the mark in the comprehensive schools. Some, who were aware that their potential and personal aptitudes were being disregarded, were not even able to take it seriously. Andy Spurgeon (highly gifted, aged 17, at school), with a measured IQ in the top 1 per cent of the population, said: 'The careers master told me, "Look, they want 50 bus drivers – here's the form." They just want to get us into jobs for the school statistics. I laughed at him.'

Andy's school did not find him easy. He had a mischievous sense of humour and a very different kind of ambition from most of the other pupils there:

> When I told them I wanted to go to university they asked, 'Have you considered other options?,' and I said, 'Well, I had thought of being a toilet attendant; you know, work up from the bottom, start as a loo brush,' and she said, 'That's glamorous!' Truthfully, I'd really like to become an actor, but I want to go to university first, so I chose a course which I knew I was going to enjoy, and which had a fairly low workload. You should have seen the careers people's faces when I told them I was going to university to do honours Philosophy.

The perceptions that teachers have of their pupils is well known to be affected by matters other than the pupil's ability. This subjective appraisal of potential also affects the advice and encouragement which youngsters receive for their future working lives. Whereas poor children may be seen as suitable for manual work, a gentle girl can be directed to something which seems appropriate to her perceived personality rather than to her gifts. Caroline Whiting is a highly gifted, quiet, and unassuming young woman. Although she was at a high-powered girls' school, like so many of the gifted girls in this sample she had not only been directed to a nursing career, but in addition had been strongly dissuaded from aiming as high as she could reach. But her delicate demeanour hid stern resolve:

> When the biology teacher saw my entry for a national biology competition, she said it was no good and full of mistakes, so I shouldn't disgrace the school by putting it in. Of course she wouldn't put it in, but I didn't listen and put it in myself. It was runner-up, so they couldn't say anything after that. If only I had been given a tiny amount of encouragement I could have done a lot better, instead of wasting my energies fighting them.

P.S. Caroline went to university, received a first-class honours degree, and is happily working as a research biologist.

Careers Education for the Gifted

How can young people who are gifted across the board know which line to take up and develop to a high level? Too many options and not enough guidance make Jack a confused boy. The mistakes which lack of guidance brings can mean not only time wasted in sampling different courses, but stereotyped misdirections, such as girls and boys being slotted into sex-role occupations; boys pushed into the professions, though they may be better suited to the arts.

The essence of being able to make the right choice is in knowing what there is to choose from, both in what is available and in one's own potential. The first priority in helping the gifted choose their career paths is to enhance their awareness of themselves and others. Right from the first years of school, career education must be concerned with self-awareness, self-acceptance, competence, positive attitudes to work, and awareness of how different kinds of work can be personally and socially significant. It is important for most schoolchildren to appreciate that the general trend of their endeavours may be for life, so the exploration of careers also means exploring different lifestyles, including leisure activities and family roles and settings. Making such decisions involves the acquisition and use of decision-making skills. Career doors should be kept open as long as possible while the student does this exploring.

The best way of putting over careers ideas, and what could be involved in following them, is to integrate them into everyday classroom teaching of all subjects. Many school lessons are already enriched by group discussions, debates, and exploratory experiences for the pupils, and many already include careers concerns. There could be added experiences for the pupils, beginning perhaps with library research, then shadowing workers in areas in which they are interested, and also their own work experience. By no later than the age of 14 children could be looking into possible career-searching activities.

THE GIFTED AT UNIVERSITY

The transition from the relatively structured and disciplined school day to the heady freedom of university life can bring adjustment problems to all students, and the gifted do not have a monopoly on them. But of those in this sample who did succumb to distress, when their whole life situation was examined, it appeared that their problems were of much longer standing and had been brought to a head by this life-change. The problems were, for example, associated with the family circumstances which had bothered the Target group in the first part of the study. Or sometimes they were associated with the pressures to achieve academically, pressures which were sometimes particularly heavy on the gifted, who were subject to the deeply invested hopes of parents and teachers. Then, having reached their goal of university, there were decided feelings of let-down, as well as a fear of being unable to keep up such a mighty impetus and results among their intellectual peers. It is a syndrome well known in business, which comes after a hard-won deal has been struck.

Those students described feeling devitalized, overcome by inertia, with difficulty in concentrating, and a lowered motivation to study. Four of the students in this sample were almost clinically depressed or anxious. In every case they had tried to cope alone or with the help of their families. Their university teachers, who clearly saw their roles as purely academic, were rather crisp when approached for help. Maybe it was bad luck; there must be others who are kinder. Only two students had approached the official university counsellor, but they felt their visits did not promise to meet their needs, and so had not gone again.

Although virtually all the gifted students had spoken of wanting to work with their intellectual peers, quite a few described an experience of shock at moving into an all-round higher intellectual gear. When coming top of the pile was no longer a matter of course, self-confidence was sometimes dented. But Jonathan Martin (highly gifted, aged 22), studying for a PhD in Chemistry, still yearned for healthy competition at Cambridge: 'I'm so specialized that I'm not really competing against anybody. If I'm top, it may only be out of a small number of people and it's a lot easier to do, so I don't feel that it counts.'

In the first part of the study, the intellectually gifted children were significantly more lively than the others in their suggestions for improving their schools, and indeed the education system (39 per cent suggested more than three changes, compared with 17 per cent). One could say that the gifted also took a more stellar, metacognitive view, because they were less concerned with detail and more with the principles of how the system functioned. They suggested significantly more organizational and curricular improvements than those of more average IQ, who were likely to suggest more personal, domestic changes (see Appendix II).

When asked about higher education, the gifted again gave a far higher proportion of lively responses and saw improved organization and management as keys to better provision. This was particularly true for the way they were examined:

Surely at university, there was no need for the old-fashioned sort of exams that we had to take for finals. After all, everybody was pretty well at the same standard. A university should be a place where the student should have some say about how he's taught. They always seem to dismiss the ideas we put forward, and find excuses as to why it wouldn't be suitable.

On the other hand, some dedicated and highly gifted students viewed their time at university as a rather nicer form of school. They did what they had to for their exams, were inspired neither by the teaching nor by the atmosphere, felt no obligation to dip into any thought-provoking or even fun areas outside their own study, and had no comments to make on the system. That rather passive group was largely made up of science students of both sexes – who also managed to avoid most of the social and emotional problems, which they left to the students of the humanities and arts.

Prestigious Universities

Every country has them: in the USA they are known as the Ivy League Universities (because of the ivy that grows on their walls), and they are private and expensive; in Britain the prestigious (yet free) universities of Oxford and Cambridge are often seen as the holy grail of education by many parents and schools, and are known as Oxbridge. Although most of the sample who were at Oxbridge revelled in the new environments, both for their personalities and their intellects, some were decidedly less than comfortable amongst the dreaming spires.

The greatest benefit for many of the gifted at Oxbridge was the easy-going approach to tuition. The more mature students, those who were competent enough to use their tutors as a resource rather than givers of instruction, enjoyed every minute of their time there. As one contented student said: 'The nice thing about being here is I've got time. I can toddle along to the library to follow an idea up, then go and have a chat to somebody or my tutor about it. I like learning like that. I find it a very constructive approach to work.'

But the reputations of those universities, and the heavy investment the students made to get there, at times seemed to have the effect of accentuating and compounding the normal problems of leaving school, the time of setting out from what is familiar and standing to some extent on one's own feet. A student's reactions to the new situation depended not only on personality, but on home background, and the type of school he or she had come from. Sometimes the social divide was great, or the competition frightening.

The incentive system in most schools is extrinsically motivated, for example, by examination grades or class prizes, and when those familiar rewards are either removed or become too distant, good school achievers can sometimes lose their way; that is, if they have not managed to incorporate their motivation to become intrinsic. This had happened to Rachel Wallace, whose enormous effort had included seven A-levels at two sittings, as well as special scholarship papers for Oxford. Though still only 17 at the time, she had secured a place at one of the most selective colleges, for which she had paid with emotional exhaustion. Once there, dogged by constant fatigue, she could not muster the strength to become involved with university life. She cried a good deal and felt that she had lost control over her work and was a failure. When she tried to tell her examiners about why she had not done well in her examinations, they said she was simply a bad examination candidate – in spite of her long string of A grades all through school.

Rachel Wallace *(highly gifted, aged 19, studying mathematics as a second-year student at Oxford):*

My ambition was to get to Oxford. But when I got here, everything fell flat. My brain went to sleep after about four weeks and it hasn't woken up since. I've worked about 5 per cent of the amount I worked before, though my tutors couldn't care less. My own tutor never looks at my work. I don't go to lectures, because I fall asleep in them. There's a lot that is quite interesting to do in Oxford, but I just go shopping, drink tea, read books, wander round the colleges – anything but work, really.

There are people here who are so much better than me that I could never have a hope of catching them up, and I no longer have the possibility of coming top, so that's rather a let-down. It seems a cheat to have to work hard to be third or fourth. The panicking becomes a way of life. I just don't know where to start. I get very bored and lonely too. I have one friend, but apart from her, nobody. Black depression is there. I just get days of it, and I try to keep myself busy, but I'm really powerless to do anything. I think it's getting worse, but I don't want to leave university. In a way it's quite cosy, and you don't have to think about tomorrow, because tomorrow you're just going to be in the same situation.

Oxford and Cambridge universities are made up of semi-autonomous colleges, each selecting its own students, and having its own social make-up. In the early 1990s the number of applications to these two universities from the private and state sectors are about the same, and accordingly each sector gains about half the places – even though the private sector makes up only a tiny portion (about 7 per cent) of the school population. One comprehensive school boy in the sample said bitterly: 'Although they say they're trying to remedy that, they should really have something like 90 per cent of state school people there, instead of less than 50 per cent.' Admissions tutors say this is due to myths about Oxbridge – for example, that they discriminate in favour of pupils from private schools – and consequently comprehensive schools do not send enough applicants. Additionally, since many of the private schools see other universities and polytechnics as only second-best, they are more likely to apply to Oxbridge as first choice. There are added stumbling-blocks for candidates whose schools have not prepared them adequately, because entry is not always entirely by state examination results. Not only are there interviews to be negotiated, but some colleges have entrance exams of their own design which need special preparation.

Several gifted and academically high-achieving Oxbridge applicants in my sample believed they had failed to gain a place because of inadequate preparation from school. There may not have been enough pupils there taking the special papers to merit the provision of teachers for the necessary tuition. Also, the gifted were in more of a minority at some schools: 'There wasn't enough competition to drive me on to do well.' Those from state schools who did gain acceptance had usually received the kind of heavy coaching that is more common in private schools. One comprehensive school boy said: 'I've almost been on a conveyor belt for two years. But I was amazed when I got to Cambridge. I was expecting all these egghead types – it's total rubbish! Most of the people are the most amazing bunch of dossers the world has ever seen. How they got there, most of them, is beyond me.' At least six students from my sample had applied with a fistful of A grades at A-level, and had been turned down. It did look as though there were some non-academic reasons for their rejections.

Those who failed to get in sometimes felt that it was not so much their own as their school's social status which had been held against them. A student explained:

'Last year, I would have told you I wasn't affected by social class, because at my comprehensive everybody was equal in a way. But then I was rejected by Oxford. It really shocked me. You get the message quite clearly here at Bristol, which takes a high proportion of public [that is, private] school types – they call it the poor man's Oxbridge. These people don't regard me as a comprehensive school person; to them, I'm just non-public school. I've found it very difficult.

The lifestyle of the prestigious universities would be daunting for socially unprepared students. These powerful effects were experienced in a tragic way by Alison Cranfield, an outstandingly brilliant girl, who had attempted to jump the culture gap. But it was too wide for her and she had slipped and fallen. Even to think of it, nearly a year after the débâcle, still brought tears to her eyes. She was a tall, sensitive, hard-working girl from the far north. Even at our first meeting, when she was 10 years old, I had noted how retiring and extremely polite she was. At Oxford, she described her fellow students as having too much money to spend: 'The boys got drunk, and the girls were too worldly.' Though her school had given her superb teaching within the syllabus and taken great pride in her achievements, they had not given her sufficient personal help to see her through the great change of pace and style which she faced alone, and neither had the university. There was no precedent in her family of university, no model to give her courage, no one to see that she was adequately prepared. She had only her belief in God.

Alison Cranfield *(highly gifted, aged 21, a bank clerk):*

I felt looked down on because of where I came from. They would tease me and imitate my accent, then say they couldn't understand me. It was very upsetting at the time, but that wasn't the whole reason I left. I failed my first-year exams because the course wasn't right for me. No one at school had ever discussed it; it was just 'OK, off you go.' My background knowledge wasn't sufficient, because I only knew what I'd been taught in school, those few books I'd read for my exams. I had so much catching up to do. I was taking French, though I've never been to France, yet other students even had second homes over there. When I left, I felt I'd let down my school and the neighbours and the church. The college agreed that it was best for me to leave. It was galling when they suggested I should have done a different course or gone to a different university.

After I got back, for the first six weeks I'd go to sleep at night and pray for the bomb to come. I didn't have the courage to commit suicide and I wanted someone to do it for me. I stayed in the house all the time because the neighbours would ask me about Oxford. But I was just ending up self-pitying, so I started going to places where people hadn't known me before. I took up new interests, started going to a drama group once a week and made new friends there. And I went to a different church.

I felt very much that what I'd done was wrong – to step out of my caste, to think that I could be like one of them. My reaction was to hate the students, higher education, and everything that I associated with Oxford. If I have my own children, I wouldn't encourage them to go on to higher education. I'd rather they were on the loose for a few years and sorted things out before committing themselves to something like that.

P.S. Alison finished training as a teacher and is now happily married and teaching.

More Support Needed

Samantha Goldman had risen in her brilliance like a shooting star, then fallen to earth again. Even in this exceptional sample, she was quite outstanding in her breadth of ability and enthusiasm for life. Her six A grades at A-level taken at one sitting were in widely varied subjects, and they had not included music, although she was also an outstanding pianist at her specialist music school, and had been expected to reach the concert platform. But it was that immense talent and vitality that had been her undoing. Once out of the supportive school structure, in which she had worked extremely hard for those results, she had been without guidance. Her enthusiasm for the enticements of university life carried her away, leaving little time for her studies. Some support and advice from the university, taking her personality and background into account, could have made all the difference to her future.

Samantha Goldman *(highly gifted and talented, aged 20, at university):*

Cambridge was my first choice, but I failed the entrance exam, probably for lack of preparation, and anyway they probably wouldn't take people from a school like mine. In my first year at London I played in the orchestra, in the second I was orchestra manager, and in the third I'm president of the music society. They still tease me a bit, like when I come in someone says 'Oh look, the working classes have arrived!' I think of myself as working class, and obviously all the rest of them do because of my accent, so they tend to treat me like a pet poodle, and it can get a bit irritating. I'm going to go back north as soon as I can.

I didn't go to the lectures after the first couple of weeks in my second year because of the musical I was directing. It just snowballed. I wrote the score, organized the costumes, and did just about everything else. I spent all day in the theatre from about 8 in the morning till midnight, and then extra hours on the phone. It's the thing I've enjoyed doing most ever, and it was a smash. But it was staged the day before my first exam and as a result I did very badly. I hope to do something like that when I leave, but I don't know how to get into it.

P.S. Samantha failed all her final exams and did return north to work as an assistant teacher at her old school. She then retook her finals, but only scraped through, took a teaching certificate, and became a primary school teacher. She is very happy and has made big changes to the school musically.

Although most intellectually gifted students are happy and do well at university, it is, to say the least, a waste of human energy that those who are more sensitive, or still immature, or who find themselves taking unsuitable courses may fail to thrive there. Though universities were decidedly not set up as caring agencies for the fragile, they do want to get the best from the students they accept, for reasons both humanitarian and economic. Gifted students come to university with the special vulnerabilities which are described in this book, of having sometimes extraordinary expectations, drives, and clarity of vision of what might be done, of being the recipients of many put-downs, of feeling different, short of praise and reassurance, and so on. They need someone to turn to who understands their situation and how they feel about it, and who can help to make them feel more comfortable in a sometimes alienating place. It may be, for example, that a small, intimate institution would be more suitable for an individual than a large university. Not only would this help the gifted student to continue to develop at his or her own pace – and eventual exceptionally high level – but there would be time for more creative, involving, and challenging activity as these students continued to grow up.

In theory, such help is available now, but is too remote and not always very effective. Greatly improving the universities' counselling services would not be an extravagant move; for example, suitable faculty members could be trained in counselling skills and paid extra for their time. Indeed, in economic terms, stemming the loss of bright young people from these costly places of study would more than pay for the extra help they might receive. It would, however, require a refocusing of university outlook.

Chapter 8
Influences on Education

The most pervasive social influence on an individual's education, which applies from birth, is family outlook, including attitude to gender. Although this applies to all children, its effect on the gifted can be both different and more powerful because the stakes are much higher. It was just because of their exceptionally high abilities that the gifted children sometimes found themselves displaced into schools into which they did not fit comfortably. In this study, parents were able to fill in many otherwise lost details about longer-term family effects, which helped to untangle the web of circumstances in which the young people grew up.

SOCIAL MORES

Social mores clearly affect people's lives in Britain, as indeed elsewhere, though they are sometimes very subtle. In this study, the unwritten social rules, hallowed by time, could radically change the life chances and progress of these young people. It was not primarily a question of money, because the families ranged form very poor to very rich, but rather people's ideas about themselves, their self-concepts. When a highly gifted boy refused to go to university (at no cost) because 'it's not for the likes of me,' he was listening to past social values, not the reality of today; but it did change his life.

The idea that gifted children from all backgrounds can make sturdy growth without special help is fading, if slowly. In many parts of the western world, diminishing numbers in many schools due to a lower birthrate have narrowed the curriculum and thinned the educational nourishment. High unemployment has meant that bright youngsters, the ones most likely to get the jobs, sometimes see little point in staying on to take more exams at school, and leave to take what work they can get. Far more children in Britain leave education at 16 (26 per cent) than in other countries, such as Japan (4 per cent), Germany (10 per cent), and the United States (10 per cent). A smaller proportion too take up further training; a great loss for late developers.

Home outlook is effective in enabling gifts to grow in many ways, which are not always obvious. It shows, for example, in the amount and quality of homework a child does (Timar and Kirp, 1988). In every country, children who are set homework, who do it, and who have it marked perform better at school than those who do none. Even though there is a wide variation in how much different schools set, parents who approve of it often see a heavy load as a sign of a caring school, and some highly successful children set themselves extra problems to do at home. Schools in poor areas sometimes make the premises available after hours for those whose homes are not conducive to study.

Family outlook and style of living was highlighted, for example, in the young people's television watching habits. When those who watched more than three hours a day were compared with those who watched less, a number of significant family aspects emerged, though there were no differences in the children's sex or intelligence. The lighter viewers were distinctly higher up the social scale, more likely to be at selective schools than at comprehensives, had longer concentration spans, and enjoyed more outside activities. When they did watch television, they preferred more serious programmes.

A modest family background could have a more profound effect on potential high achievers than on those of average ability. This was because they were more likely to change their educational environments and thus have to swim in a somewhat different social sea. The move could come in childhood via a scholarship from the local primary school to one which was selective, private, specialist, or boarding, or it could come later with entry to one of the more prestigious universities. Whenever it happened, the gifted individual would be well aware that it was made because of his or her brain power or talents, and that his or her social background was not the same as that of most classmates. Most did settle well, some being explicit: 'I couldn't be bothered with anybody who was prepared to exclude me in terms of background. People put far too much energy into maintaining distinctions and barriers.' Others, though, shied away from confrontation: 'Going to Oxford, you meet people who are definitely in a class above you. They are friendly enough, but never too friendly. Well, that's fair enough, because they're of that class and I'm not.'

The difference between state and private schools in all countries of the world is not only material but social. A highly gifted boy at a Liverpool comprehensive school described the gulf: 'I've only ever met boys from private schools in passing. You can spot them straight away. It's two different societies, them and us really.' It was echoed by an equally able boy from the other cliff: 'One would assume that if people cared enough, they wouldn't send their children to those extremely limited state schools.' The snobbery at some of the private schools could be hard to take, as one girl found who had clearly let her school down: 'At speech day they only called out the names of the girls who'd made it to Oxbridge, not those of us who'd gone to other universities.'

Fish out of Water

Their lower social status was held to be responsible by at least six unquestionably gifted youngsters who had not been accepted for scholarships to selective private schools. This seemed to be the case for Karl Sutcliffe, for in terms of measured academic potential, he was more than merely suitable for selective education. Indeed, the secretary of the school he had applied for had told his parents that he had done extremely well in the entrance exam. Karl concluded bitterly that he had not been accepted because his 'face didn't fit', and in truth, there were very few boys like him there. He felt that this blow to his ego had caused him to lose interest in schoolwork, causing his mother many tearful nights. But he was determined that never again would he be socially rejected. He was a dominant young man who would interrupt many of my questions to redirect me as to what I should be asking. Socially, he saw himself as having already made progress, being 'mentally upper middle, but held back by my parents', a shop assistant and a mechanic. He was trying to smarten himself up, beginning with an expensive sweater. I feared for him as destined for embittered middle management, his enormous intellectual power dissipated in pub philosophy.

Karl Sutcliffe *(highly gifted, aged 22, a bank clerk):*

People I know socially talk behind my back, but I tolerate them, put on a show. They've got a use, and perhaps one day I'll need them. I'm going to make something of myself. For the next couple of years, I'm going to follow the bank's career structure and then get myself in a situation where I can go out and say, 'That's the job I want; I'm having it.' I'm going to educate myself, but not in formal education – I am in life – I'm trying to diversify my interests. I'm going to start playing golf, because these are things you need, like joining the boss on Sunday in a game. Try and get myself in with the right people, that's what I'm aspiring to do. One day I'd like a nice castle with a moat in Surrey, or some old county, as an investment. I can get rid of my accent; I can carry that off. I'm not thinking about elocution lessons; it would sound odd to the people I'm currently in contact with; it's got to be a gradual thing. Mind you, the way really is to tie yourself to the top of the Empire State Building and say, 'World, listen to me.'

Paul Nash had the opposite problem in a sense, and found his life was 'schizophrenic'. Because his local education authority had forbidden any child to be advanced at school, he had ended up with a free place at an expensive boarding school. His home was small and drab, a little bit run down, on a housing estate of hundreds of others like it. The other boys at school were often from rich families, who he felt rather looked down on him, so he would not bring them home. In spite of having been at the school for seven years, he had clung to his original strong local accent, perhaps as the bit of him that he still owned. Although his examination results were outstandingly high, Andrew refused to try for Cambridge, fearing yet more snobbery, and so felt that he was letting everyone down. 'Despair' was the word he used to describe his frequent long spells of depression, which were sometimes so bad that he felt he would never re-emerge. He saw himself as trapped, not knowing which way to aim. He felt he would have been much better off at a mixed-ability day-school, especially one with girls in it.

The effect could be almost as distressing when the move was from private to state school: 'Some of the people at school, they make you think that you're just a turd on the sideboard because you're middle class.' Another even came across it at Cambridge: 'I'm meeting people for the first time from comprehensive schools. They seem to be such nice people.

In fact, I'm the only public [private] school person in my group, and they think it's very amusing, but they don't hold it against me – I don't think.'

Suspended between those different social worlds, Yvonne Barnett was never quite sure where she fitted in. Coming from a poor home which was also emotionally disturbed, she had been given a scholarship by her local education authority to an expensive boarding school. Her experiences had left this highly gifted, sensitive, and beautiful young woman with a problem of insecurity. Her mother said: 'We thought it was a good idea at the time, going to that posh school, because she needed the push and the competition. But then she saw how the other half lived and she couldn't compete. We did have such hopes for her.'

Yvonne Barnett *(highly gifted, aged 22, out of work)*:

I've got a very mixed-up family background, but it means I can cope very well, because I've been through that and nothing else ever seems so bad. When I first went to the school, my accent was really strong, and kids used to rag me and make me talk so they could laugh. I got very jealous that some of them could buy anything they wanted and had loads of clothes. Also, I'd never done French at junior school like the people that had been to private schools. Consequently, I was hopeless at it. I would never bring anyone home. They would have been embarrassed at coming to such a little house, and my manners were so different. I don't think I should have gone. When I heard about my local comprehensive, what they've learnt, and the kind of courses they were applying for, it made me really jealous.

P.S. Yvonne left university in her second year, worked as a waitress for several years, then took some business courses. She is now a thriving young administrator for a small firm.

Derek Girling had an IQ over the top of any scale, and the ability to do almost anything, had he not been intellectually crippled by the social shackles in his mind. He often said, 'Well, that's the way I like to put it – blunt like a working man.' He had left school at 16 with all A grades at A-level – 'in my worst subjects'. But:

At the time of the choice to do Oxford or Cambridge, I believed that I wouldn't have got in, mostly because my father wasn't a suitably employed person. That would make a difference to my credentials; they'd ask more of me than somebody whose father was, say, a doctor. That's how I feel. I would like to have gone in a way, but I don't think I'll lose out by what I'm doing.

His mother filled in: 'He'd mixed with them boys for six years at school, and he wasn't that struck, especially the moneyed ones. He didn't want to mix with them for another three years. He's much happier on the ground with "real people".' Indeed, he was working for an electricity company, doing a part-time degree, wiring houses, 'knowing what it's like with his finger-ends frozen, trying to dig a solid piece of ground'. His mother approved, adding:

> Bringing my kids up, I've had some brick-bats from neighbours, because I let them play out and get dirty, and because I had a piano for them instead of new suits and posh clothes. It really hurt at the time. But I looked at them and they were happy, and they were thriving. They were achieving what was in them. You're not a bad mother if you don't have the latest microwave oven.

P.S. Derek eventually gained a first-class honours degree in engineering and is rising steadily up the career ladder in the electricity industry. He and his girlfriend have bought their own home, and have, he said, 'found out what it's all about'.

However, some of the young people were clear that social divisions were here to stay and would affect everyone's life chances no matter how gifted. This was expressed vehemently by Samantha Goldman (highly gifted, aged 20, studying science at university):

> It's in everything, absolutely everything. All your life chances are restricted if you're born into the working class. You can never escape from it. You can never completely con yourself or anyone else in trying to change your class. You're born and brought up into a certain set of people, who have certain attitudes towards society, each other, and education in particular. It makes communication between the classes quite difficult in either direction. You can see it happening around you. For instance, in the staff-room [of the primary school] where I teach, teachers think that children are stupid because they come from the council estate. They use it to explain why a certain child's misbehaved in a classroom, though it's probably just that he thought their lesson was boring. You can even see it in marking the work, because I went through a lot of their exercise books, and if they had the right name

or the right accent or the right dad, they tended to get a better mark than I would have given them, not knowing who they were.

GENDER

Very many studies have shown that from earliest childhood, boys receive more encouragement than girls to be independent, be self-reliant, and assume responsibility, which alters their approach to both school and work. In this study over 30 per cent of the boys, compared with 5 per cent of the girls, found their greatest satisfaction in achievement, a basic difference from which many others stemmed (see p. 117). In addition, the boys were more ready to see their success as due to their own ability and hard work, whereas the girls often looked upon it as something outside their control – luck – though they regarded their defects as their own faults. For girls, being successful can still be a threat to their self-image of femininity, a threat which a gifted girl at university in this study kept at bay by her display of good-girl behaviour. Her only hobbies were knitting and sewing, and she insisted that I inspect her neat, child-like bedroom – dolls, teddy bears, and slippers in their places. She said: 'I do care what other people think of me, and I always try to be nice.'

In this study, there were significantly more boys in co-educational comprehensive schools, which they disliked twice as often as the girls did their schools, significantly more often selective and single-sex, where they worked more diligently. Parents agreed and were significantly more satisfied with their daughters' schools and progress there than with their sons' schools and performance. At GCE level, the first hurdle of state exams, this seemed justified, since the girls passed more subjects, but the crunch came at A-levels or Highers – when the boys obtained twice as many A grades. Somehow, maybe like an oyster with a grain of sand, the boys' dissatisfaction had produced the pearl at the vital time.

More boys had gone on to university, more girls going to colleges and polytechnics. So, in spite of all the girls' hard work in well-run schools, and the parents' protestations about equal aims for their sons and daughters, both the girls and their parents appeared to be satisfied with a less intellectual form of higher education for their daughters than their sons. Some of the girls even spoke of being discouraged by their teachers, who sometimes pointed those of the highest intellectual ability to college and polytechnic rather than university. Every one of the girls in this sample who had gone to university had been at an all-girls school for most of her school life, and every one of the seventeen boys who had gone to university from a comprehensive school had studied science. This extraordinary division may be coincidence, because the sample is not large, but it is in line with evidence from much larger studies.

Equal Opportunities

When asked whether boys and girls should have the same opportunities in life, virtually all parents said they should. But deeper questioning and observation sometimes exposed the old division – science for the boys and arts for the girls. In fact, three times as many boys as girls specialized in science, and more than twice as many girls as boys in arts subjects. The parents of the girls were decidedly keener to have music appreciation taught at school, and indeed five girls went on to study music, though no boys did. For all girls at school, as they get older, the likelihood of being taught science by a woman, and so seeing a woman in a scientific role, becomes less. In 1985, for example, 56 per cent of 10-year-olds in Britain were taught science by a woman, but the proportion fell to 31 per cent for 14-year-olds, and was only 14 per cent for A-level physics pupils.

However, not all the parents would even pay lip-service to the idea of equal opportunities. Julie Knight dressed with care and style, smiled as she spoke, and at 16 was much sought after by young men; her father fielded the constant phone calls. Her mother and father fulfilled their gender roles to an extreme; her mother said little and always agreed with her husband, who pronounced with great authority. Their messages for Julie's future were clear.

Mr Knight considered it was a complete waste of time for girls to have anything to do with science. 'Let's face it,' he said, 'you can be all the women's lib you like, but there are no jobs for girls in science.' Arts was the subject for girls, though it was not important for boys, because of the job situation, and anyway: 'The female mind works more on intuition, and the male reasons things.' Consequently, although Julie had been a keen scientist, her father had directed her to take French, History, and English, adding: 'Well, she's going to get married anyway and have children, so there's not much point in her studying further.' She dared not tell him how she felt, but said to me in an impersonal way: 'People should have more say in their own careers, because it's their life.'

It was more complex for Gina Emerson, a girl who seemed to have every facility to do what she wanted. She was intellectually quite outstanding, had been to one of the most exclusive girls' schools in Scotland, and lived in a large, beautiful home where there were many good books. But her brilliance had added greatly to the intensity of her gender conflicts. Her father, who loved his daughter dearly, was a somewhat old-fashioned man, brought up in a patriarchal system. His expectations of his daughter, which had been tragically compounded by her mother's death, included the old-style female role. From childhood, her conflict between trying to please her parents and wanting to enjoy the excitement of using her mind had brought her guilt and distress.

Gina Emerson *(highly gifted, aged 19, studying English at university):*

When my mother died, it changed everything instantly. I was suddenly responsible and in charge of things. I was 16. I spent nine months at home before university and got the frustrated housewife syndrome. Mummy's friends became my friends, and I took over some of her voluntary social work with them, which is all right up to a point. Daddy said I was having a kind of marriage without the good bits, just doing the housework.

Rationally, I know I don't have anything to be depressed about, but I still cry quite a lot. And when I cry, I really cry. I can't turn to my father, because either he'd not understand why, or he'd feel guilty, thinking it was all connected with Mummy's death. At university I see my boyfriend, it's wonderful. But though I'm quite happy to be superficially cheered up by him, I feel kind of guilty because it's not really a solution to my problem. During these holidays I've only been out twice, and after both times father said, 'You left all this washing-up to do, and I had to do this, and we didn't have enough potatoes on Saturday night,' or something. I want to be a student, and I've got to be a housewife too. He doesn't ask my brother because he's away at school: he's different somehow. Day to day, I never seem to have enough time to do the ironing or the meal or whatever.

I suppose I am growing up a bit, though, because I'm feeling more responsible. When I go back to university, I tell my father he's got to feed himself properly, leave him instructions as to how to do his washing, and ring him up to check if he's all right. I picture myself marrying an alcoholic or something, and having a really tough life, but satisfied because I've redeemed that person.

Should Girls and Boys Be Educated Together or Separately?

It is a strange twist of fate that the gifted are far more likely than other, more average children in Britain to go to single-sex schools. This is because they are more likely to be selected for highly academic schools, which are usually single sex. Although single-sex education was common even 25 years ago, it now seems a little odd, and did not help the very bright children to make easy relationships with the opposite sex. In fact, when asked what they would have preferred, only 14.2 per cent of all the sample would have chosen single-sex education, and those were mostly girls (23 per cent of the girls), who felt that they could be placed at a disadvantage with boys in the class. They often looked forward, however, to a more balanced life at university, though it did not always happen: 'I'm living in an all-girls hall of residence, so I've never really spoken to boys.'

Those boys (9.2 per cent) who did prefer single-sex education still worried about missing out on the social aspects of growing up, and with reason, because it usually affected them more. It was described by many boys: 'There's a certain sort of veneer you get at an all-male school. Everybody was always quick to put everyone else down and quick to make jokes at each other's expense. You come out very hard-bitten, cynical, and quite quick, but very dry. It would have been a lot better if it was mixed.'

But some of the boys could see what the girls feared: 'At my comprehensive, the girls did very badly in science, though they were probably about even in the arts subjects. I'm sure they would have been better off in an all-girls school.' But the price the girls had to pay for their greater opportunities there was at times decidedly Victorian:

> We weren't allowed to talk to the boys, even though the boys' school was next door, and you got a bad mark against your name if you got caught. The only allowed times were either in a joint choir that came together once a year, or in the orchestra. In the sixth form you did have some lessons with them, but our biology mistress said that all boys were very bad and they would want to get you 'into trouble'. Girls from my kind of school may flip when they get to university, and be off with the boys every night.

As some prestigious, highly academic boys' schools are now admitting very bright girls into their sixth forms, several girls in this study had the experience of both girls' and boys' schools. However, they were not always made to feel at home.

Rachel Wallace *(highly gifted, aged 19, studying mathematics at university)* was one:

> At the girls' comprehensive school, they just didn't seem to have the same enthusiasm and competition. But when I first went to the boys' school, they'd say, 'Good heavens, a girl doing physics – can't possibly be right.' There were four girls in the class and the teacher used to just teach to the boys, and if we didn't know anything he used to say, 'Oh, don't ask. Don't ask.' Even on my school report he wrote that I asked too many questions. He didn't want to know the girls. He just talked to the lads.

But for girls from the more rigid type of selective girls' school, the new mix could come as a great relief, as Gina Emerson found:

> The boys' school was much more relaxed; no uniform or regulations about bedtimes, which were ridiculous for 18-year-olds. Before, the mistresses used to get so uptight about petty things, like, 'Your hair's sitting on your shoulder and it's not tied up with a blue ribbon'; they think it's the end of the world. It could go on for a fortnight – 'That wicked girl in the second year.' You go to bed at night, and you've got to face it all the next morning, and you haven't been able to tell anyone or go home and get away.

Many gifted young women, enjoying an education and positions that would have been denied not only to their grandmothers but to their mothers, took it all as their right, with never a backward glance. Some at university saw the feminist groups there as irritations and felt that they were spoiling the female image with their aggressive behaviour, often dissociating themselves from any taint of relationships with them. About a quarter of both sexes thought that feminist 'extremists' had gone too far. As one girl put it: 'It's quite funny, at the beginning of term the feminists put little leaflets in all the fresher girls' pigeon-holes asking, "How do you feel about being one in four at Cambridge?" I'm very happy: I like it like that.'

In the last decades of the twentieth century, then, the forces of prescribed gender roles were still seen to be moulding the lives of these gifted girls and boys.

FAMILY PROGRESS

Opportunities in education have been improving over the generations across the western world, especially in Britain, but some families have managed to make better use of them than others. One of the advantages of this long-term study has been that the accumulating influences of family outlook on the education of this sample could often be identified. It showed very clearly in looking back at the almost parallel lives of two Liverpool families.

Across three generations, the two families had a great deal in common, though they had never met. The four sets of grandparents had been poor, unskilled, and minimally educated. Then, caught up in the benefits of the post-war welfare state, their children, today's parents, had been selected for free grammar school education, and each now had a highly gifted son. Both boys had been to state primary schools and had been picked out as gifted by their headteachers, but each family had reacted differently, and the boys' stories forked. Both boys had then aimed for Cambridge University, but one made it and one did not.

Neil Cope's family took a fatalistic attitude to life. His parents' feeling of lack of control over their own destiny was not far removed from that of their own parents. Against their deep doubts, they had accepted the headteacher's advice and sent their son on a scholarship to a private school. Neil's father had obviously been a very bright boy: 'One day I came home and said to my mother, "I've got eight O-levels," and she said "Great," and carried on with the washing. It just didn't mean anything to her.' But in spite of their grammar school educations, neither he nor his wife felt capable of making decisions about their son's education: 'We feel the teachers should guide the children, because our own education wasn't sufficient for us to do it. So when Neil was 10, they took it out of our hands. Yet making him so different, he had such a difficult time.'

Neil Cope *(highly gifted, aged 20, studying chemistry at university):*

Nobody at the school came from my area of Liverpool, and I felt a bit inferior because of my accent. I also got bullied because I was getting my homework in on time and they weren't. Some of the boys there really weren't very good. I knew I was intelligent, but if I didn't do well, then nobody else would know. That's why I got my head down and worked, and also I'd be letting a lot of people down if I didn't.

When I went for my Cambridge interview I felt slightly out of place, because I thought a lot of the people there would have money, and I didn't, but I really wanted to go when I saw it. For a lad like me, I'd have to do better than a person from Harrow or Eton, and if I had been at a comprehensive school, I would have had to do very much better still. If I hadn't tried, then I would have regretted it for the rest of my life, and at least I know now that I didn't get in because I wasn't good enough – or at least I wasn't good enough on the day.

Although he was from the same social background, the attitude of Alastair Lund's family was completely different. He came from a line of fighters. His parents declined exactly the same advice from his head-teacher, instead sending him to the local comprehensive.

Alastair Lund's mother:

We had great pressure put on us by the headmaster of the primary school for Alastair to go to the independent school, but we wanted him to be in a more natural environment. Obviously there were children there who weren't interested in learning, but we backed Alastair to rise above that, and he did, staying with his own age group. I can't complain of his results at all, with fifteen O-levels, can I? But at the independent school they were geared to the Oxbridge exam, and there were no facilities at all for that at the comprehensive.

At the last minute, we went to Cambridge as a family, and Alastair and I hoofed it round at least twenty colleges to see which ones would take him without special entrance papers. Some, like Magdalene, wouldn't entertain boys from comprehensive schools. He had to go through very rigorous interviews, and he's very modest. I don't suppose he told you that he was head boy in both his schools, and he got an A grade in O-level computer studies without any lessons. We're just wait-ing to go to the Palace for his Gold Duke of Edinburgh Award.

My father was a man of great strength of character. When he was a boy, he ran away from home to avoid working in the copper mines in Anglesea. He told me he walked barefooted through the snow to the nearest port, saving his good boots strung round his neck – it was in January – and signed on as a cabin-boy in a sailing ship. They went round the world for about twelve years, and when he came back to the village he found his mother had died of a broken heart, the year after he'd left. He bought her a decent headstone. He'd gone from being the dogsbody on board ship to being the captain.

Alastair Lund *(highly gifted, aged 20, studying engineering at university):*

In the sixth form at the comprehensive, I admit I became rather intolerant. I know that sounds big-headed, and I'm sorry. They weren't talking about anything that was worth talking about, it was all, 'Did you see *Top of the Pops* last night?' and 'Do you want to come out to the pub tonight?' There was nothing else. I desperately wanted somebody else to talk to. And that was really bad. In the end, I just switched off a bit. Since I left school, I haven't really maintained much contact with them at all.

I've had no social problems at Cambridge, but then I keep away from the droves of Sloane Rangers. One of my closest friends is from a public [private] school. I keep telling them about people in Liverpool and how they speak. I took a Scouse [Liverpool dialect] dictionary down with all our words, spelt in the same way they would be pronounced, and also a book of short stories written in this sort of dialect. They find it quite hilarious, especially if they hadn't met any before.

Moving up in the World

It was clear that many of the parents and grandparents of the young people were very bright, though relatively uneducated. So often in their youth they had been keen to study, but their chances had been blocked. Sometimes the route to higher education needed several generations to cover. Very few of the parents in this sample who had left school at 15 still assumed that their offspring would do the same, and most made every effort to help their children to post-school education.

For some, usually the mothers, their own experience had added considerable impetus to their efforts for their children. In the first part of the study, the mothers who had joined the National Association for Gifted Children had been significantly more dissatisfied with their own education, at whatever level, than the mothers of both the Control groups. As one of them said: 'I passed for the grammar school, but my mother, who was traditionally Irish, didn't think it was a good idea for a girl to start there and go on to university. And so I wasted all those years after I was 11. It's made me more determined that my children are going to have the best.'

There were some remarkable stories of how families had changed their lifestyles across just a couple of generations when the opportunities for betterment were presented, after perhaps hundreds of years at a basic level. One mother said: 'My mother went into service at about 15, so she had no education. But when I failed my eleven plus, I wasn't allowed to forget about it. My brother, though, he graduated and got a PhD.'

The rise of Angus Cameron's family was exceptional. All four grand-parents were Scottish crofters, but it was the men of his father's line who had pushed upwards. His father's father had struggled via night-school to become a school teacher, then his own father had become a qualified chemist through apprenticeships and night-schools. Now Angus, as gifted as his forebears had been, had reached university. The family had become middle-class city folk. His father described how Angus had found school:

Here in Edinburgh, Angus went to one of the largest comprehensive schools in Britain, in an area which has a reputation for being one of the roughest, dirtiest areas in Scotland. They speak fairly rough Scot-tish, 'Dinnae ken, Jem' sort of thing, and my two spoke in a rather posh accent. We all had a rough time, with anonymous phone calls at home. It was a bit hurtful, but Angus is quite a tough character, and fortunately he got into the really top class, and emerged unscathed out of a school like that, with excellent results. His sister suffered a lot, though.

In the old days, difficulties in obtaining education had often been due to financial poverty. Taking up a 'free' grammar school place meant buying a uniform and games kit, paying for outings, etc., and was more than poor people could manage. A Welsh mother described the situation: 'I was brought up in a mining valley in the depression. My father was out of work for six or seven years, which is why I left school at 15, having matriculated a year early, though my parents would have liked me to have gone on. My brother got a county scholarship to university. They wanted us to get out of the mines.' Sometimes, though, determination paid off to some extent, as one father described: 'My father was a brilliant scholar who was forced to leave grammar school at 15 to earn the family bread. He got a degree and a PhD on his own externally at London University in economics, though it was never really any use in his career in the bank, so he stayed frustrated there all his working life.'

Girls, a generation ago, not infrequently had to give way to their brothers' education: 'My father's attitude was that education for a woman was a bit of a waste, and he took a very detached view of me then as just a girl. But my brother obviously had to earn a living and keep a wife, so he could go on to college.' Several of the mothers had actually been told to fail their exams: 'My mother told me to fail the grammar school examinations, because being a divorced parent at that time, she couldn't afford to send me, although I was the top of the class. I've had a raw deal.'

But it could also be teachers who halted both boys' and girls' educational progress:

> The day before we were due to sit the scholarship, the headmistress came in and said that too many people had passed the prelim., and that these girls, even if they took the scholarships, wouldn't pass. She read out about ten of our names, and I was one of them who weren't to take the exam. I had a sister just two years older who did go to grammar school and she's done very well. She ended up at university. I still feel cheated.

Teachers, however, were less likely to discriminate for reasons of sex than of social class, which is how this father lost his chance:

> I was at a small village school with just two teachers, and if your face didn't fit with them, you didn't get your rightful chance. Three or four in the class that were nice were given lots of extra tuition and pushed to get to the grammar school. The rest of us were nowhere near ready for taking that exam. When one of the 'outcasts' actually passed for the grammar school, the sheer amazement on the headteacher's face was something I remember even now.

In spite of difficulties for poorer children, passing the eleven plus to the free grammar schools provided the opportunities for many to move up educationally and socially. Mary Owen's mother, who is now a college lecturer, had that springboard:

> Thanks to the 1944 Education Act I went to the grammar school, but my parents hadn't a clue. They were very nice and supportive – honest working class. There was never really anywhere at home to go to be private, to do my homework, or to think things. We all lived in one living room, and I used to do my homework on the bus. All the middle-class kids, whose daddies worked in offices, tended to be in the A form, and the rest of us were second-best in the B form. I didn't know how

to cope in the system, and I was terribly overawed by these middle-aged, Oxford-educated ladies. The only thing you could do with all that din at home was paint and draw – the soft option – so at 13 I went to art school part-time. Quite a lot of the people who were gifted that way did the same.

Gordon Bailey's four grandparents and his own parents had had minimal education. Although his mother did win a place at the grammar school, she was not told about it for years, as her parents wanted her to be useful about the house. She said: 'My father wouldn't even let me go to the girl guides, because he thought it was middle class, and that I might have met people there who would give me ideas beyond my station.' But she and her husband were determined that their children should have something better. It was a long and difficult trail for them to find out about schools and scholarships, but now two sons were at Oxford with open scholarships, and the third, Gordon, was on the way there, though it was at times a little rough. Gordon was at a selective school: 'At school there's a really awful middle-class social circuit, which excludes working-class boys like me. Of course they wouldn't exclude me if I tried hard to be like them, but I don't want to be. There's very little mixing really between the social classes, which is a shame.'

THE EFFECTS OF PRESSURE

Strong pressure on the gifted to strive to their utmost came from three sources: from the family, from the school, and sometimes from within the child while parents looked on in amazement. It is a danger for some gifted children who become seduced by the social rewards of learning – those of honour and improved self-esteem – that their zeal can become excessive, virtually taking over their lives. For a few schools, it did look like a means of collecting the hunting trophies of examination successes, and both schools and parents did take advantage of it, when it would have been better for the pupils to have been helped to develop other areas of themselves, such as making relationships. (See The Cost of High Academic Achievement, p. 116.)

There are parents from every walk of life who want their children to fulfil their dreams, and are prepared to spend great amounts of energy and money to make them come true. A handful of the gifted young people in this sample seemed to be squeezed to the last drop of effort to do better and better. If they could achieve the results without much obvious effort, it was not good enough; they had to be seen to work for them. For such parents, a 'good' school always 'stretched' their children and had a record of high exam success and Oxbridge entrance. Some of the private schools had obligingly directed themselves into turning out well-primed exam-inees, though parents were usually aware of their children's lack of all-round education: 'I wasn't happy with the fact that he didn't have a cultural education at school, and in the fast stream you miss out on all the sports too.' A father who had knowingly over-pushed his son was sympathetic: 'I pitied him going there, but I had to take him away from the other school because they'd gone on to mixed-ability teaching, which is absolutely diabolical. It would certainly have ruined him, because he would have taken the opportunity to just drift along. But he never did make any friends.'

Some children, however, were strong enough to throw off parental pres-sure, as the mother of a gifted girl described: 'She once told me that she concentrated on music because it was one way of getting Daddy to herself; he would do music with her endlessly, because he loved it. Then she stopped because she was terribly afraid he was trying to make her into a professional musician, and she knew she didn't want to be.'

But others, for whom the pressure had accumulated to an insupportable level, might suddenly opt out of school – making a leap to freedom and fun, as a boy at a high-pressure school explained:

In the final year of the sixth form, it came to me in a flash why certain people would jack it in, just suddenly get fed up of the whole thing, and leave school. I know quite a few people who've done that, only a few months away from their A-levels. It's disillusionment, when they've spent all their lives in education and it doesn't seem to be getting them anywhere. Some of them went to [community] colleges, taking another two years, when they could have finished them in four or five months at school.

Sometimes a young person was subject to all three pressures, like Mark Stubbs. Unlike many of the boys at his high-pressure school, who resented the limitations of the curriculum, Mark was filled with pride and delight at being there. The very action of striving, which was much stronger than a normal desire for achievement, seemed to give him great satisfaction. He smiled with pleasure as he described the demands his mother made on him, and the firmer his teachers were, the better he liked them. His wide range of reading matter was chosen carefully, for educational value rather than pleasure.

At 9 years old, Mark had seemed to me to be withdrawn, with noticeable difficulty in making eye-contact. At that time his one great joy was his little dog, and his pleasures were divided between 'going for walks with my dog' and 'playing indoor games against myself'. By the time of the follow-up, he had developed an academic, professorial manner, considering small points in detail before allowing himself to move on, and often returning to earlier questions when he felt his answers had been less than satisfactory to himself. He rebuked himself several times for being 'lazy'. He was an only child, obviously the apple of his parents' eyes, but he still wanted to be made to improve himself. I found him sensitive and sympathetic, but he had yet to feel moved, he said, by any artistic experience.

Mark Stubbs *(highly gifted, aged 20, studying physics at university):*

In the express course at school, you learned something once and then you were expected to remember it. It was good for me. The only disadvantage was that we didn't have time to go over much work. I was pretty near the top all the way through, because it was hard to slack at that place. There was a lot of pressure to get good marks every half term, and you really had to work to try and improve each time. I enjoyed the pressure. Most managed to cope, though a couple of boys cracked. The science teacher tended to mark me down a bit if I didn't do everything word perfect. He'd probably give me a B instead of an A, because he knew I could do the stuff and wasn't really trying. It was good for me because it pushed me on. They only do that for people who they think could be getting full marks every time, and I was around the top in both arts and sciences.

Mother always says, 'You should have done better,' whatever I do; she's never satisfied and always finds something wrong. I only got two A grades and a B at A-level, though I did get to Cambridge, but she said, 'Why didn't he get three As at A-level and a scholarship?' At school, it was better for me when I got the cane rather than detention, because then my mother wouldn't find out about it. There's no way I could hide the fact when I arrived home late at 5 o'clock, whereas if I'd had a caning, I could hide it. She'd be very angry and I'd get an extra punishment from her, then she'd keep it going over dinner with sarcastic remarks. That sort of thing would go on for a day or so.

Sometimes I get angry about my work and call myself a fool, saying, 'Look at this work. You've only got ten for this work. You should have got at least fourteen. Absolute fool.' After a little while I calm down, realize what I've done wrong, and try to mend my ways. With friends, I try and assess what's wrong with me and then try to change, force myself to be different from what I really am sometimes. If I wake up in the morning and think I've actually learned something the day before, that I'm actually wiser, that gives me a lot of pleasure.

But it was not always possible to tell the direction from which the pressure came – how much from the young people themselves and how much from outside. For example, Stuart Carter's determinedly achieving parents were both scientists who said they simply could not imagine a family where people were concerned about the arts. Neither could Stuart, who spent all his energy on scientific study, to the clear detriment of his emotional development. His self-esteem appeared to hang on the academic rewards he could present to his parents. But his father said that any problems were inherently Stuart's own: 'The relatively academic education he's had and his choice of subject [computer science] are absolutely ideal for a person like him, and have gone some way to minimizing the effects of his personality.'

Stuart Carter *(gifted, aged 22, a computer programmer):*

I always want a piece of paper to be proud of at the end. If you've done a subject for a few years, and you end up with nothing, apart from knowledge – which of course is valuable in itself – it doesn't give you as much to be proud of. Even a school exam which says, 'You got such-and-such a percentage,' it finishes off the achievement. I've been work-ing fifteen years continuously in education, and now I'm working as a computer programmer. But I need a rest. I'd like to be a bit irresponsible occasionally, not in the nasty sense, but I want to feel that there is a lighter side to life. Other young people seem to have it.

Pressure from home was also imposed on young people who were seen as gifted, but who were not, so the children could not live up to it. Marion Steele's environment had been carefully structured for climbing the aca-demic ladder. Both her teacher parents had pushed her hard to study, as had her old-fashioned grammar school. She was dutiful, worked hard, and had done extremely well with her above-average abilities, getting into a polytechnic. But within weeks of leaving home she had fallen in love. When she and her fiancé were no longer constrained by home and school to put in the extra work necessary simply to pass, they had promptly failed their first examinations. It was love on the dole for them. When I arrived on a glorious summer's day, Marion was watching a television soap opera behind curtains closed against the sun – held down by books. She knew what it was all about: 'I really need to be forced to work and I missed that pressure when it was gone. When I didn't pass my exams, the course leader had me in his office and said, "If I were you, I'd do the decent thing and withdraw now. You've got nothing up here" [she pointed to her head]. I've got to pay back the grant now.'

Describing the pressure she had been under, Louise Brinscombe said, 'My Mum was never satisfied,' though her mother put the blame in an unexpected place:

I joined the Society for Gifted Children after reading an article in a magazine, because Louise fitted in with so much of what it said. When she was very small she did all sorts of unusual things, like teaching herself to read at 3. But if I hadn't joined this Association, and then been part of this survey, I wouldn't have really felt that she was very bright. I was sorry I did, because then I put a lot of pressure on her, and I think that's one of the reasons why we're not close. My expectations of her caused quite a bit of antagonism with the teachers too, because I thought she could do better, when from their point of view she did quite well. If I hadn't known she was quite bright, I would always have been pleased and encouraging to her when she did quite well. Perhaps it's an emotional thing, a problem that I've got, that I still find it difficult to say I'm pleased with her. I feel as if she's resented me expecting too much . . . I suppose, though . . . in actual fact, your survey didn't have anything to do with it.

Pressure from home could alienate gifted children from their parents, but it could also hold them captive. Alec Spicer's quiet personality appeared to have been additionally subdued by his mother, who had brought him up with an intense concern for what she saw as right and wrong. Consequently, he had put his very high intelligence to use by studying at home, while his school fellows were out enjoying themselves. After a handful of A grades in his A-level exams, then university, he had returned to the nest to carry out her moral teachings by becoming a policeman.

Alec's mother had placed him in an intolerable intellectual dilemma. If he had followed his school excellence at university with a first-class degree, he would have been obliged to leave his home to work in the city and would have been in danger of not returning. So, quite unconsciously, he had lowered his final marks, and so was able to continue to live with his mother. She told me:

> I was 42 when Alec was born, and he's always been with adults. He didn't have many children of his own age as friends – well, not any that we wanted him to play with. Not because of social status, but because of standards of behaviour. His only friends were the son and daughter of a minister actually, but they were little devils. I wouldn't let Alec go into a house where I felt the influences were bad. I wouldn't let him eat school dinners, because they fed them on fat, so I always gave him sandwiches. He didn't like school dinners anyway.

Pressure from School

The Assisted Places scheme is a British government measure, introduced in 1980, to provide fees and other expenses for low-income parents who want to send their bright children to private schools. By 1987, 26,961 children had taken up assisted places in 227 private schools at a cost of £56.5 million to the taxpayer. Some private schools fill more than 40 per cent of their places this way. However, the recipients are now seen to be mostly the children of middle-class parents, such as teachers, who would have helped their children educationally without the scheme; very few places have gone to children from homes with poor educational provision (Edwards et al., 1989). Several children in this study had received this award, which involved all of them in lengthy travel to school that took a heavy toll on their energies and relationships.

Neil Cope's father described with evident distress what his son had gone through:

> Neil used to leave home at seven, then do two hours' journey each way by public transport. Then, he'd have homework on top of that – about two to three hours a night, every night. He used to have to turn in Saturday mornings as well, till 12. That's six days a week, four hours a day travelling. When he was tired, or when there was something emotional he couldn't deal with, he used to just cut off completely and sleep. In the school holidays he'd just sit and not do anything, or read a very light book.

Being gifted, Peter Amos, also a recipient of an assisted place, had no difficulty with the academic work, but because of it had carried an exceptional physical and emotional load from the age of 11. Although there was a very similar school near by, his parents had chosen the distant one in their pride at his 'place'. He said: 'I have to catch three buses each way, about three hours' travelling a day. I do about two hours' homework every single night, and weekends too. It's too much, I could do as well without that amount of homework.' Coming from a working-class home, Peter felt different from the other boys at the private school – 'There are one or two other boys at school like me, but not many' – and after a lot of talk he eventually said he would have preferred to be in a mixed-ability, co-educational school where he could be more involved, and probably happier.

He was a slight lad, who at 15 could have passed for much younger. He did what was expected of him and slept a great deal. In talking to him, I was sometimes concerned that he could not work up enough energy to respond to my questions. He found it quite impossible, for example, in spite of a great mental struggle, to say what was attractive or unattractive about himself. His father said that if told to, he would put the kettle on, but would not check whether it had water in, and laughed that this was typical of the professorial mind. To me, Peter was emotionally impaired, but it was hard to tell whether it was a defence against his hard world, or simple exhaustion.

Though it had taken a different form, school pressure on Emily Saville (aged 15) had also taken a heavy toll. She was undoubtedly well above average, but neither quite up to the school's aims, nor up to the performance of her highly achieving older sister. On the surface, she was the most positively happy schoolgirl one could ever meet, insisting how much she loved her school, how dearly she looked forward to going to it every day, how many friends she had there, and how superb it all was. She played the violin in two school orchestras, the piano in between times, and lacrosse for the school. But the protestation was too much. Her mother described what would happen:

Her sensitivity is acute, far above the norm, quite extraordinary. She hated the school to begin with, though it's small and friendly; a lovely school. But she felt she was in prison. She became claustrophobic; you could see her clamminess and her heavy breathing. She couldn't stay in the classroom and had to be sat near an open door. Then there was an awful phase when she couldn't go out to play, even down to the bottom of the school field, without being absolutely terrified.

The way that school measures things, she's middle of the road. One night before an exam, she had a giggling fit, which I think was hysterics. I heard this terrible noise from her room, went up and found her with tears rolling down her face, and she was saying, 'Well, I just can't remember. I can't remember.' She couldn't stop. It went on and on. She sometimes tidies up the counter of a shop she happens to be in. She's been thanked once or twice. It's all things like that that make you think that she's very insecure and wonder why. She seems so happy and uncomplicated.

Pressure from Acceleration

The easiest and most frequently chosen way of raising the level of education for intellectually gifted pupils is for the school to advance them a year or more. This procedure has many names, such as 'skipping a class' or 'being put up', but it is sometimes now called 'vertical enrichment' or 'acceleration'. It is the favoured procedure for some educationalists, who believe that the emotional problems it may bring are exaggerated.

However, it was clear from this study, in which the children's continued personal development was examined within their wider environments, that very few had benefited from being accelerated at school. Seventeen of the 169 young people either had been accelerated or were young for their class. Many had found that this presented them with such difficulties that it was at times detrimental to their greater well-being. Acceleration may even have been responsible, as some parents thought, for lowering their children's final examination marks.

A team in Baltimore, working on the Study of Mathematically and Scientifically Precocious Youth begun in 1971, have been influential in promoting 'speeded-up' learning for recognized high achievers (Stanley, 1986). Over the years they have amassed a great deal of data about school progress, and they found more positive benefits from that action – possibly because the children were not questioned in fine detail, and they were of course a different sample. The Study was originally set up to find high mathematical achievers, but the organization has since changed its name to the Center for the Advancement of Academically Talented Youth (CTY) and its outlook to talent-searching all kinds of abilities; it has broadened its scope to help a very wide range of gifted children (see 'Useful Addresses').

Psychologically, acceleration focuses a child firmly in the direction of improved learning achievement, which is indeed the purpose for which the children are moved up. The major reason given by schools for acceleration is that it will alleviate the children's apparent or anticipated boredom with the work their age-mates would be doing, and so will encourage their educational enthusiasm. But in my study, those of identical ability who had not been accelerated were not at all more bored in school than those who were. Quite the contrary – gifted pupils with same-age, non-gifted classmates became far more involved in the non-academic aspects of school life. They had significantly more friends, enjoyed school more, and had achieved at least as well academically.

Only two of the young people who had not been accelerated would have preferred it, at least in their area of high ability. Stephen Kaye (highly gifted, aged 14, at school) was in a difficult position, and in his case it looked as though acceleration or some other form of enrichment for mathematics would have been a great help. He explained:

Most of the things I've been taught in maths I knew anyway because I was very interested from a young age. The lessons are OK, but the work is boring. I used to finish it quickly, but then I ended up getting more and had to redo the same work over and over again. So now I spin it out. Sometimes I do what everybody else will be doing next, so when they come to it I just have to wait. The problem is that I can do it more quickly because I know it better, but because of that, I end up doing more work instead of less. It's the others who ought to be doing more really, because they're learning it and I'm usually not.

I wondered why his school would not allow this quiet boy to work on his mathematics in the school library, instead of having to endure that classroom tedium day after day.

Parents who had to watch their highly gifted children struggle socially among older pupils often suffered with them, and would say: 'He didn't tell us what he was going through at the time. He had a few stomachaches and things like that on going to school, you know.' They often felt obliged, though, to take the opinion of the 'experts', the teachers. A mother described how her highly gifted son had been unhappily accelerated by two years: 'Both the head and the deputy head wanted it. They said, "If he can't make it, who can?" ' But it did not always have even the supposed benefit of giving extra time for work, as one accelerated boy said: 'I didn't try for Oxbridge because it would have meant staying on at school, and even though I was so young, I'd had enough.'

Of course, parents and teachers did not always agree, as one mother complained:

Although Iain passed the entrance exam to the grammar school a year early, the junior school headmaster wouldn't allow him to go, on the grounds that he would be socially immature. We, his parents, would have liked him to have had the advantage of the extra year later in his school life, but they made him repeat that year and take the entrance examination again. It was degrading to him in a way, because it was a feeling of failure. Now we know that the headmaster's judgement on his social standing in his class was wrong and Iain is too mature for his year.

In making the decision to accelerate the children at school, both parents and teachers acted in true sincerity and in a way that seemed right to them at the time. No one, though, had asked any of the children what they themselves would have preferred – I checked on that. But the decision was never taken lightly, as a father explained: 'We did a lot of heart-searching, then and now. It was a great pity in some ways; he wasn't mature enough. When he was 16, there were men of 19 in the sixth form. He played football very well. People used to talk about it, this tiny little boy who played like a tank.' He was, however, actually of normal size for his age.

Growing-up Effects of Acceleration

For some of the highly gifted pupils, normal growing-up problems had been exacerbated by being accelerated in school, as expressed by a 14-year-old girl: 'Some of my class at school have changed beyond recognition, leaving me behind. They like going out and drinking and things like that, and only last year they were staying in, or just going round to each other's houses, having a laugh. I don't think I've changed so much.'

Talking to the whole family, two sides to the story could be seen. Robert Fraser was a tall, 15-year-old, highly gifted youth. He had an air of supreme self-confidence, anticipating the success he considered his due. However, he spent little time in study, and saw his modest exam results as unimportant, consciously relying on the powerful reserves of intelligence he knew he had to bounce him over the next more significant hurdle. Though socially there had been no problems with his classmates because of his acceleration at school, it was different at home. Yet his father's strictures ran off Robert like water off a duck's back.

Robert's father understood the problems of his son's two-year advancement in school:

> He feels he should be able to go to places for 18-year-olds like the others in his class and be treated like someone of that age. But though he seems very mature in some respects, in others he's still a little boy. There's been a lot of trouble because of the influence of his peers. This final year, it's not been easy at all, because I'm not very good at keeping my temper. When I see that he's playing around, and he pulls the wool over his mother's eyes, then of course, it starts a row.

From Robert's point of view, however, life with his parents seemed to be even more of a struggle of being misunderstood and having his maturity underestimated than it was for other adolescents who had not been accelerated. As he said:

> Growing up has only been difficult at home, not elsewhere. My friends are all older than me, but they're quite proud to know me. My parents don't understand; when all your friends are going out, you want to go out with them. Next year I'll be learning to drive, and after that I'll have the use of my parents' car. And it won't just be the odd day trip here and there; it'll be a long weekend away. Being young in the class like me is quite a rarity, quite special. But there was a bit of resentfulness from some people who thought I might have taken their place by going to that school early. It's done me more good than harm. I think anybody would jump at a chance of missing a year at school.

Even in a selective school, where the whole class of similar ages works at an advanced level and differences in maturity are less of a problem, advanced intellectual stimulation can still be at some cost in relationships outside school. This was described by Vincent Jacobs (gifted, aged 16, at school):

> Old friends at other schools still haven't taken their O-levels, and I've done them already. Now, I'm working for my A-levels and then there's the six years for medicine. I know I've got to slog for the future, but I feel as if I've lost my youth. Life comes in one headlong rush; it's going

to hit you in the face tomorrow, and you don't have any time to take stock of what's happening.

His extreme acceleration had put a considerable strain on the natural pace of growing up for highly gifted Damien Bradley and may well have left him unhappy for life. During the first part of the study, when he was 10 years old, his father had described him as an outstandingly happy child with many friends, though that had not been my impression of Damien at the time. I had noted his withdrawn manner and how his eyes seemed to lack the responsive sparkle of fun and challenge in the testing sessions that virtually all the 210 children in the sample had shown. In fact, he already looked bored with life. His intellectual ability was so advanced that in spite of being at an academic secondary school, he had been accelerated nearly two years – and then placed in the express stream. The result of putting him among much older boys, with regard neither for him as a developing person, nor for the two years of learning he had missed, had lowered both his expected examination results and his sense of worth in himself. To try to right the difference, he had taken a year off between school and university, so that he was now almost the normal age and size for a student. But the psychological pattern had been set. He had very few friends or outside interests at university, and it was probably too late to right the balance of his life.

Damien Bradley *(highly gifted, aged 18, at university):*

Being smaller at school, I wasn't going to stand any chance physically. I was never good at sports, and I was hopeless at athletics and gym. It used to embarrass me. At the time, I used to think of it as just me, but later on I realized it was probably that I wasn't as well developed muscularly – mind you, I've never found sport that important, so it doesn't bother me. If someone said, 'Why are you so small?,' I used to just laugh. It just became a joke, so I had to beat them verbally and usually it worked. It got to such a stage where I would do it to just anyone – put up a defence straight away. It's automatic now. I've taught myself not to get angry. I get bored sitting around the university, but then, I've always been bored. I don't think it's been any advantage, being younger, apart from the fact that I've had a year out. It wasn't right at all. I'd have been much happier in my own age-group. I wouldn't do it to my kids.

Being smaller than one's classmates affected girls too. Her mother called

Julia Morley (gifted, aged 16, at school) a 'nine-out-of-ten girl', as she had never quite reached her potential. She had been advanced a year, but as she continued through her girls' selective school, her marks sank lower and lower. She was socially immature in the class, and had considerable relationship problems – the older girls would give her the brush-off very crudely. She told me: 'I was always very self-conscious about looking younger, especially at first, and I was very small compared to the other children, although not compared to my own age-group. I still think of myself as short, even though I'm average height.'

It was not a sudden move-up at school which had disturbed Rachel Wallace, as she had been taught with classmates older than herself through almost all her school life. Her examination progress had been accelerated to an extraordinary degree – much to her parents' approval. She had taken three A-levels at 15, moved schools, and taken a different four the following year. She described with pride how she had worked so hard that a teacher told her she'd been up till 2 in the morning marking the extra work Rachel had volunteered, and had begged her to slow down. Yet separately, both Rachel and her parents told me that she had not been fully stretched! Her mother described some of the results of the pressure on this brilliant girl, who was now at Oxford, as planned.

Rachel Wallace's mother:

She's obviously outstanding in her abilities, and therefore she couldn't find her intellectual peer group, except somewhere like Oxford or Cambridge. There's no one round here able to have a conversation at the intellectual depth she wants; she's a very deep-thinking girl. She's told me that her mind thinks independently of her – it goes on racing and racing, and you can't stop it; it's got a life of its own. Sometimes she hates herself with a deep anger, and she can attack herself, which is very difficult to handle. She scratches herself and makes herself bleed, and then this morning she was banging herself. I wonder whether it stems actually from when she was very tiny and she couldn't do the things she wanted to. Her arms and legs wouldn't do what her gifted mind ordered, like she couldn't control the pencil and so on.

We had an incident with her. I can't remember what started it now: it all happened in the middle of the night. First she sat on the landing and threatened to throw herself downstairs. We tried to talk to her to calm her down, and eventually she went outside into the garden, barefoot in her nightdress, sat down in the flower-bed and screamed. When Rachel screams, she really can; she used to do it as a baby in her temper tantrums. She screamed about three times at the top of her voice, so much so that several sets of neighbours phoned the police thinking murder was happening, and three police vans arrived outside. One of them talked to her; I don't know what he said, but eventually she came in, somewhat subdued, and went to bed. It was obvious she's been under enormous pressure.

Rachel Wallace *(highly gifted, aged 19, studying mathematics at Oxford):*

I've had no regrets about being accelerated; I found the work interesting, and I might have been bored if I'd been further down. I came out equivalent with girls of 11 when I was 7, but they thought they couldn't really put me with others of that age, so they went half and half, and I was two years ahead instead of four. I had absolutely no confidence at all, and I didn't have any friends. The others would spend their time teasing me because they said it was fun – 9-year-old little girls are so cruel. I don't think it was my fault, or that I was spoilt.

It didn't make it easy for me to grow up, though I think I did gain something while I was going through that. Even though I now have friendships that I feel sure are not going to disintegrate, at the same time, there's always the lurking fear that they don't really like me, that they're only tolerating me. It's not really rational, and I'm quite negative about myself. To a certain extent, I've been a bit depressive and melancholy in temperament from the time I was very young. My mum tells me I used to come home sometimes from school crying my eyes out, being so unhappy. I don't remember that.

It can only be concluded that moving children out of their age-group did not appear to be the best for the majority of the gifted young people in this sample. It should be restricted to the physically fit and the emotionally stable; and even then, only as a last resort.

Chapter 9
The Challenge

Wherefore have these gifts a curtain before 'em?
WILLIAM SHAKESPEARE, *TWELFTH NIGHT*

In looking at the influences on the attitudes and behaviour of some gifted and non-gifted children across ten years of their growing up, this study is able to offer some insight on what helped some of the children to develop to extremely high levels of ability, and is able to suggest ways of helping others. Were all children to be able to apply their abilities in a competent way, one would expect to see a notable rise in the overall level of their performances, as well as in their happiness. But this calls for a greater flexibility and sensitivity towards the individual child than many schools and parents seem to offer at present.

ASSESSING INTELLIGENCE

In the first survey, many myths about intellectually gifted children had been exposed as false. Physically, other than being more likely to wear glasses, they were the same as other children. A high IQ of itself had not appeared to cause the children any problems, but other people's attitudes towards their gifts, as well as unhappy home circumstances, could affect them emotionally. The real differences between the gifted and the others clearly lay in their abilities, particularly their concentration, memory, and sensitivity.

Current research in developmental psychology is moving away from dependence on specific measures, such as tests of abilities or classroom experiments, towards more naturalistic assessments. I chose a combined approach of in-depth interviews with observations, and also measurement of the young people's intellectual, artistic, and emotional life. However, the intellectually gifted present special problems of measurement. Firstly, an extremely high intelligence is rarely fully exercised and so cannot be observed in action in the everyday world, and secondly, there is uncertainty at the very highest levels about what intelligence scores are describing, and whether the scores go high enough. In fact, sixteen of the young people in my follow-up study hit the ceiling of the tests, since it was not possible to score more than 100 per cent.

One could measure in more general ways; for example, using the developmental stages described by Jean Piaget. But recent research has shown that not only are most young children more advanced than the ages he suggested for these stages, but the gifted are considerably more advanced than that. In spite of considerable statistical analysis, this long-term study provided evidence not of a sequence of stages particular to the gifted, but simply of their speedy progress through most normal milestones. Even that distinction faded when they left childhood, and in the context of their environments they showed great individual variation in their continued development and behaviour. Fortunately, learning is a lifelong process, with neither early experience being immutable, nor later experiences being only superficial (see Freeman *et al.*, 1991).

The two intelligence tests used in this research provided different viewpoints, one measuring only with patterns, and the other with some learned, school-type material. But such tests were not designed to find out how a score was reached – only to compare a child with others of the same age. Clearly, not all the intellectually gifted young people who did so extraordinarily well on either or both tests were always using that level of ability in daily life, not least because they had been differently affected by their circumstances.

Throughout the study, the young people of the highest IQ appeared to have a higher speed of perception, as well as better memory and concentration than the others. Those who were emotionally well balanced were more likely to describe using more efficient methods of thinking and learning, and to make the best use of their personal styles. But even when they used poor study strategies, the highly able were usually able to achieve high levels at school by relying on their excellent memories. Their teachers did not seem to be concerned to improve their learning methods, and parents were at a loss to know how to help. However, personal study skills can be extremely important in learning, and this was shown acutely when the external structure was lost, as when moving on from school to university.

LESSONS FROM HOME

Almost all mental life is socially influenced. Learning how to assess the capacities and predict the behaviour of other people calls for sensitivity and awareness, and is an important part of intellectual as well as emotional development. How an individual tackles a problem, even in everyday life, may change radically with the social context. For instance, it is well known by both parents and teachers that what a young child appears to be capable of doing alone at school may not hold true for home, and vice versa. This study provided many clues to ways in which parents had been able to help their children develop to a very high level, and when they were analysed statistically two highly significant aspects of home educational advantage emerged – parental involvement with the child, and provision of the means of learning.

1) Parental Involvement

There is no single type of parent–child interaction which is critical to the development of children's high-level abilities. It is complex because parents and children all have their own intellectual capacities, as well as their own personalities. But genuine, regular interaction of parents and children is decidedly effective. It starts with 'conversations' with babies and moves on to a variety of mutually pleasurable activities and experiences, such as listening to music and exploring interests. For example, a child may be interested in sea-shells. Giving him or her a book with pictures is very nice, but how much better when parents and child set off to look for sea-shells together, using the book as a guide, maybe with a picnic, and certainly with enthusiasm. The beneficial difference in outcome of that kind of involved approach was plain to see in this study.

It was also clear that the way parents conducted their lives was a very powerful influence in teaching their children: it was example and not expectations which made all the difference. Parents act as models for their children, and in their love, the children neither simply imitate them nor even swallow their ideas whole, but rather, using mental schemas and strategies, each child absorbs and then evolves its own values from what has been seen and experienced. The parents who had the most positive effects on their children's high-level development were not those who told their children what to do, but those who did it with them.

2) Provision for Learning

The second key to the development of children's potential is provision with which they can learn – both physical equipment and adequate tuition. Would-be artists need far more than a few scraps of paper and a pencil stub, a mathematician needs a teacher, a linguist has to hear the language, and a budding violinist needs a violin.

Children need to be taught specific skills and be given the opportunities to practise them. For example, it has been seen many times (Smith, 1990) that when children are learning to read, those who read out loud to their parents regularly at home have markedly higher reading attainments than those who do not. The ways which are the most likely to enhance children's high-level learning, which will last through life, are not, however, dependent on a great deal of money. Education authorities in many parts of the world provide extras virtually free, even if parents have to seek them out. The public library service is but one shining example. But parents have to be both willing and able to make the effort for their children to take advantage of the opportunities around – and some parents in this study who had very little money showed that this was entirely possible and greatly advantageous to the children.

STRESS

It is a vicious circle; when a child is exposed to family stress he or she may become emotionally disturbed and thus 'difficult', the extra attention the child then demands causing further detriment to the parents' own relationship, bringing the child guilt. Over time, the emotional turmoil can eat away at the child's feelings of worth, the burden continuing long after the initial problem has gone. But when parents become irritable, aggressive, and quarrelsome it does not impinge equally on all the children in the family. Boys are more susceptible to family discord than girls

(Quinton and Rutter, 1985), and highly able children are probably more sensitive to it than others.

In the first part of this study, the children with exceptionally high IQ scores were found to be as emotionally stable as the others, and had no distinctive personality traits. However, they were described independently by parents and teachers, and measured on tests of social adaptation, as being more sensitive, and this aptitude had clearly stayed with them as they grew up. The children who had been described and measured as with some emotional disturbance had ability levels spanning the whole sample range. Their problems were mostly those of family disturbance, such as strictness, which had hampered their emotional – and sometimes intellectual – growth in terms of developing adequate resourcefulness and feelings of competence.

But that distress had not acted like the grain of sand under the shell of the oyster – none of those unhappy children looked ready to produce any pearls of art or poetry. In fact, they had generally achieved less well than those of the same ability who had enjoyed peace of mind. Though there were hopeful signs that some had begun to grow out of their childhood problems, others, such as some young scientists, appeared to be entrenched in a poor self-image for life. I hazard a guess that in spite of their innate brilliance, they will not mature into Einsteins or Linus Paulings.

The gifted in the sample spoke of special pressures, such as feeling obliged to conform to the average by way of teacher 'put-downs', and the influence of their classmates. Even greater pressure, though, came from parents and teachers who, maybe for their own vicarious satisfaction, pushed them very hard to achieve. Some youngsters did their best to oblige, subduing their personalities (if not their souls) in blinkered striving for academic excellence. For them, healthy emotional development, including the freedom to play and be creative, was severely curtailed; the glazed look in their eyes said a great deal as they worked doggedly on to achieve their A grades.

The evidence of how these young people received and reacted to the special stresses of being gifted is here in their own words. The message for those who are likely to bring that stress about, teachers and parents, is that such pressure usually has the opposite effect from what was intended; the children often achieved less well. Far better results in human terms were found when children, however brilliant, were treated with respect, allowing them enough responsibility to make many of their own discoveries and decisions. However, there were others, especially those in the arts, who seemed to have an inbuilt impetus, a spark, a 'psazz', which could light up their personalities, bringing them great inspiration and success.

Defences

It is often possible to help people become aware of their own emotional defences, especially if these are not too well entrenched. The helper has to be sensitive enough to discover the ways through, even though such defences can take many and surprising forms. Certainly, it is always easier to see other people's than one's own.

In their exceptionality and their sensitivity, the gifted sometimes construct complex, inhibiting psychological defences against expected hurt. A common variety is to hide behind academic, intellectual walls of their own making, implying that they are too clever to have normal relationships with ordinary people. Alternatively, they present themselves as being bored at school, and so never learn the routines of learning discipline, which can be difficult to pick up later, and so this defensive boredom becomes a downward spiral, getting worse and worse.

The defences are built to ward off the particular painful situations in which the gifted can find themselves. They may, for example, be particularly stressed by the never-ending very high expectations of others, even though they are capable of meeting them, because they too have a need to relax from giving a superb performance every time. These expectations are especially difficult to produce if either their gifts are developing at uneven rates or, as often happens, they are receiving less praise for their achievements than other children. In this study, there was the boy who produced three funny 'books' a day, when the teacher wanted a serious effort, and so had them torn up in front of the class (see p. 122). Having to keep quiet about one's surging ideas all the time is more than distressing; it is destructive of future ideas.

The poor feelings about themselves that can result from such situations, and the defences the gifted put up against further possible hurt, can be alleviated. This can be done both by skilled counselling by people who understand the gifted, and by enabling such children to mingle with others of the same ability. It is true for everyone that to be with others like oneself is not only more comfortable but reaffirms one's personal outlook and sense of reality. Especially during adolescence, when the developing sense of self is being revised and remoulded, it allows the gifted to stride out intellectually, while continuing to learn how to make relationships. Being with their intellectual equals also lets the intellectually gifted see that hiding behind their brilliance is a false defence. They find out that even among young people of the same ability, emotions still foul up relationships, and that intellectual activity cannot be the sole or even the dominant criterion in life.

It has been suggested that boys with sensitive artistic traits, which are regarded in the West as feminine, may only be able to find their comfortable mirror in similar males, and that this might be a possible reason for homosexual relationships. But the great majority of the highly sensitive, artistic, and aware young people in my study who felt they were different from others had simply grown up with it as a part of their personal make-up. It did not seem to have affected their sexual identity.

Where pressure on these gifted young people was unyielding, the study all-consuming, the incompatibility of their new surroundings too strong, or their own sensitivity too difficult to handle alone, they did have emotional problems. The gifted too need time to 'stand and stare', to find out about life at their own pace and in their own ways. To be healthy, there has to be a balance in everyone's life, and for the gifted adolescent that includes good relationships, developing interests outside study subjects, and taking part in school and many other activities.

LESSONS FROM GIFTED LEARNERS

All schools aim to set up educational experiences designed to develop the minds and behaviour of pupils in certain ways, and a school which is beneficial and effective shows it in the care the teachers provide. It shows in their concern for the way the children learn, which includes the means of teaching, such as feedback on pupils' work, as well as what is taught. It shows in the encouragement for pupils to be involved with the design of their own education, both in and out of school. It shows in the atmosphere in the school building, both physically and emotionally (Mortimore, 1988).

But even with the finest educational provision, the results may not be as intended. Children are never passive recipients, whether they appear to conform or not, but are constantly adjusting their mental outlooks to their new experiences, either unconsciously or by deliberately altering their behaviour to fit in, as a gifted child may in a class of more modestly able children.

An education for the highly able should not be, as it so often can be, a matter of acquiring astounding exam successes early, culminating in a PhD at 20. As with all children, it should encourage a genuine feeling for learning and considering, and should stimulate curiosity – 'knowing how' rather than 'knowing that'. In the long run, the goal of education must be to equip all children with the means and motivation to continue learning after they have left home and school. The only way to find out whether the gifted do need a change in their education is to look in detail at how they are managing with what they are receiving now.

In the identification of high ability, tests or expert judgements should always be employed with an observation of the way a child learns – looking at the process as well as the product, within the context of the child's development. This is commonly done, for example, in identifying musical talent. Such all-round assessment avoids the educational wastefulness of either going over an already familiar area – a strong possibility with a speedy learner – or assuming a foundation of knowledge which is not there – as with children who have jumped a class or two. But most teachers are neither trained to find out developmental details, nor always have the time to do so. An extremely helpful move, especially in secondary schools, would be for pupils to be sure of frequent one-to-one interviews with a specially trained teacher or counsellor; one who also keeps good contact with the parents.

These counsellors should also have understanding of the kind of pitfalls they may encounter and the special ways of looking at life which are described in this book. Regular visits would enable an advanced child to find out, away from the subject teacher, about different areas of interest with a view to future occupations. The gifted have special needs for guidance, as they can be not only advanced in their learning capacities but exceptionally able across the board, or, more than other children, lopsided in their development. Comparison of age norms on measures of social and emotional development, as well as in specific subject areas, can provide valuable clues.

For most normal schools, however, it is not always possible to meet the needs of these special children, especially those who have non-school-type educational needs. For instance, most academic school education is biased towards verbal skills, rather then the visuo-spatial ones such as fine art or sculpting. But there are very many different places outside school to which children can be directed to learn new skills, for example, places of work, specialist out-of-school activities, museum visits, archaeology digs, and even spending time in other kinds of schools.

Adaptable Intellectual Learning

The human brain has an almost infinite capacity for activity, and as relatively little of it is used in everyday life, the potential for improvement is vast. The difference between a novice and an expert is that the expert has a much broader knowledge base on which to use the same level of intelligence, and this holds for the process of learning as it does in other areas. What the novice learner has to acquire is not only more information, but also the increasingly complex procedures to apply it to a greater variety of problems. Any expert action, such as high-level examination achievement, requires both knowledge and the means of using it. In well-practised everyday activities like making a phone call or driving a car, everyone makes use of such expert actions. It is even possible to develop general, adaptable, expert strategies for problem-solving. Professional administrators have a selection ready to apply in very different fields of activity and situations. This is why a competent manager can move with good effect from, say, a factory producing glassware to a business buying and selling cloth.

One can think of children as novices and adults as experts, although gifted children may become experts well ahead of their years. However, it is arguable that even though a child may give adult/expert-type perform-ances, such as Mozart's or Mendelssohn's early compositions, they are in fact the products of infant prodigies and do not compare in depth to those of the same or other composers in their adult years (Radford, 1990).

Fitting the teaching to the learner's state of development and style of acceptance is a much better way of ensuring adaptable learning than fitting the learner to the teaching. However, it is impossible for any teacher to do this in a class of individuals. The alternative approach is in the style of teaching which allows ideas to remain open and flexible as they form and settle in the child's mind. New information can become rigidly held when the child does not quite grasp it because of inattention or narrow teaching. The mental structure in which the learning is housed has to be very rigid or that fragile stuff will be lost and forgotten. That is why the rigid learning strategy of rote-learning is so popular; it holds the straight information in a place where it may be stored and retrieved. Multiplication tables are usefully stored in this way. But a more flexible approach based on deeper understanding of principles is essential for real competence and high-level functioning.

Those selected by virtue of their ability to do well in examinations are a particular group, with very specific mental skills, and they do not represent all gifted individuals – Picasso could barely read and yet was obviously highly intelligent as well as being an artistic genius. Highly achieving examinees must be able to concentrate and remember large amounts of material, as well as having access to the advanced skills of drawing their ideas together in the examination time. This is not simply exam techique, such as answering the question accurately and timing answers, but concerns the use of superior mental facilities. There were in fact clear reasons why so many of the young people in this study had achieved at such exceptionally high levels.

To begin with, they did have the potential – sheer intellectual ability – to work at a gifted level. As very young children, they had often begun to acquire the essential broad knowledge base, usually because they wanted to know things and searched them out. Their parents told me and I saw what they were doing for myself in the first part of the study. Their home educational environments had usually included the necessary means for learning, including material provision, the example of their parents' behaviour, and the good communication that parents, teachers, and child often shared, which was a statistically significant feature throughout the study.

As they grew up, the more successful young people had found personal ways of organizing their powerful mental abilities, which were different from those of the less successful. They were more aware of, and made more use of, their personal learning styles. To help their understanding and remembering, they used methods such as searching the material for its principles, then focused more on the substance than on the tiny details of what they were learning. This helped them not only to reproduce the material, but to elaborate on it. They were also more aware of the nature of the problems they were tackling, and through that awareness were already a long way towards solving them. The less successful had remained with more immature, less effective, shorter-term techniques, like memorizing their lesson notes and hardly ever looking things up in books or using other resources.

In addition to their own efforts, the teachers and parents of the most successful youngsters had mostly judged their potentials accurately, and had helped and given them encouragement. For the high achievers, there was often a mutually rewarding situation both at home and at school, the young people feeling comfortable with their desire to learn and parents taking pride in this. But the less successful pupil was less likely to enjoy that kind of harmony, sometimes seeing school lessons as irrelevant to his or her personal needs and future life.

However, what teachers have always said – that hard work brings results – is undoubtedly true; a significant proportion of keen pupils of moderate ability (mostly girls) had studied as well as they were able, and with good results. The strength and direction of their motivation were influenced by its goals of doing well academically, and what that meant to them. When intellectually gifted children are unmotivated, it may be that they are either avoiding threats to their self-image from possible failure, or aiming for different goals from those which have been chosen for them. For many of the highly successful examinees, the goal which had influenced them was not just the examination successes but the acquisition of knowledge, and the promise of further use of that learning. This goal was appropriate for their abilities and interests, and they had worked towards it with efficient study strategies. Were less able or less motivated youngsters to be offered lessons which appeared to them to be personally valuable and meaningful, these would be more likely to inspire them to take part in them.

Enhancing Learning

The academically successful do not have sole rights to the learning methods they use. These can be employed in normal teaching and learning. The essence of teaching children how to learn is in recognizing the individuality of each child, so as to find and strengthen each one's personal style. Because new learning depends so much on how prior knowledge has been stored, simply telling children what to learn is not always adequate. They need to relate the new to the old, in ways which are meaningful to them, from their own perspectives. This can be very straightforward, such as teaching geometry in terms of football pitches and the movements of the football (Claxton, 1990).

However, a high proportion of all the young people felt some lack of communication with their teachers. Improving that situation should be a priority in finding out about the children's learning styles. It is not as difficult as it might seem – when they are asked, most children are able to tell the teacher how they like to learn – though some may need a little help to think this through and find it out. Discussion of the different ways of learning and thinking, guided by teachers or parents, is a valuable method of helping children to reach understanding about themselves. Nor is the problem of organizing a classroom to suit individual modes of learning entirely insuperable. It is, after all, the same problem that all teachers face, with more or less success, every school-day. The answer lies in a variety of lesson presentations. This not only helps children to pick up ideas in tune with their personal learning style, but also encourages them to adapt to different approaches to a subject.

To enhance learning strategies, younger children may be helped by talking through ideas or even acting out possible ways of approach to a new area. To do this, they must be really involved. In history, for example, children can discuss or act out basic information such as the coming of the plague to a medieval village, how it affected individuals, and how they might be likely to behave, then compare their present-day thoughts with what really happened. Children can think up and try out different aproaches to the subject area themselves. For example, they could take an aspect of technology, consider different ways in which it impinges on their lives, and then follow the trains of reasoning as far as they can in many directions. Once acquired, flexible learning and thinking strategies – on a sound knowledge base – can be transferred for use on other, similar subjects with problems of increasingly greater complexity (De Corte, 1990; Watts, 1991). As with the highly successful examinees, a positive outlook on learning, with a well-practised and flexible mind, allows almost any child to apply and adapt a range of intellectual skills correctly in new situations.

Teachers and parents should also try to become aware of their own repertoires of teaching strategies. These might be, for example, a heavy reliance on the instruction of children to remember rather than interpret. Or adults might have a poor ability to cope with redundant noise, so that they demand constant silence from pupils. The strategies which adults teach children to learn by may not in fact be the best ways for their recipients, which is another good reason for keeping things flexible.

There is evidence that children who believe their abilities are fixed fail to aim as high as they could, particularly if they see themselves as not very bright (Chapman and Lambourne, 1990). Enhancing children's sense of competence is possibly the most basic way of improving their potential for learning – especially for girls and children from ethnic minorities – and should include practical help in improving their learning strategies. Self-rating is the first step towards self-reflection and control. It helps any child (or indeed adult) towards a positive and realistic understanding of his or her own ways of thinking and learning. A very effective technique is to guide children in rating their own performances and products as they work through practice problems, instead of depending on a teacher's marking.

Another way of bringing direct rewards and so improving a pupil's learning is by the teacher's positive attitudes. This does not mean false praise, but seeking out aspects of what the children are doing for constructive comment. It helps the children to develop stronger feelings of proficiency in learning, which in turn makes them more likely to invest energy in it, enjoy it, and do better. Once in motion, the upward spiral raises the probability of success, since enhancing positive feelings also improves the motivation to learn.

Because the gifted have the potential to move into higher levels of intellectual thought they should, at least as much as any others, be practised in the thinking strategies of analysis and evaluation. This would involve immersing them from the very start of school life in ideas which are complex, sophisticated, and stimulating. To do this implies that they must be recognized as sufficiently able to tackle those tasks. This does not mean wholesale intelligence testing of all school entries, but rather that the teacher takes a more intellectually challenging approach to children's learning than is generally so at present, and offers this possibility. It can come from the bright child, as when 9-year-old gifted Chloe asked me, 'Why should I believe in history? All those things which people say tell us about long ago, perhaps they were false clues left for us to find. And God, why should I believe in God?'; so we talked about assumptions, motivations, and faith.

A common example of unchallenging learning is in the teaching of reading. It is not unusual for very advanced early readers to be kept at the same pace as the rest of the class. One mother spoke for many, as 23 children in this sample were said by their parents to have read something by the age of 3:

> When she went to school at 5, we were told that she was too young to read. I went up to school and said, 'This is ridiculous, she's reading *Black Beauty* at home. Why can't she read at school?' The teacher said, 'Oh, I don't believe all this.' So I said, 'Right. Pick any book off your bookshelf, fetch her, and find out for yourself.' So he did, and she read it through, but it still didn't make any difference, she still had to read at the level they decided. They couldn't see that she was getting frustrated.

Using a more challenging approach, the teacher would first have had to recognize the little girl's ability, then encourage her to have a stab at a higher-level text. He would also have had to spend a little time with her, talking about what she was reading, getting her to elaborate on it – 'What happened next?' – and relate it to other ideas she might have – 'Was this like the story you read before about the prince?'

All children need plentiful practice in sizing up tasks, analysing problems, and assessing goals, as well as attempting solutions. Practice for these basic learning strategies, like looking for similarities and differences, is not difficult to find. It is readily available in everyday commercial puzzle-books for children. More specific techniques of improving ways of thinking and learning for older students can be found in self-help books (for example, Buzan, 1988).

Developing good thinking and learning strategies does not imply that a conscious decision should be taken every step of the way. It is usually more a matter of being able to draw on past experience so as to be aware of different possible ways of proceeding. For example, reading a science textbook calls for a more considered, stop-start approach than the relaxed, flowing enjoyment of an easy story-book. Many youngsters do not know that the two types of text call for different approaches and processes. In describing their study methods, the poor examinees in my study often closeted themselves with their textbooks and notes and simply read them, many times, as though they were novels. They described how hard they found it to absorb the material. No one had ever helped them to learn how to use analysis and comparison of the information, and then how to fit the principles into an overall pattern – to learn strategically.

But even good learning techniques can be misused, like the very effective method of taking notes by writing down key words or 'outlining', which takes hours of practice to set up. If the system has not been well learned, the effort at remembering the technique can overload the working memory. For example, a student trying to use it inexpertly in a lecture, unless he or she is intellectually gifted, cannot pay attention to both the technique and the information at the same time, and may not only miss some of the information but also become disheartened from using the method (though it is still a valuable skill).

Since motivation for learning varies with the success and failure of endeavour, accurate feedback is vital. But even with good feedback, the first attempts may not be satisfactory, or the chosen course of action may begin to fail after a time, and sometimes it may seem that endless encouragement is called for. The insight gained into the ways in which most of the young gifted people in my study had used their minds has shown that when they had the knowledge, the practice, and the confidence to act in their own way, they were extremely effective. And their methods are open to anyone.

Creative Thinking

Creative thinking takes the products of learning and analytic thinking to their highest levels. But it is also a basic, everyday activity which includes almost any decision – should you wear the red or the blue blouse with the green sweater? We can learn from those who do it well that creative thinking skills are improvable and teachable, in a similar way to those of adaptable learning, by using appropriate strategies and styles, if with a touch more feeling. The difference is in the way both sides of the brain are used. Traditional teaching and school problems usually exercise the analytical, left side of the brain, and more creative thinking makes more use of the global, more fun view of the right side. Making better use of the whole brain enhances all academic learning, because each side helps the other to develop and function (Torrance and Rockstein, 1986).

However, many of the lively minded pupils in the study were seen as nuisances when they attempted to think creatively in the classroom. They described non-creative classrooms which they hated – authoritarian, rigid places, working by the bell. There, they had felt themselves to be disregarded as emotional people, because the teacher was more preoccupied with discipline and the giving out of information, or when marking a piece of work, was only concerned with presentation and missed the child's ideas. As one boy said: 'Formalized learning stops your creativity.' But there were creative classrooms which were seen to be places where thinking was valued as much as memory, and pupils felt themselves respected as individuals with 'permission' to experiment with ideas. The most appreciated teachers were creative facilitators – the agents of change – and not just authorities with the right answers. Their teaching was always held in high esteem.

The evidence from the study shows up the need, especially in some ardent young scientists, to encourage high achievers to use their brains in a more balanced way. For some of them, the fact that the rich, non-school side of their lives was pushed aside impoverished not only their creative thinking, but also their feelings of self-worth. It made them feel like learning machines, grinding on for the glory of the school and maybe parental aspirations, rather than for their own fulfilment. If the gifted are to prosper in a balanced, creative way, they may need to ease up on the purely academic side and increase their social and leisure activities. But to do this they need the help and support of parents and teachers, in part to overcome their own urges for hard learning. Especially for the highly able, this would not result in lower examination marks, but probably higher ones because of their wider experiences, their greater maturity, and the depth they would bring to their answers. It would also be expected to bring them greater personal strength and happiness.

In all educational processes, there is some conflict between two natural yet opposing tendencies – either to open up the world, which involves some anxiety, or to stay sheltered in what is familiar. But scholarly, conforming children, who are socially unsure of themselves, can find the anxiety overwhelming, and so may only accept learning which seems to be safe – that is, from a safe source such as teacher – and will question little. Such children need more than normal emotional support to be able to generate their own ideas. The atmosphere in which to think and learn best is one which is secure enough to allow the individual to feel sufficiently confident to take risks. Jung (1964) described how people often erect psychological defences to protect themselves from 'the shock of facing something new', due to a 'deep and suspicious fear of novelty'. The simplest way for children (and adults) to modify their anxiety about new learning is in play, a strategy of analogy, which makes the unfamiliar familiar.

However gifted they may be, young children's natural approach to a new experience is one of play – a wonderfully flexible and creative aspect of intellectual development. Play is an activity which is not obviously goal-directed, and may merely recreate what has been observed, but it is imaginative when the child brings in novel settings, times, and characters. Indeed, educators can use the level of children's play as an assessment guide to their development.

Play can be seen from either a cognitive or an emotional perspective, though of course there is overlap between the two. Piaget saw it as vital to the developing intellect, in the process of assimilating new information into the old. Emotionally, it is a social learning tool, and can also be a cathartic activity for young and old. Children use it to comprehend social behaviour by replaying what they have seen others do, as well as in coping with their own fears and fantasies. When the quality of children's imaginative play is poor, it is a matter for real concern.

It is a sad truth that parents and teachers who are ambitious for an intellectually highly able child can place too much emphasis on measurable achievement, and may regard play as a 'waste of time', prohibiting it until formal learning – the real business of the day – is finished. Even very young gifted children are often unconsciously perceived as quasi-adults, with little need for play, so that the only approved and provided-for learning experiences they receive are relatively sophisticated and often 'bookish'. It cannot be assumed that all children play freely and imaginatively; cross-cultural studies indicate that in some cultures, and with culturally disadvantaged children, such play hardly ever occurs. Even among children who have facilities and encouragement, there are very different levels of the frequency, amount, and quality of play.

The conditions for worthwhile play are the same as those for good learning: an educational atmosphere in which there is permission to experiment whatever the outcome, emotional support, the relevant learning materials, and a living cultural tradition from which to draw and on which to build. Play at home or at school helps children to know something of the talents they possess, such as singing along with a recording or a sense of visual perspective in setting up a model, and also to experience those talents, giving them greater control and productivity over them. It is also fun, and makes learning more attractive.

Examples of creative teaching techniques might include asking a child to think up alternatives to what appear to be unchanging situations, such as, 'What would happen if everyone worked at night and slept by day?' Another might be working towards uses for apparently useless ideas, which a class could think up together, such as, 'What would happen if colours changed without warning?' Encouraging creative thinking means giving children 'permission' to play with ideas, however odd, without criticism for a while, and giving time for them to ferment. It is that precarious balance between psychological safety and freedom which allows the child to feel both secure and free enough to take the chance of putting forward unusual ideas. The encouragement to tackle problems creatively is germane to all subjects in the curriculum, through the original thoughts and creative productions of the children themselves. For creative thinking, the emphasis has to be on the process, rather than on the end-result. It starts with the knowledge and feeling, then the doing, and only then the product.

Whether at home or in the classroom, the very essence of gifted pupils' creative behaviour is at risk through conformity to social desirability, when they have to find a means of being socially acceptable. In the delicate position of being unappreciated, not only are their potential contributions easily diminished or dismissed, but they may feel that there is something wrong with them.

Talent in the Arts

It is strange, in an age when all children are considered to be potentially creative, that so much artistic education is uninspiring – whether it is stilted painting techniques or glued-together egg boxes. As a judge of a British national poetry competition to which there are about 35,000 entries a year, I found it dispiriting to read so many poems on 'The Daffodil', 'The Wind', 'The Fog', 'The Autumn', 'The Summer', etc., etc. So often, too, the poems were obviously half-written by teachers, the entries from different schools being clearly influenced by the same wooden touch.

In my study, the beginnings of future artistic talent usually started as play, as Bloom (1985) also found. At 10, for example, Anna Markland (highly talented, aged 20, studying music at university) had thought the audition for the music school was great fun. However, as Thomas Edison is often quoted as saying, genius is 99 per cent perspiration and 1 per cent inspiration, and this was true for all these artistically talented young people. Their outstanding performances had inevitably meant hard, time-consuming work to acquire the artistic knowledge base and to practise it. Their aims and their motivation were high. They had good support, though, from positive feedback from the performance itself as well as from teachers and parents.

None of the sample made it to a high artistic level on their own; support was essential all the way, however much effort and teaching had to be found as the difficulty of performance increased. Sometimes the whole family's energy became funnelled into supporting it, at times to the detriment of other possible activities. The parents of the creative youngsters had always encouraged their children's curiosity and taken it seriously. They had read to their children and taught them what they knew almost from birth, and as they grew up, often took to learning along with them.

Developing artistic talent is not dissimilar from adaptable intellectual learning – to find the style which suits the individual. When work needs inspiration, such as creating a book or a painting, one can help by trying to recreate environments in which inspiration has come before. This may involve arranging props to act as stimuli, such as working with a particular pen, or in a particular room or chair. Sometimes getting into the creative mood can involve an idiosyncratic ritual, like a preliminary walk in the park, a cup of coffee, or sitting on a hard chair. Some people can only work creatively at certain times, such as the early hours of the morning. The important thing is that the environment for creativity must be as free as possible from anxiety, which is why the surroundings should be familiar.

Another effective technique is quiet meditation, which even schools can make provision for. It involves trying to empty the mind, thinking of nothing, but being aware of everything. When the mind can be free of conventional associations, fresh ideas can emerge. The more successful creative young people were more able than the others to manipulate their environments to that effect, keeping unwanted, distracting sensations at bay, controlling the level of redundant stimulation. A common example was to take a break from the mental struggle, empty the conscious mind by doing something completely different, then re-enter the growing web of associations with refreshed perspective and strength. Another method they used was a change from a higher to a lower level of thinking, such as a move from considering general concepts to concentrate on details, and then going back to concepts.

In creative thinking, it is necessary to keep in close touch with the elements of the problem, and yet be sensitive to one's own thoughts and feelings about it. Creative people do need a global knowledge of their field to give consistency, as well as intuition. They need that information to work with, which can be frustrating for the gifted child who has not lived long enough to acquire it. But there are differences in subject area. Whereas creative scientists will make more use of the analytical control needed for verifying facts, creative artists make more use of intuition, because their need is not so much for consistency as for emotional control. Possibly because of this heavy emotional load, creative artists have to have a higher tolerance of stress to keep their equanimity, because for them, unlike the scientist, there can be no retreat into impersonal data.

The gifted do have something rather special, something the world needs, and they also have as much right to fulfil their all-round potentials as anyone else. The unbalanced, uncreative stuffing of some of this sample with examination material did not allow them to develop in a balanced way. If we are really aiming to enable children to do their best, we have to help them understand how their talents function so that they may have greater control over them. The answer to the question as to whether the gifted and talented need a change in their education is: 'Yes, they do – urgently.'

AN EDUCATION FOR THE GIFTED

An appropriate education for every child means that each one's abilities have the chance to develop fully – and that includes the gifted. As the twentieth century draws to a close and new ways of life and technology become more commonly available, people have a greater need to use the abilities they were born with more flexibly in many different situations. The way we educate our children and inspire them to approach new developments will form the basis of future society.

Special educational needs are those which call for something different from what is normally provided. A school's provision for the needs of any particular group, though, depends on outlook as well as the patience and enthusiasm of the staff, to help children make the most of their experiences. Gifted children are exceptional in their abilities, and because of their special vulnerabilities and strengths they have special needs. But it is not easy for most schools to know how to cater for them, and too often their exceptionality is seen primarily as an ability to absorb lessons quickly and easily – achievement rules. But the evidence from my study has shown that there is much more to being gifted than having the potential for achievement.

Anyone who is exceptional is bound to be affected both in the way he or she sees life and in the way he or she is treated, and if highly able children are to develop their potential, their teaching must be in tune with their abilities. Because their educational needs are at times at variance with those of the rest of the class, teachers in more formal schools may need extra information, maybe from the children's homes, to help them recognize and care for these children. But they do sometimes recognize giftedness in under-performing children by a feel for how such children handle language, general knowledge, and problem-solving. There are gifted children, though, who keep a low profile in class, appearing to be average (like conforming little girls), but who can readily be identified as gifted through psychological tests. Overall in this study parents were found to be very good at identifying giftedness, and most were first-class guides to their own children.

Special training of teachers for teaching and guiding the learning of gifted children is still unusual in most of the world. Perhaps that is why the intellectually gifted are so often only directed by teachers towards examination achievements. The teacher, though, is in a position to enhance creative thought with an open, questioning, and challenging style of teaching, providing a safe haven in which the gifted might try out their intellectual wings. The open approach asks that the teacher should give minimum directions to help children think about the subject, instead encouraging their ingenuity by asking the kind of questions which will enable them to go beyond the worksheet, the textbook, and the 'correct' answer. Problem-solving is also a diagnostic measure for the bright – their intelligence will show up in their answers.

Teachers are often concerned that their job is to teach, and not to deal with the psychological problems of their pupils. Yet adults are children's main source of their good or bad feelings about themselves, and it was clear from my study that children want their teachers to care about them as whole people who have worries about exams or a dislike of sport, not to mention a divorce or a new baby in the family. Very few of the children in the study, of any ability level, received much psychological help from their teachers.

Praise seems to be in short supply in schools, yet it has long been recognized that the carrot is more effective than the stick in producing better work, and this is especially important for the gifted, who can miss out on congratulations when expectations of them are very high. Sarcasm often seems to come to a teacher's lips more readily. What the young people said they were in need of were teachers who would work with them, rather than for them. They often described how their ideal teachers would be as concerned with the structure of their learning and their ability to cope as with the passing on of information. But there was also evidence that with a teacher's enthusiastic help, sometimes unusual subjects could be studied in ordinary schools.

It can be said that if educational provision were truly child-centred, there would be no reason for special concern for any exceptional group. Yet how can children be provided for appropriately, when their special nature goes unrecognized? Whatever their talents, those who are exceptionally good at learning will do it faster and at a greater depth and breadth than other children, which has implications for teaching:

- *Faster learning*: a large differentiation in pupils' learning speed is difficult for teachers to manage. It interrupts the timing of lessons and classroom activity. The gifted also sometimes skip sequences in the learning process prepared for them, particularly the mathematically able. A change of subject, such as art for the mathematicians, is often more beneficial than simply supplying more of the same kind of learning.

- *Depth and breadth*: extending and enriching the subject area is essential for the gifted. This needs to be done by going over the area in finer detail and relating it to other areas.

School Provision

Selection is contentious and not a matter for individual schools to decide. Even in its simplest form, when just a few children are grouped together they begin to form their own in-group, psychologically excluding others. Separate education for the gifted over the whole of their school lives, though, may be complicated by relationship problems, such as growing up without the facility to mix easily with others of less ability and education. Nor is it always necessary.

However, there are just a few kinds of gift or talent which do seem to call for full-time specialist education. These include music and the performing arts, notably ballet, though in the USSR and the United States there are also schools for other specialities, such as technology and languages. It is true that when highly able children are grouped together for teaching, they do make better progress in their school work, and most of the young people in this sample said that selection for most teaching would be their preference. This did not seem to be a matter of intellectual snobbery, because they usually liked mixing socially with people of many kinds, but rather that what they found to be the slow pace of normal classroom learning was irritating and held them back. With so much teaching aimed to the centre of the ability range, such children must indeed waste some of their time in mixed-ability classes.

The key to educating special groups in a school is flexibility and organization. Flexibility could be as simple, for example, as the trust which allows a child who has finished the lesson early to leave the classroom to work in the library, or a school starter to choose his or her own reading book. The organizational methods most frequently used to help the gifted within a school are acceleration, part-time withdrawal, and enrichment.

Acceleration

Most of the growing-up problems for all but one of the seventeen youngsters who had been young for their class at school appeared to have been exacerbated by it. Having to make relationships every day with classmates who were emotionally more mature was confusing, and also aggravated relationships at home. Nor did it even seem to benefit the young people academically; some had done less well in their examinations than had been expected, certainly with regard to their measured intelligence. Just four of those who had been advanced had managed to organize broader, non-academic educational experiences for themselves as leisure activities. Though there may be situations in which it seems to be the only way out, any child who is accelerated will need extra emotional support. It could only be concluded that, unless a pupil is not only highly gifted but mature for his or her years, school acceleration is probably not the best option.

Part-time withdrawal

The idea of taking children of below-average performance out of normal classes for remedial teaching is generally accepted, as is their need for special education, which overrides that of keeping them with their class-mates all the time. The teacher or a psychologist usually decides if it is to be done, and it is integrated into the child's school curriculum. The main problem the children may then face is difficulty in catching up with what the rest of the class had been doing while they have been out – not something that would be likely to cause problems for the gifted.

In the United States, it is not unusual to find gifted children in 'pull-out' classes. But there, as in Britain, teachers fear that if some children are selected as brighter than the others it will detract from their relation-ships with their classmates, promoting jealousy and élitism. Deeper still, perhaps, is the implicit threat to the teacher's competence. Such feelings may be quite unconscious, but many teachers cannot help but feel slighted that somehow, by virtue of some of the children being withdrawn from their class for something 'better', they themselves are seen to be not good enough. The intellectual reasons many teachers give for opposing this idea, such as disruption to routine and missing ordinary lessons, are not necessarily the real ones.

But American experience shows that it all depends how this is done – on the outlook and practical approach of the school system (Cox *et al.*, 1985). For example, if the gifted are taken somewhere exciting for a geography field trip, it is reasonable for the rest of the desk-bound class to feel envy – not least because they could all probably benefit from the trip. And yet it does happen that way. But withdrawing the gifted for specialist tuition in mathematics or a foreign language is less likely to be envied. One added danger is that withdrawals of the intellectually gifted are often likely to be made during 'unimportant' lessons like physi-cal education, which they need as much as any other child. Enhanced academic achievements in the gifted have been reported from such classes, as well as improved self-confidence and more positive attitudes towards school and schoolwork. Handled sensitively, it does not seem to have the effect of upsetting the others in the class.

Enrichment

Enrichment is the butter between the bread of a standard school curriculum. But it is not a complementary diet, an attempt to build up the protein that may be missing from home. Enrichment should be a natural, everyday part of the school-day for all the children there. It can take the form of school outings, experts coming in to school to teach, laboratories being left open at the weekend for keen physicists, time to spend trying novel ways of approaching a technical problem, and much more. It should never be confined to the very able, but be a part of every child's right within education. For the gifted, though, it is a particularly important aspect of their developing mental life. Enrichment is the vital stuff of a truly enhancing education for those who have the capacity to grasp the gist of the subject they are learning, relate it to other areas, and play with ideas in the processes of creativity.

Giving children who are exceptionally able in any area the opportunity to work intensively at their own pace may mean that they need a higher (not a lower) degree of supervision. But that care need not always be by teachers, since parents and experts can step in with specialist knowledge. If there are just a few children who are similarly head and shoulders above their classmates, working groups of different ages can be made up within the school, as is often done already for, say, a specific project.

Vacation courses are a very enriching opportunity for the gifted to be with other people like themselves, so that they can relax and drop the energy-consuming defences which they normally use for support. Gifted children who are able to take part in summer schools, whether private or provided by education authorities, have described with pleasure and relief how it was for them to meet and be with others of their own kind. For the duration of the course, the children can become enthusiastic with an energy which is daunting to the teachers in charge, but discipline problems are rare, and the overriding feeling is one of working together.

Mentoring for the gifted is a form of enriched learning. It is one of the oldest instructional models, in which a more informed and experienced adult acts as an expert counsellor to a younger protégé, in the same way that Socrates was a mentor to Plato. It provides a highly specialist form of education for youngsters whose needs cannot be met within the educational system, such as observing and assisting an adult in their daily work, maybe a lawyer, an administrator, a sculptor, or an engineer. It is not an apprenticeship, nor does it indicate long-term commitment; it is rather a more diffuse relationship in which there must be respect on both sides for it to work. Because of that personal relationship, though, mentors have to be very carefully chosen to be trusted with youngsters.

One problem which comes from improved teaching for the gifted is that the disparity between them and the rest of the class is likely to grow. This can be handled well by outside-school meetings of such children with others like themselves. These meetings need not be for selected children, but open to all who want to join in. Youngsters who find them too difficult or boring will normally drop out. Every neighbourhood, no matter how apparently culturally deprived, has its share of interesting things for children to see and do, and interesting people to meet (Freeman, 1991). This kind of enriched learning, which takes place in many settings, is difficult to measure in conventional academic terms, though improvement in school achievement usually follows. The wider advantages, such as improved relationships with other people, and the flow of ideas, are usually easier to see.

PSYCHOLOGICAL GUIDELINES IN THE WHOLE EDUCATION OF THE GIFTED

The real challenge in promoting the special education of highly able children is to alter government and school outlooks. The consequences would be of practical value for all children.

The objectives in the lists below are the best that can be hoped for, though they are clearly not obtainable all the time by all educators, whether teachers or parents. They offer a focus for a style of education which is not theoretical, but has been taken from the practical evidence of this research, often in agreement with the findings of other researchers all over the world. They are perhaps an ideal, but one for which it is important to strive.

Competence in Teaching

1 Teaching should be geared to the ability of the child.
2 Particularly for the highly able, teaching must be intellectually sound and also challenging.

3 The way pupils learn, their personal style, should be taken into consideration by providing a variety of approaches in the style of teaching.
4 Learning material should be appropriate and adequate. Most schools in my study had enough basic resources, but some used them far more efficiently than others.
5 Competence means a firm yet flexible hand on the reins, from both class-teachers and headteachers. The pupils need to know where they stand and what is expected of them in order to aim for agreed goals, with a consequent higher chance of success.

Encouraging Motivation in Learning, Thinking, and Creativity

1 Doing things with children is much better than simply telling them what to learn.
2 The pupils should be the focus of their own education; too many in my study felt like ciphers in the system.
3 What is taught should be relevant to the pupils' values and interests, both to their present leisure activities and their future vocational possibilities.
4 Schools, particularly those selecting the intellectually able, should be aware of the possible abuse of academic values which can result in sterile learning and inhibited emotional development. Teaching orientation can be changed from concern with the accumulation of information to its more creative use by a more questioning approach.
5 Enthusiasm in teachers for their subject was very much appreciated, and had the effect of inspiring the listeners to greater efforts.
6 Praise is far more effective than punishment or sarcasm.

Adult Involvement

1 Concern for the all-round welfare of children always brings positive results.
2 Accurate and regular feedback to children on what they attempt is vital for their guidance.
3 Parental involvement includes helping school learning, as well as at home.
4 Adults and children working together increases their mutual respect,

including that for children of different abilities and backgrounds. The positive attitude it engenders improves learning.

5 Adults who tried to hide their human side were less trusted by youngsters, who warmed to those who were relaxed and let their own failings show. A sense of humour in teachers is a great and very much appreciated gift.

Educational Guidance

1 Helping children to get to know what they are good at, and helping them to do it, is a vital part of good education in school.

2 Vocational guidance cannot start too early. Although this is important for all children, it is especially so for the highly able. Their future contributions are a vital part of a nation's resources, and to disregard such potential, as so often happens, is both wasteful and destructive. It can diminish both the satisfaction of the young people and the future strength of the whole community.

Appendix I
The Questionnaires

This is a summary of the basic questioning of the young people and their parents. Most of the points were quantified by rating and also acted as stimuli for further, spontaneous investigation, though some were simply noted. There were additional communications of phone calls and letters. All the interviewing was audio-taped and transcribed on to computer for further analysis, both statistically (factor analysis, analysis of variance with orthogonal comparisons, non-parametric methods) and by many readings of the text.

THE QUESTIONNAIRE FOR THE YOUNG PEOPLE

Education

- Views on own education, both academically and socially, and how they would like to change it. Preferences for mixed or pre-selected teaching, single or mixed sex, corporal punishment.
- Your teachers: rapport, academic feed-back, how they saw you, preferred style of being taught, easy-going or firm teacher.
- Preferred style of studying: project work, working alone, talking about it.

- Vocational guidance, help in choosing, personal advice, problems at school.

Self

- Personal interests, boredom, creative activities outside school.
- Reading – newspapers, books for pleasure.
- Television: how much, temptations, preferences.
- Self-concept: your attractive and unattractive points, awareness of others, attraction to others, same or different from others, ambition.
- Empathy: sensitivity, empathy, role-playing, independence.
- Communication: talk a lot, life always fast enough.
- Emotion: anger, loneliness and depression, growing-up experiences, relationships.
- Mental life: cognitive style.
- Memory: what kind and when it worked best.
- Concentration: revision patterns, style of remembering, length of concentration, attention to more than one thing at once, mental processing.

Opinions of the World

- The present state: drugs, the bomb, violence, unemployment, politics, equal opportunities, homosexuality.
- Beliefs: religion, prayer, reasons for living.
- The future: how life on earth is likely to change, can you help change it, best about living today, your personal pleasure.

THE QUESTIONNAIRE FOR THE FAMILY

About Their Child

- Health: allergies, coordination, sleep.
- Behaviour: liveliness, sensitivity, independence, obstinacy, talkativeness, perseverance, differentness, growing up.
- Educational progress: handwriting and spelling, relationships at school, progress at school.

Educational Preferences

- Single or mixed sex.
- Attitudes to the arts and sciences.
- Style of teaching and discipline.
- Hopes for child's future.

Parents' Education

- School, age of leaving, satisfaction, career, recognized influences on child.
- Grandparents: their educational and social experiences, influences, politically or religiously active.

Own Activities

- Interests: music listening and playing, reading.

Home and Neighbourhood

- Style of living, neighbourhood.

Appendix II
The British Educational System

SCHOOLS, EXAMINATIONS, AND THEIR BACKGROUND

From the mid-nineteenth century, British education began to emerge as a force for national power. But progress was slow. By the 1920s, the great majority of children received narrow, often irrelevant, lessons in the elementary schools. Even the state secondary schools, based on the mores of expensive private schools, generally looked down on demonstrated intellect and on the sciences, which were associated with trade. Instead, they emphasized the humanities (especially dead languages) and 'character' building, for both girls and boys (Musgrove, 1971). Only one in a thousand reached university.

The Eleven Plus

The eleven-plus examination was one of the grandest experiments in education the world has ever known. Beginning in 1945, it was an examination intended for every child to take at 11 years old, and it still operates in pockets of the country in the 1990s. Its entirely splendid aims were to select children to be educated at secondary level according to their 'age, ability and aptitude', and to refocus education on the needs of industry.

Although a technical option was originally planned, in the end around 25 per cent of all children were selected for academic study in the grammar schools, while the remaining 75 per cent received a more practical training in secondary modern schools (Vernon, 1957).

Many good things came out of that sorting system, most notably the concern with ability rather than money, effectively slicing through some of the rigid social-class barriers of the time. It offered bright, working-class children the opportunity to attend the grammar schools, up till then largely middle class. In the 1930s, of all the children with IQs in the top 1 per cent, only a third of those with unskilled parents had gone to the grammar schools, compared with 96 per cent of equally able children from professional homes. Once there, pupils had the chance of going on to university and to enter the professions. Indeed, several British Prime Ministers, including Harold Wilson, Margaret Thatcher, and John Major (Wyn Ellis, 1991), found political fortune from a background of eleven-plus success in the grammar schools.

But the children who 'failed' their eleven plus and were assigned to the secondary moderns very often responded by lowering their self-esteem and their expectations. Parents rarely tried to contest the Local Education Authority's decision, and though some could send their children to private schools, most had no choice. The profound after-effects of that major life pronouncement of 'pass' or 'fail' at 11 years old still influence the self-concepts of the many millions of adults who took it, and also their children.

There were many problems of incorrect placement of children, whose fate was usually decided on the basis of a single day's effort at the age of 11. Moreover, the local tests were not standardized. Children in one area might be selected on an intelligence test, but in another by achievement in English and mathematics; some even ran officer-training-type activities. In addition, the number of grammar school places varied widely across the country: in Gateshead in the north-east it was 8 per cent and in Merionethshire in Wales 60 per cent.

Nor did class bias and prejudice really die out as had been hoped. Middle-class parents were far more likely to seize the new opportunities, and working-class parents too often did not. One mother in the follow-up spoke for several parents when she told me:

My mother won a scholarship to the grammar school, but was too poor to take it up. It blighted her life with resentment, although she would never actually say it out loud. She was always very keen for all of her kids to do well. My father was almost illiterate – he still can't do joined-up writing – and his parents condoned him missing school to earn his living. But he was thrilled to bits when three of the four of us passed the eleven plus. But once we got on well in the grammar schools, he bitterly resented that we appeared to be cleverer than him. He made sure none of us stayed on at school. My mother didn't fight about it; he was her life.

Even during the heyday of selection, however, gifted children were not necessarily well catered for. Each type of school treated all its pupils as though they were of similar ability. The gifted mistakenly put into secondary modern schools were clearly in an untenable position, since neither suitable academic provision nor enrichment were available to them, and their expected performance was of a low level. But even at the grammar schools an enriched curriculum was unheard of, and provision for the top academic pupils there simply directed them to more, higher-level examinations.

Schools Today

It became clear in time that the eleven-plus system was too unfair and wasteful to be continued. Today, about 80 per cent of pupils in Britain go to all-comer comprehensive schools, which began to replace the rigid eleven-plus divisions in the 1950s. In theory, they provide a social and intellectual mix where pupils can move through different scholastic levels to suit their developing abilities. Indeed, a much larger proportion of children are academically successful today than in the age of the eleven plus. But still, comprehensives in middle-class areas are far more likely to provide capable staff, adequate facilities, and an encouraging ethos than those in working-class areas, which may suffer from limited opportunities and social problems.

About 7 per cent of the UK school population, more or less the same proportion as in the USA, is in private education. Confusingly though, in Britain the most expensive private schools are called 'public' – a hangover from as early as the fifteenth century, when they did indeed provide free public education for poor, bright boys. The remaining 93 per cent of children attend a variety of schools, which still include grammar and secondary modern schools.

Public Examinations

At the time of the follow-up study (1984–8), the major public examination in England, Wales and Northern Ireland, the General Certificate of Education (GCE), was taken in individual subjects at two academic levels by about half the school population. O-level (Ordinary) GCE was usually taken at about 16, and A-level (Advanced) at around 18. These A-levels are of a highly specialized nature and consequently of very high standard in comparison with the school-leaving examinations of other countries. A minimum of two A-level passes is essential for university entrance, and taking more than three is unusual. In Scotland, O-levels are being replaced by Standard Grade, and the school-leaving examinations at 17, which have a broader spectrum approach than A-levels, are called Highers. Universities ask for between three and five of these for entrance. Through this selection process, only about 14 per cent of British youth was then qualified to go on to full-time higher education after school.

But age is not the only determinant of these exams; in 1987, of the nearly 500,000 candidates at O-level, 434 were found to be under 15, and 30 aged between 9 and 12. There were even two children of 11 and 9 who acquired A-level passes.

Up to 1988 there was also a lower-level examination, the Certificate of Secondary Education (CSE). In 1985, about 57 per cent of the population acquired just one O-level, or its equivalent of a grade 1 CSE, and 28 per cent got five or more O-level passes (*Social Trends*, 1987).

The O-level and CSE exams were replaced in 1988 by the new, single General Certificate of Secondary Education (GCSE), still taken in individual subjects and available to all ages. The new qualification, however, is the result of many kinds of assessment, most notably a concern with what pupils have accomplished over a two-year period, rather than what they can do in a series of two-hour examinations. In theory, it offers a fairer assessment of all children's progress, and it could be beneficial to the gifted, perhaps bringing back the joy of discovery to their lives. The danger is that teachers might take the guidelines as directives and keep children at the average pace for which the system is essentially designed.

THIS SAMPLE AT SCHOOL

Schools Attended

Of the young people in my study, 14.2 per cent had been to grammar schools, and about equal numbers of the others were divided between comprehensives (40.2 per cent), private schools (39.6 per cent), and secondary modern schools (1.8 per cent). This disproportion in relation to the general population was because they were a high-ability sample, and were therefore more likely to go to selective schools – either to free state ones or to private ones on scholarships. Very few of their parents positively chose comprehensive education, though when they did, it was more for social than academic reasons.

Looked at in another way, most (72 per cent) of the high-IQ group were at selective schools, proportionately fewer (45 per cent) of the above-average-IQ group, and fewer again (36 per cent) of the average-IQ group.

Examinations and Grades

Tables II.1 to II.3 give details of levels and numbers of examinations passed.

Table II.1 *Level of Examinations Passed*

Mean IQ	Level of exams passed
151	Degree
142	A-levels
127	O-levels and CSE
113	CSE only

Table II.2 *Numbers of O-levels Passed*

Mean IQ	No. of O-levels
150	10–12
140	6–9
130	1–5

Table II.3 *Numbers of A-levels Passed*

Mean IQ	No. of A-levels
147	4–6
142	1–3
121	0

The high-IQ group achieved proportionally many more A grades in all school exams (see Table II.4). This was especially significant at A-level, where 42 per cent obtained between one and three A grades, and 10 per cent between four and six A grades (see Table II.6).

Table II.4 *Grade As Achieved at O-level*

IQ group	Grade A (%)
High	71
Above average	59
Average	27

Not all the young people in the sample were old enough to take their A-levels, but the proportions of those who did are analysed in Tables II.5 and II.6.

Table II.5 *Passed A-levels*

IQ group	One or more (%)
High	49
Above average	30
Average	21

Table II.6 *High-IQ Group's Total A-levels at Grade A*

Grade A (%)	No. of A-levels
42	1–3
10	4–6

However, there were differences between the results of the girls and boys at A-level, cutting across the IQ groups, the boys obtaining relatively more A grades.

Table II.7 *A-level Results, Girls and Boys*

A-levels at grade A	Girls	Boys
1	10.0	1.8
2	6.7	9.2
3	5.0	11.0

Table II.8 *Total Numbers of O-levels and A-levels Passed*

IQ	O-levels				A-levels		
	None	1–5	6–9	10–12	None	1–3	4–7
Average	36%	36%	26%	2%	83%	14%	2%
Above average	30%	25%	34%	11%	68%	25%	8%
High	18%	4%	54%	24%	41%	24%	35%

Table II.9 shows types of subject taken by the different groups. The brightest children, in IQ terms, tended to take science rather than arts A-levels, or a mixture of the two.

Table II.9 *Subjects Taken at A-level*

Group	Science only (%)	Mixture (%)	Arts only (%)
High IQ	41	49	10
Above average IQ	17	?	?
Average IQ	7	?	?

Reactions to Teachers and Schools

Table II.10 shows pupils' understanding of teacher assessment of their abilities.

Table II.10 *Q: Does Your Teacher Think You Are Bright?*

Group	Yes (%)
High IQ	76
Above average IQ	21
Average IQ	7

Table II.11 shows how the whole follow-up sample answered the question on possible changes to their schools.

Table II.11 *Q: What Changes Would You Like to Have Seen in Your School?*

Type of change	%
Organizational	37.9
None	27.8
Curricular	20.7
Domestic	7.7
Staff	5.9

References

Abroms, K.I. (1985) 'Social giftedness and its relationship with intellectual giftedness,' in J. Freeman (ed.), *The Psychology of Gifted Children: Perspectives on Development and Education*. Chichester: Wiley.

Albert, R.S., and Runco, M.A. (1985) 'The achievement of eminence: a model based on a longitudinal study of exceptionally gifted boys and their families,' in R.J. Sternberg and J.E. Davidson (eds) (1986), *Conceptions of Giftedness*. London: Cambridge University Press.

Bastick, T. (1982) *Intuition: How We Think and Act*. Chichester: Wiley.

Bloom, B.S. (1985) *Developing Talent in Young People*. New York: Ballantine Books.

Buzan, T. (1988) *Master Your Memory*. London: David & Charles.

Cattell, R.B., and Cattell, M.D. (1973) *High School Personality Questionnaire*. Illinois: Illinois Institute for Personality and Ability Testing.

Chapman, J.W., and Lambourne, R. (1990). 'Some antecedents of academic self-concept: a longitudinal study,' *British Journal of Educational Psychology*, **60**, 142–52.

Claxton, G. (1990) *Teaching to Learn*. London: Cassell.

Cox, J., Daniel, N., and Boston, O.B. (1985) *Educating Able Learners: Programs and Promising Practices*. Texas: University of Texas Press.

De Corte, E. (1990) 'Acquiring and teaching cognitive skills: a state of the art of theory and research,' in P.J.D. Drenth, J.A. Sergeant, and R.J. Takens (eds), *European Perspectives in Psychology*, vol. 1. Chichester: Wiley.

Deslisle, J.R. (1985) 'Vocational problems,' in J. Freeman (ed.), *The Psychology of Gifted Children*. Chichester: Wiley.

Edwards, T., Fitz, J., and Whitt, G. (1989) *The State and Private Education: An Evaluation of the Assisted Places Scheme*. Basingstoke: Falmer Press.

Entwistle, N.J. (1987) *Understanding Classroom Learning*. London: Hodder & Stoughton.

Erikson, E.H. (1963) *Childhood and Society*. New York: W.W. Norton.

Eysenck, H.J. (1985) 'The nature of intelligence,' in J. Freeman (ed.), *The Psychology of Gifted Children*. Chichester: Wiley.

Freeman, J. (1976) 'Developmental influences on children's perception,' *Educational Research*, **19**, 69–75

Freeman, J. (1979) *Gifted Children: Their Identification and Development in a Social Context*. Lancaster: MTP Press.

Freeman, J. (1983) 'Environment and high IQ – a consideration of fluid and crystallised intelligence,' *Personality and Individual Differences*, **4**, 307–13.

Freeman, J. (1984) 'Talent in music and fine art,' *Gifted Education International*, **2**, 107–10.

Freeman, J. (1991) *Bright as a Button*. London: Optima.

Freeman, J., Span, P., and Wagner, H. (1991) *Actualising Talent*. Gottingen: Hogrefe.

Gardner, H. (1985) *Frames of Mind: The Theory of Multiple Intelligences*. New York: Basic Books.

Goertzel, M.G., Goertzel, V., and Goertzel, T.G. (1978) *300 Eminent Personalities*. San Francisco: Jossey-Bass.

Howe, M.J.A. (1989) *Fragments of Genius: The Strange Feats of Idiots Savants*. London: Routledge.

Howe, M.J.A. (1990) *The Origins of Exceptional Abilities*. Oxford: Blackwell.

Jung, C.G. (1964) 'Approaching the unconscious,' in C.G. Jung (ed.), *Man and His Symbols*. London: Aldus Books.

Luria, A.R. (1984) *The Working Brain: An Introduction to Neuropsychology*. Harmondsworth: Penguin. (Originally published 1973.)

Mortimore, P. (1988) *School Matters*. London: Open Books.

Musgrove, F. (1971) *Patterns of Power and Authority in English Education*. London: Methuen.

Nisbet, J., and Schucksmith, J. (1986) *Learning Strategies*. London: Routledge & Kegan Paul.

Perkins, D.N. (1981) *The Mind's Best Work: A New Psychology of Creative Thinking*. Cambridge, MA: Harvard University Press.

Piaget, J. (1971) *Structuralism*. London: Routledge & Kegan Paul.

Quinton, D., and Rutter, M. (1985) 'Family pathology and child psychiatric disorder: a four-year prospective study,' in A.R. Nicol (ed.), *Longitudinal Studies in Child Psychology and Psychiatry*. Chichester: Wiley.

Radford, J. (1990) *Child Prodigies and Early Achievers*. Hemel Hempstead: Harvester Wheatsheaf.

Rutter, M. (1985) 'Family and school influences on cognitive development,' in R.A. Hinde, A.-N. Perret-Clermont, and J. Stevenson-Hinde, (eds), *Social Relationships and Cognitive Development*. Oxford: Clarendon Press.

Schofield, N.J., and Ashman, A.F. (1987) 'The cognitive processing of gifted, high average, and low average ability students,' *British Journal of Educational Psychology*, **57**, 9–20.

Selfe, L. (1983) *Normal and Anomalous Representational Drawing Ability in Children*. London: Academic Press.

Sisk, D.A., and Rosselli, H.C. (1990) 'Leadership: a special type of giftedness,' in Calvin W. Taylor (ed.), *Expanding Awareness of Creative Potentials Worldwide*. Utah: Brain Talent-Powers Press.

Smith, T. (1990) 'Parents and preschool education,' in N. Entwistle (ed.), *Handbook of Educational Ideas and Practices*. London: Routledge.

Stanley, J.C. (1986) 'Fostering use of mathematical talent in the USA: SMPY'S rationale,' in A.J. Cropley, K.K. Urban, H. Wagner, and W. Wieczerkowski (eds), *Giftedness: A Continuing Worldwide Challenge*. New York: Trillium Press.

Sternberg, R.J. (1986) *Intelligence Applied*. San Diego: Harcourt Brace Jovanovich.

Stipek, J.J., and Weisz, J.R. (1981) 'Perceived personal control and academic achievement,' *Review of Educational Research*, **51**, 101–37.

Stott, D.H. (1976) *The Social Adjustment of Children*. London: Hodder & Stoughton.

Terman, L.M. (1925–9) *Genetic Studies of Genius*, vols I–V. Stanford, CA: Stanford University Press.

Timar, T.B., and Kirp, D.L. (1988) *Managing Educational Excellence*. The Stanford Series on Education and Public Policy. Lewes: Falmer Press.

Torrance, E.P., and Rockstein, Z.L. (1986) 'Styles of thinking and learning,' in R. Schmerk (ed.), *Learning Styles and Learning Strategies*. New York: Plenum.

Vernon, P.E. (1957) *Secondary School Selection*. London: Methuen.

Vygotsky, L.S. (1990) *Mind in Society: The Development of Higher Psychological Processes*. Cambridge, MA: Harvard University Press.

Wallace, A. (1986) *The Prodigy. A Biography of William James Sidis, the World's Greatest Child Prodigy*. London: Macmillan,

Watts, M. (1991) *The Science of Problem Solving*. London: Cassell.

Wiltshire, S. (1987) *Drawings*. London: Dent.

Wyn Ellis, N. (1991) *John Major*. London: Macdonald.

Useful Addresses

European Council for High Ability (ECHA)
Bildung and Begaben
Wissenschaftszentrum
Ahrstasse 45
5300 Bonn 2
Germany
Tel: 49 228 30 2283
FAX: 49 228 37 65 54

Arranges workshops, conferences, publications, information centre, International Diploma on the Education of the Highly Able, international research, exchanges, etc. They have national correspondents to direct enquiries to local oragnizations for the highly able in 25 countries, some outside Europe.

European Council of International Schools
21b Lavant Street
Petersfield

Hants GU32 3EL
England
Tel: 0730 68244

International Data Base on High Ability
Deutsches Institut for Internationale Padagogische Forschung
Schlostr. 29
D–6000 Frankfurt/M 90
Germany

The Young Person's Institute for the Promotion of Art and Science
Tel Aviv University Dept. of Psychotherapy
Technical College
32 University Street
POB 17074
Tel Aviv 61170
Israel
Tel: 03 415 776

Education Otherwise (UK)
Alternative education organiser
25 Common Lane
Hemmingford Abbots
St Ives
Cornwall
Tel: 0480 63130

For help with teaching your child at home.

Prof. Dr Elvin Kalinin,
Chairman of the Organising Board INTELLECT
Aspec: 119034, r. MockBa
KypcoBoH nep. 17
Moscow
USSR

The Schools Psychology Service can test your child's abilities. This tested evidence can be useful in getting the local authority to recognize special needs. Contact your own local education authority.

The Potential Trust (Summer schools)
Kingston Stert
Chinnor
Oxfordshire OX9 49L
England
Tel: 0844 51666

Irish Association for Gifted Children
Royal Dublin Society
Science Section
Thomas Prior House
Dublin 4
Ireland
Tel: Dublin 68 06 45

Robert Mulvey, Principal
Craigmuir International School
Edderston Road
Peebles EH45 9JD
Scotland
Tel: 0721 29566
FAX (0721) 29548

This is a school for the all-round education of the highly able.

National Association for Gifted Children (UK)
Park Campus
Boughton Green Road
Northampton NN2 7AL
England
Tel: 0604 792300

The association is a registered charity which has great experience of clever children and runs courses and holidays for them. They can put you in touch with your local branch, if there is one, or help you start one.

National Association for Curriculum Enrichment
Nene College
Moulton Park

Northampton NN2 7AL
England
Tel: 0604 715000

Produces materials for enriching teaching.

French National Association for Gifted Children
34 Rue Paul Deroulede
54520 Nice
France
Tel: 93 88 4016

Portuguese Association for Gifted Children
Centro Portugues para Criatividade, Inovacao e Lideranca
Rua Jorge Barradas, lote 1
Apartado 4535
1511 Lisboa Codex
Portugal
Tel: 705192–7
FAX: 70 00 59

Spanish Association for Gifted Children (CREDEYTA)
Diagonal 482
08006 Barcelona
Spain
Tel: 237 56 22

NORTH AMERICA

Center for the Advancement of Academically Talented Youth (CTY)
N. Charles and 34th Street
Baltimore
Maryland 21218
USA
Tel: (301) 338 6340

World Council for Gifted and Talented Children
Secretariat
Prof. Dorothy Sisk

Lamar University
PO Box 10034
Beaumont
Texas 77710
USA
Tel: (409) 880–8046
FAX: 409 880 8404

Arranges conferences and publications.

American Association for Gifted Children
15 Gramercy Park
New York
NY 10003
USA
Tel: (212) 473 4266

The Association for the Gifted (TAG)
Council for Exceptional Children
1920 Association Drive
Reston
VA 22091
USA
Tel: (703) 620 3660

National Association for Gifted Children (USA)
5100 N. Edgewood Drive
St Paul
MN 5512
USA
Tel: (612) 784 3475

Dr David Weikart
High Scope Foundation
600 North River Street
Ypsilante
Michigan 48198
USA
Tel: (313) 485 2000

Mary Lynn Baum
President, Gifted Children's Association of BC
PO Box 35177 Station E
West 42nd Ave
Vancouver BC
Canada
Tel: (604) 266 6624

Judy L. Lupart
Director, Centre for Gifted Education
University of Calgary
Faculty of Education
2500 University Drive NW
Calgary
Alberta
Canada T2N 1N4
Tel: (403) 220 6280

ASIA

Gifted Child International Network
PO Box 639
Greenhills 3113
San Juan
Metro Manila
Philippines

AUSTRALIA

Australian Association for the Gifted
Darling Downs Institute
School of Education
PO Darling Heights
Toowoomba, Queensland 4350
Australia

CHIP Foundation (Children with High Intellectual Potential)
Prof. K. B. Start

29 Ross Street
Toorak
Victoria 3242
Australia

SOUTH AFRICA

Dr John F. Knel
Pretoria
Centre for Gifted Children
Private Bag X382
Pretoria 0001
South Africa

Index

Aug 18

July 14, 1998   — called
                        Bob Gooch
    8:30 - 11:30   3hrs

July 21, 1998

8:30 - 11:30   3hrs

July 27, 1998
    9 - 3   6hrs — talked
                        with B. Gooch

Aug 4
    9:20 - 12:50
                3½ hrs

Aug 11 - 11 - 3:30   1hr Bob Gooch
        4½ hrs